I0225294

Blazing the Trail

Celebrating 90 years of
Black Golf in Southern Africa

BRINGING DOWN APARTHEID

Barry Cohen

© Copyright Barry Cohen

Published and printed in South Africa, 2019

ISBN: 978-0-620-82779-9

Content lovingly crafted by the team at
www.myebook.online

Photograph on front cover:

Golfballspilewithcopy-spaceisolatedonwhitebackground high©viper-agp - stock.adobe.com

Photograph on back cover and spine:

Golf wood with a golf ball and golf tee:
© rosieapples - stock.adobe.com

All rights reserved.

No part of this publication may be reproduced or transmitted in any form or by any means, electronic or mechanical, including photo-copying, recording or any information storage and retrieval system, without prior permission in writing from the author.

FOREWORD

Tokozile Xasa

The Honorable Minister of Sport

The story of South Africa cannot be told fully, without the inclusion of the contribution of sport in breaking racial barriers. At the heart of the cultural boycott under apartheid was sport as a tool to bring the might of apartheid to its knees. Who can forget the mantra of the South African Council on Sport (SACOS) coined by its then President, Hassan Howa that there can be "no normal sport in an abnormal society"? As Sport was used as a tool to breakdown the apartheid system, it has continued to be utilised as a tool for nation building and social cohesion post the 1994 democratic era. The story of it is interwoven in the national psyche and fabric of the South African society. In this story lies 90 years of the story of black golf, largely undocumented and untold. It is our firm conviction that against all odds, the story of black golf in South Africa must be told!

The fabric of black golf is interwoven with attempts by the South African apartheid government not to allow black golfers to compete against their white counterpart and on the international stage, consistent with the 1956 Apartheid Sports Plan. In many ways the contribution of black golf in highlighting the injustices visited upon black sports men and women cannot be overstated. Several black golfers of the day, went on to be the poster boys of the horrors of apartheid sports policies and practices.

There are so many interesting stories. The story of Bambata Boodhun, Peter Louw, Cox Hlapo, Edward Johnson-Sedibe, Ismail Chowglay, Papwa Sewgolum, Vincent Tshabalala, Lewis Chitengwa, and others, was mainly unknown until this book, and it is a huge amount of credit to Barry Cohen that he was able to piece together not only their story but the tournament statistics given that no records have surfaced. There's more to be done on this journey of recording these stories. We need to also remember the story of black women golf pioneers like Mary Mofokeng, who largely remain unacknowledged and uncelebrated.

Not only are their stories extremely interesting, but through their perseverance they enabled the anti-apartheid sport movement to draw the attention of world sports fraternity to these injustices and what was happening in South Africa. Collectively, they contributed immensely towards breaking down the sporting barriers and helped eliminate apartheid. It is important to record what occurred during apartheid, and for the voices of the oppressed to be heard. The story of golf, and how black golfers rose from humble beginnings to challenge the might of the golfing titans, and compete on an equal footing.

The way one generation passed the baton onto the next generation and inspired millions of struggling black people through the exploits, as read widely in their newspapers. The story is not only the thrilling blow by blow tournaments, but the narrative of how they rose above the challenges, only for those in authority to react and try and stop the sweeping winds of change. The book is a huge contribution in our quest to record a true and complete reflection of all of South African Sport and therefore an invaluable contribution to assisting us in righting the wrongs of the past as well as unearthing the unsung heroes and heroines to enable us to honour and applaud their contribution to a new nation we are today.
I implore all South Africans to read this book!

Honorable Minister of Sport Tokozile Xasa

Sally Little

Two-time LPGA major champion

As a young South African girl playing professional golf in the apartheid years, I faced a number of obstacles. I was boycotted and humiliated all over the world. In many instances, I was kept out of tournaments, not being allowed to pursue my passion.

BLAZING THE TRAIL tells the heartfelt stories of the many incredible athletes who just wanted to play their sport and pursue their passion, but instead were used as pawns for political purposes. The stories are compelling, the history fascinating, and kudos to Barry Cohen for bringing both to light.

BLAZING THE TRAIL is a wonderful tribute to those forgotten champions and an inspiration to us all.

Sally Little

Rajen Sewgolum

Sewshanker 'Papwa' Sewgolum's son

People of colour are taking up golf in their droves – the so-called rich person's way of doing business spearheaded by President Ramaphosa. But up until now, there are only whispers about the great black golfers. Who were the black iconic golfers followed by millions during the 50s – 80s? Apartheid and its repercussions are topical daily on radio shows and newspapers but this is a story which has never been told ...

The fabric of black golf is interwoven with attempts by the South African apartheid government to prevent golfers of colour from competing against white sporting South Afri-

cans and on the international stage. Finally after becoming the figurehead of the anti-apartheid sport movement, golfers ensure that the tail wagged the dog. There are so many interesting stories, BUT ONE IN PARTICULAR, my dad, Sewshanker 'Papwa' Sewgolum, against all odds, won the Dutch Open playing in only his second white-tournament, and a total of three times in four attempts. Then after being allowed to play in the white-Natal Open he demolished a top field, and two years later when he was again allowed to play, beat the world number 1, the white-champion, Gary Player, head-to-head, only for the apartheid government, after a failed assassination attempt, to ban him from tournaments in South Africa, and then withhold his passport to prevent him playing abroad, such that he died impoverished.

They said we couldn't do it .... but we became the symbol of the anti-apartheid sport movement, exerting pressure to have South Africa banned from the Olympics, sport boycotts, and our golfers banned from competing in various countries, such that the world took notice and came to our aid.

This book is written in a popular, conversational style. It's easily understood by those who don't know much about golf, yet the book's message is of hope and perseverance. It tells the story so that these golfers and their struggle are not forgotten, and in so doing, creates black golfing heroes to inspire the youth, whilst recording the lost history of those who were disadvantaged during the Apartheid years.

Rajen Sewgolum

Introduction: The journey

Sport in apartheid South Africa (SA) was a powerful medium used to achieve the ultimate objective for a non-racial democracy in the politics of liberation.

It is a misnomer that rugby and cricket were the prime sport movers involved with the dismantling of apartheid, athough they generated substantial pressure internally on the government from local fans, and during the 1970s and 80s when demonstrations came to the fore in England and New Zealand.

In fact, it was black SA golf which first drew international condemnation during the 1960s, leading India to have SA thrown out of the Olympics in 1964.

Then during the 1970s and 80s numerous SA golfers were banned from playing in Europe, such as in Sweden, Netherlands, Tunisia, Greece, Denmark, as well as African countries, with tournaments called off in Scotland and elsewhere, and anti-apartheid demonstrations against SA golfers, especially Gary Player, in Britain, Ireland, Australia, New Zealand, and the USA, whilst pressure was applied to Jack Nicklaus and Lee Trevino not to participate in the Sun City Million Dollar events.

Meanwhile, 'Papwa' Sewgolum became the first symbol of the anti-apartheid sport movement in 1963 after receiving his trophy in the rain. His treatment by the authorities during the 1960s and 70s continued to receive substantial coverage in India, the UK, and elsewhere.

At the same time, the story of black golf and records of tournament results have never been told or recorded, this book is an attempt to relate their place in history, from the story of the first dominant Indian golfer, Ramnath 'Bambata' Boodhun in the late 1920s, to the rise of golf clubs for black, Indian, and coloured golfers; Sewsunker 'Papwa'

Sewgolum, his rise to international fame and torch-bearer of the anti-apartheid sport movement, and his main rivals Ismail 'Boy' Chowglay and Simon 'Cox' Hlapo who went before him, and Vincent Tshabalala who triumphed in the French Open and then sensationally refused to partner Gary Player in the World Cup. Likewise, Edward Johnson-Sedibe, Richard Mogoerane, administrators such as Peter Louw, and finally Lewis Chitengwa, who first beat Tiger Woods to the world junior title, and then won the South African Amateur, as well as many others.

Although this history was unrecorded and untold as minutes and records were not kept, the interesting point is that golf has been very popular with black communities since the 1880s as many of these golfers were employed as caddies and spent the entire day at the golf course where they learnt to play.

The development of black golf is one that appeals very strongly. How could it be otherwise when in South Africa almost directly we start to play the person closest to us during a round, more often than not, is a caddy of colour. And it is from the caddy ranks, almost invariably, that the black golfer springs pre-unification.

What is also interesting is that many employed the unique 'caddy' grip which was later popularised by Papwa Sewgolum and Ismail Chowglay where they applied this reverse grip to hit the ball.

This then is their untold story:

- how apartheid stopped these champions from displaying their talent to the world, and how this was broken down at home and internationally leading to unification,
- the parallel black Tournament Players Association (TPA) tour and tournament statistics,
- an in-depth look at all the players of colour, giants of the game in Southern Africa.

*Author's note: Terminology relating to a description of people changed over the years as we progressed to a free democracy. I have used the terminology prevalent at that time, such as piccanin, non-European, non-white, Bantu, native, white, coloured, Indian, coolie, and blacks. Further, the terminology 'black' may also refer to all people of hue other than white. No offence is meant.

Table of Contents

List of Acronyms

CANSA	Cancer Association of South Africa
DISGA	Durban Indian Sports Ground Association
EP	Eastern Province
EPGU	Eastern Province Golf Union
EP(N-E)GU	Eastern Province (Non-European) Golf Union
GC	Golf Club
GU	Golf Union
NE	North Eastern
NUSAS	National Union of South African Students
OFS	Orange Free State
OFSGU	Orange Free State Golf Union
PE	Port Elizabeth
PE(N-E)GU	Port Elizabeth (Non-European) Golf Union
PGA	Professional Golf Association
RAF	Royal Air Force
SA	South Africa/n
SAA	South African Airways
SACOS	The South African Council of Sport
SAGF	South African Golf Federation
SAGU	South African Golf Union
SANROC	South African Non-Racial Olympic Committee
SA(N-E)GA	South African (Non-European) Golf Association

SASA	South African Sports Association
T(N-E)GU	Transvaal Non-European Golf Union
TPA	Tournament Players Association
UDI	Unilateral Declaration of Independence
UK	United Kingdom
UN	United Nations
US	United States
WP	Western Province
WPGU	Western Province Golf Union
WP(N-E)GU	Western Province (Non-European) Golf Union
ZPGA	Zimbabwe Professional Golf Association

CHAPTER ONE

In the Beginning

It is good to have an end to journey toward;
but it is the journey that matters,
in the end.

Ernest Hemingway

Southern Africa has produced more Major winners since World War II apart from the United States (US), despite the fact that there are fewer than 500 golf courses, and only 160,000 registered golfers in SA, that is less than one per cent of the world's golf courses, and yet it continues to punch far above its weight in global golf.

The question on everyone's mind is how is it that this miniscule percentage of golfers could win 30 Major titles, and have four players ranked at various times as world number one? Even more telling is that South Africans had to travel abroad to win these golf majors. Still, golf continues to dominate the sports headlines almost weekly as our players are in contention on both the US and European tours?

Bobby Locke, with his innovative way of hooking every shot, won the British Open in 1949, and then being hugely disadvantaged because of his height, Gary Player came to the fore and took over the mantle with his victory in 1959, winning against the odds as he was the focal point of the dark days of anti-apartheid demonstrations. He was followed by Nick Price, born in Durban but playing out of Zimbabwe, and Ernie Els, the 'Big Easy', all of whom at one stage or another were probably the world's number one golfers. Likewise Major winner, Maud Gibb (playing out of England at that time), and later Sally Little, who as a 20-year old in 1971 went to take on the Americans as she had beaten all the local opposition, and won two Majors on the

Ladies Professional Golf Association (LPGA) tour.

The list of contenders who did not quite succeed but finished in the top three is also littered with famous Southern Africans, who have, nevertheless, cemented their legacies. These include Sid Brews, a major runner-up in 1934, Denis Watson penalised two-strokes for waiting too long before his ball dropped into the hole, thereby losing the US Open by one shot, Rory Sabbatini and Tim Clark, both runners-up, Mark McNulty, Bobby Cole, Harold Henning, and David Frost.

They all laid the foundation for the rise of a generation of 'born free' golfers, headed by Trevor Immelman, Louis Oosthuizen, and Charl Schwartzel, all of whom became Major winners, and a top three for Brandon Grace, with the result that today, almost without exception, there is a South African golfer in contention in the final Sunday round of a Major.

Yet there is a troubling trend. Without exception, every Major winner Southern Africa has produced has been white!

Black golf, which was unknown abroad, nevertheless flourished alongside their white counterparts during this time on a so-called 'parallel golf tour', and it is time to tell the untold story of black golf, the champions and their identities, and how the apartheid government did everything to prevent these winners from competing on the international stage.

The belief that people of colour did not play golf during the 20ᵗʰ century is another apartheid myth, with Ramnath 'Bambata' Boodhun being the first South African player of colour to participate in the 1929 British Open.

And yet, the abundance of extraordinary black golfing talent that has flourished in this country – before, during, and after apartheid – serves notice that golf is anything but a white man's sport and that SA is well poised to produce a local 'Tiger'.

The jury will always be out on whether 'Papwa' Sewgolum had what it took to win a Major in different circumstances, but the reality is Southern Africa has yet to raise a 'black diamond' – a black golfer who has the ability to win at least one of the quartet of annual blue-chip major tournaments.

It seemed that Zimbabwe's Lewis Chitengwa was the 'black diamond' for whom Southern Africa had been waiting, but tragically he passed away aged 26.

CADDIES – THE FIRST BLACK GOLFERS

The first golf club in the colony of SA is purported to be the Cape Golf Club (later the Royal Cape Golf Club) and established on Waterloo Green at the Wynberg Military Camp in November 1885. The layout of the course is not known but from the photographs it appears to be laid on open veld with minimal trees in a straight line out and in. It is certain that playing conditions, at their best, were rough and ready.

However, this was not the first golf club with a membership as there is a report, dated 30 May 1878 in The Natal Witness, of a golf club, the first of its kind, having been started at Cronstadt (Kroonstadt), 'the materials from Edinburgh having arrived, and members in full swing'. This is confirmed by a letter to the editor of the Friend of the Free State and Bloemfontein Gazette dated 17 June 1880 from an enthusiastic golfer from Cronstadt describing the fledgling Cronstadt Golf Club.

Subsequently, in 1890, T.W. Hoseason was reported to have laid out and started the Kroonstadt golf course where the Post Office now stands.

One imagines that Hoseáson would have known of the founding of the club some 12 years previously and would have mentioned this to R. G. Fall in 1930 when he wrote about the founding of the first club. It can only be assumed that the club started in 1878 did not last long and that by the time Hoseason arrived in Kroonstad in 1889 the first club was long forgotten

The first reported medal competition was held in August 1886 at Wynberg where General Torrens, acclaimed as the founder of golf in SA, went on to win with a gross 94. This (or Cronstadt) was possibly the start of black golf as no doubt Cape Coloured, Indian, and Malay caddies were trained and employed to caddy the golf bags or simply carry the clubs and balls of the white golfers. Thus caddies were introduced to the game of golf.

As such, golf started for people of colour with caddies using rolled bent wire for clubs and katoki or bluegum seed-pods or the like for golf balls.

Most of the caddies, unlike their white counterparts, played with a reverse grip, which became known as the 'caddy grip'. The reason was because while they were idling their time waiting for a 'bag', they would set up some holes using empty tins placed in the ground in the smallish area allocated to caddies, and challenge each other. Using their very lightweight bent wire, with the 'clubface' rolled up, the only way they could get the 'ball' into the air quickly was to use the reverse grip, which later became famous as the 'Papwa grip'.

While carrying the bag is part of the caddy's more traditional role, their actual job description is a whole lot more complicated. The caddy's primary job is to replace divots, repair ball marks, rake bunkers, and attend the pin.

But their real skill in caddying lies in helping their golfer to determine the distance to the pin; in advising them on club use and informing them how their game is holding up, as well as how they think it could be improved.

They are a confidante, playing partner, right-hand-man, advisor to the golfer, and the close ties between golfer and caddy are testament to the difference they can make to a game. In short, they can make the difference between winning and losing a tournament, and in a competitive sport, that means everything!

However, they do not form part of the social circle of those playing, for instance they could not sit down with their players at the halfway clubhouse, and instead were given a halfway allowance to go and eat with the other caddies out back in a lesser environment. Also, they were not allowed in the clubhouse after the game for refreshments and relaxation.

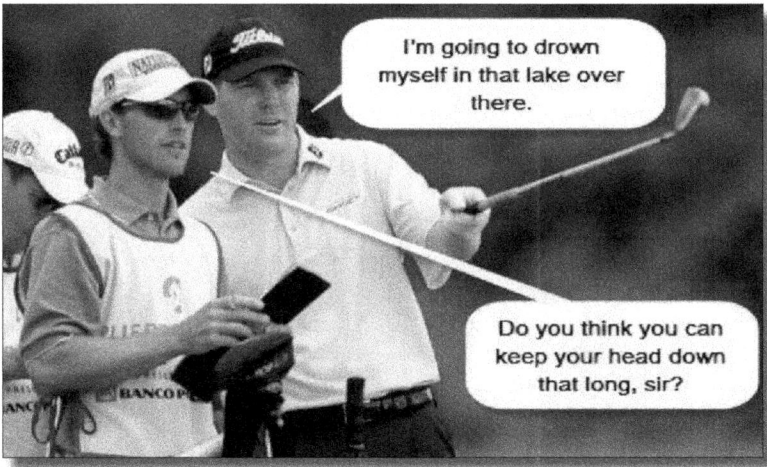

At an amateur level, caddies work out of golf clubs, and as stated, walk round with golfers carrying their golf bags, helping them with their game, and are thus paid in cash at the end of each round they work

In a professional setting, this changes. A player will

often keep their caddy all year-round, and in addition to a standard salary, dependent on how much the player is making, the caddy is usually given a cut of the winnings.

Caddy work takes place in the day, but weekends are the most popular time for the game to be played, and at club level this is the most profitable time for a caddy to work. Weekday work is available but is far more uncertain.

A caddy is not an employee of a club. They are classified as an 'independent contractor', meaning that they are basically self-employed and do not receive any benefits or perks from his association with the club; 'something which needs attention given that they arrive early from 6am and often leave after 6pm, and without whom the club would flounder'.

In 1948, the caddy fee was around one shilling and sixpence (R3), and when they had no work; caddies often used their time to hunt for lost golf balls, which they then sold for extra cash.

However, for many, the caddy's duty is 'show up, keep up, and shut up' as some players don't want to hear about club selection from caddies because it's the players' decision, sometimes though, they will ask advice about reading putts and course layout.

This was employment for the uneducated masses, and remains today a source of employment to the extent that there are programmes available today to help train caddies.

Most importantly, caddies must be alert at all times. Any penalty caused by the caddy is added on to his/her golfer's score. The caddy should be aware of his surroundings at all times, especially when players are hitting. Standing in other golfers' lines of putting or lines of sight while they are hitting a ball is discouraged. Also, the caddy is expected to understand the rules and point out any rule-breaking on the part of the golfer, such as knowing the maximum amount of clubs a player is allowed to carry.

A caddy on the Professional Golf Association (PGA) Tour, Miles Byrne, became famous when he forgot to count the clubs in Ian Woosnam's bag (only 14 allowed) before the final round of The Open. His mistake cost Woosnam a two-stroke penalty and the major championship.

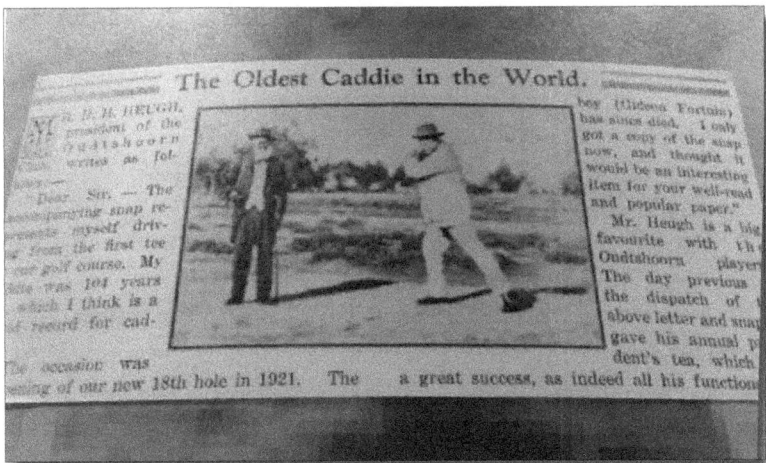

The Oldest Caddie in the World.

INDENTURED

Much like the Indian population who came to Durban in the late 1800s as indentured labourers to the local European sugarcane fields, so it was happening among the Africans in their tribal lands.

In 1909, Julius Jeppe was contemplating the formation of a Country Club and construction of a golf course in Waterkloof. Jeppe was a mining and property magnate who was in partnership with Sir Abe Bailey, and owned a 'shooting lodge' on the site of the present Pretoria Country Club buildings

In April 1910, 300 members formed the founder members group. Some of the advantages offered by the Pretoria Country Club were: 'The use of a Club House with Billiard Room, the use of a lake, tennis courts and croquet lawns, and an eighteen holes golf course'. For his pioneering role in the development of Johannesburg, Jeppe was knighted in 1922.

By 1927, the Country Club (probably other clubs) indentured caddies by going to local chiefs and reaching an agreement. It would appear these indentured youths did not have much say in the matter, but they were gainfully employed, bringing back money to their community, and at the same time, being schooled.

In conjunction with the Native Affairs Department and the Bantu Chiefs, groups of between 50–70 youngsters aged 14–20 were sent to the club from Sibasa in the Northern Transvaal on an annual basis.

Sibasa was named after a well-known Northern Ndebele or 'Black Ndebele' Chief Sibasa of the Lidwaba clan. Sibasa was one of Chief Musi's five sons and lived in present-day Mokopane (Potgietersrust), where their mother tongue is Northern Ndebele.

On arrival, they were given a uniform comprised of

shorts and a shirt for summer, and a warm jersey and blanket for winter. They were housed in the compound and fed by the club.

Every evening school classes were obligatory for every caddy, with lessons provided by a school teacher employed by the club. Their monthly wages were between 12/6–1 pound (R11.70 - R18.00), depending on their age.

When not caddying, they had to carry out light duties such as weeding, mowing, and watering the greens and tees.

Out of the 1/6p (R3) caddie fee paid by the member per round, the club retained 1/3p (R2,50), and the caddies each received threepence (R0,50), plus whatever tip the member chose to give them, which was usually sixpence (R1) per round.

At the end of each month, they were encouraged to put some of their earnings into a Building Society Savings Bank. On expiry of their 12 months' indenture, these savings plus accrued interest were paid to them, and most took home suitcases, clothes and blankets plus anything from 20 – 40 pounds (R360 – 720) on average in cash.

The retention by the Club of 1/3p per round on every round played, more than compensated in the aggregate for the expenditure on their wages and food, so that the work they did on the course – which was quite considerable – cost the club nothing.

However, this was not how the black caddy, coming from the bush, saw his duties or the game of golf as seen in the following letter:-

This letter came to the notice of Sir Thomas Graham following the South African (SA) Open championship held at the Royal Port Alfred Links in 1922 when a large number of raw recruits were obtained from the Peddie tribe to be trained as caddies. One boy set his views down in a letter to a friend of his. The letter reads:

Eastern Province
22nd April, 1922.

Dear...,

Your letter came while I was away, so I could not answer it sooner.

I note what you have to say about the scarcity of green mealies and the difficulty of getting meat. We too, have had a bad time of late. The mealies are getting ripe and hard, and the chances of stealing sheep are very small. However, Mr. ...sowed his mealies late this season, so his crop was younger and sweeter than the other farmers, and while he was away in King Williams Town we finished them all. Just before we went away we managed to get an old ewe that was left behind in the veld by Mr ...'s farm, but it was very thin (ibintye kakula) and had very little taste.

Just after that the chief called us together (all the young boys), and told us that the Government were going to give the mad white men a holiday at a place called Port Alfred, and that these mad white men would play games with little balls and sticks with heads on (intloko yegqudu). He told us that every year the Government gave these mad men a holiday, but each year in a different place. After explaining these things to us we went to this place called Port Alfred, where there is a great live water. This water has no end or banks. When we arrived it was moaning (incwina). In the night the wind began to blow, and this water became angry and roared (ukugquma) and we grew afraid, but it could not come up on the hills.

Next day we were all taken before a white man, who gave us instructions. He told us the mad white men would hit the little white balls with the sticks until they rolled into small holes made in the ground, and that we must carry the sticks and watch the little balls; but must keep very quiet and not talk because this would make the white man very angry. We were given a new name and a piece of tin with a string to hang the tin tickets around our necks. My new name was "Two Hundred and Five".

The mad men then began to come out of a very big building and called "Two Hundred and Five". I went up to him, and he gave me a bag full of these strange sticks with knobs on – some iron knobs and some wooden knobs. He placed a little ball on the grass and told me to watch it. He struck the little ball with a long stick with a wooden head and it went a great distance. I ran after the ball and picked it up and brought it to him. He grew very angry and said "damn fool", and hit at me with the stick. I was afraid and wanted to run away, but "Thirty-two" told me this white man would kill me if I did so. These white men say very little while they are knocking the balls about, but when they get tired they go to the big house on the hill and drink fire-water, and then they make much noise and all talk together. We were never hungry, because, although we could not go away to get food, as we did not know when they would want us to carry the sticks again, a white lady (she must have been a chief's wife) would bring us food – meat, bread, fruit, and some strange things we had not seen before, but they were all very nice.

We learnt many words of these white men's language, such as "Damn, Hardlines, Putter, Bunker, Goodshot" and so on. I must stop, because my paper is finished. I hope you are well.

Your friend,

....

*I forgot to mention that 'Thirty-Two' told me that the mad white men would be quiet for a year for they will spend their time in speaking lies to each other about what happened at Port Alfred.

FIRST CLUBS FOR BLACK GOLFERS

The first club for black golfers was founded in Natal, when the Durban Indian Golf Club was formed in January 1927. This small nine-hole golf course not far from the Durban Club's course at Greyville between Mansfield Road School and the racecourse was situated at the Indian Recreation Grounds (Currie Fountain), later the Mecca of non-racial sport.

Curries Fountain got its name in 1878 when a terrible drought hit Durban causing a severe shortage of water. This prompted Councillor H.W. Currie to sink an artesian well in search of water in the area below the Durban Botanic Gardens, and where he struck water, and the well-named Currie's Fountain, delivered 50,000 gallons of water to the town every day through pipes laid for the purpose.

'Curries' was a name associated with the days of vibrant struggle, particularly in the 1960s and 1970s, influencing the interaction of black people within a socio-political and cultural environment in Durban and SA. The anti-apartheid formations and political activists held many gatherings, meetings and rallies, sometimes under the pretext of organising sport and cultural programmes. Some of the major political events included a strike against land tax in 1913, when 6,000 people assembled to listen to Thumbi Naidoo, a political activist and friend of Mahatma Gandhi, the burning of the Dompas Campaign in 1959 led by Inkosi Albert Luthuli, the launch of Cosatu in 1985, and the re-launch of the Women's League in 1986.

The golf course was opened in the first week in June by the late Advocate Albert Christopher under the auspices of the Durban Indian Sports Ground Association (DISGA) with a membership of nine; at the opening tournament in July 1927 there were 57, and a year later there were over 100 members. The Durban Indian Golf Club did have some 'Africans' as members although the majority were Indians.

As the ground was swampy and boggy, a considerable amount of money was spent on French drains to clear the surface water and portions of the land that had to be filled with refuse and top soil dressing to make the fields playable.

The golf course consisted of just nine holes covering a distance of 1,884m. Par for the course was 34. It overlapped with the cricket, football and tennis playing fields, which effectively meant that golf could be played mainly on Sundays when it was free from the other codes not using the area. Membership enrolment fees were two shillings and sixpence (R4.70). Monthly subscription fees were one shilling (R1.80). Mr T.S. Rarbhoo had the honour of being the very first Club President.

The players, mostly caddies, were very keen indeed playing mainly every Sunday because all the members worked during the week, even though in conservative SA, it was frowned upon to play sport on a Sunday instead of setting the day aside for religious observance.

It was obvious that many of the members had played good golf previously. In the first year, there was one member off scratch, five with a handicap of one, six off three, and eight off four, with 60 competitors playing in the first club championship in 1929 won by E. Marrian, from R.L. Boodhun[1], the club secretary and Ramnath Bambata's brother.

No doubt the handicapping may have been a bit lax, and the allocation of par not entirely up to modern European standards.

However, it must be remembered that the course, as was the case with every other non-European course in SA, was bad, very bad, and a hole 225m in length might be well worth a bogey of four.

Durban Indian Golf Club Championship, 1929. Winner, E, Marian (left), runner-up, R. L. Boodhan (right)

---

1   The correct spelling is Boodhun as in all official government records, not Boodhan, however, as recorded in the photo..

Convenors of the Durban Indian Golf Club

Top Row: J. Mayhoo Maharajah, C.M. Singh, N. Maharajah, C.B. Singh and R.L. Boodhun[2] (hon. secretary). Bottom Row: J.B. Maharajah (hon. treasurer),. Moosa (captain), T.S. Purbhono (president), M. Mohammed (vice-president). In the Durban Indian Club there is one scratch player and five with a handicap of 1, six, with 3 and eight ith 4. In the club championships, now under way, there are 60 competitors, 20 to qualify for the final stage.

---

2   RL Boodhun – the honorary secretary was Bambata's brother.

November 20th, 1920.   SOUTH AFRICAN GOLF.   27

Durban Indian Golf Club.

Golf is making immense strides amongst the Indian community in Durban. The club started with a membership of nine; at the opening tournament in July last there were 57, and at present there are a hundred players on the membership roll. They have a small nine-hole course at Currie's Fountain, no so very far away from the Durban Club's course at Greyville, between the Mansfield Road Government School and the Racecourse. Nearly all the golf is played on Sunday, because all the members are engaged during the week and have only one day upon which to play golf. The nine-hole course is only 2,093 yards in length, and the bogey score of 34 is easy of achievement. The photo was taken on the opening day last July. In the fourth row from the top are to be found five of the vice-presidents, J. B. Singh, M. Mahomed, M. E. Pillay, D. A. Ally and P. Ranjohn (Nos. 2 to 5, and No. 7 from left). In the fifth row from the top are J. B. Maharaj (hon. treasurer), P. Moosa (captain),

A. Sookdeo (vice-president), Mrs. A. Christopher, Mr. A. Christopher (Patron), T. S. Purbhoo (president), R. B. Bamhata (hon. member, assistant to Jock Brews at Durban, and a first-class professional player whose ability is known throughout the Union; he will most likely go over to Britain to take part in next year's Open), R. L. Boodhan (hon. secretary), next but two C. R. Singh (vice-president). Several competitions have been played, the prize-winners being B. D. Singh (first on left, sitting; Pres. Purbhoo's Knock-out Trophy); bogey, L. C. Freddy, 6 up ("B" div.); opening competition, 36 holes, M. Abdoolwahaab, 133, bogey 136 (No. 4, top row); C. B. Singh, runner-up, Purbhoo's Trophy (No. 6, second row); bogey, J. N. Maharaj, 4 up (No. 8, second row); P. Mooca, runner-up, opening competition (No. 2, fifth row). In winning the "A" div. competition last month, J. N. Maharaj, handicap 4, went round in the bogey 68 (32 and 36).

On 31 March 1954, the Club changed its name to the Durban Golf Club. The Club was never in a position to reject an application for membership in regard to race or colour, such that in April 1980, it was to accept and welcome a 'white' member.

PIONEER: RAMNATH 'BAMBATA' BOODHUN (DIED 1934)

Boodhun was born in Durban, his parents came from Bihar state in India and arrived as indentured labour to work in the sugarcane fields. He lived in Madras Road, Riverside, at the end of the Durban Country Club course (later Royal Durban) situated within the Greyville racetrack.

Mohandas 'Mahatma' Gandhi

Up the road is Pietermaritzburg, where, in 1893, a young Indian lawyer was thrown off a train for having the temerity to hold a first-class ticket — which he had paid for. So began a lifelong campaign against injustice by the wealthy Hindu lawyer *Mohandas — later "Mahatma" (great soul) — Gandhi,* as he experienced the harshness of the race laws. Indians in South Africa were termed 'alien.

Ramnath 'Bambata' Boodhun was named after Chief Bambatha kaMancinza and the 1906 'poll tax' rebellion which saw 3,000 – 4,000 Zulus killed, and regarded as the start of the 'anti-apartheid' struggle.

Born not far from the Royal Durban Golf Club, it was natural that he should, as was the custom for all young Indian boys of that quarter, become a caddy. His exceptional smartness, no less than his aptitude for the game, shown at a very early age, attracted the attention of George Fotheringham (SA Open champion 1908, '10, '11, '12, '14), newly out of Carnoustie and the first professional engaged by the Durban club.

Fotheringham took him into the shop, where he learnt to make and repair clubs, and he became an excellent club-maker and 'carried' for Fotheringham in all his matches. Boodhun copied the style of George Fotheringham, such that he became a pocket-size edition of that great exponent.

He continued in this position for the next 20 years, later as an assistant first to Bill Horne, and then to the new professional of the club, Jock Brews (SA Open champion 1921, '23, '26, '28), who went on to play in The Open championship in 1926.

He considered Fotheringham to be the finest player that was ever in SA. His game developed under somewhat difficult circumstances considering the rigid 'colour' bar in colonial SA, his shot-making was absolutely uncanny, and on those occasions his mashie-work and putting had to be seen to be believed.

His weight was just over 45kg, yet his driving was as long as anyone else, professional or amateur in the country, with the possible exception of Jock Brews and Bert Elkin of Pretoria at their very longest.

Even as a boy of 15, it was a common amusement among those who knew to back 'Bambata' against up-country visitors who prided themselves as to their ability. 'The little Indian never lost!'

He had a set of clubs initially consisting of a ladies brassie, an old light cleek, and a mashie, yet he would average 72 around Greyville Golf Club. He was a natural player, and he created some astonishing scores including a 67 using only a 3-iron. Consequently, he had many local successes.

The Wonderful Golf of Ramnath B. Bambata.
By R. Muir Ferguson.

Because of his popularity among golfers in SA, the club eventually gave him the privilege on the Durban Links to play and coach before 9am, and he also coached at Beachwood Golf Club

Thus it happened that, in those many years, he played all the leading amateurs in the country. In all that time he only lost 'betterball' matches – and very few of those.

In this connection, an amusing incident once occurred. Mr J. Barry (one of the best of SA golfers and sportsmen) offered Bambata, in the days of their early acquaintance, 2s 6d for every hole Bambata won. He came in roaring with laughter and paid Bambata his 17 half-crowns.

For some time there were concerns that Bambata could

only play in Durban, and that he would be unable to compete elsewhere. As a result, he travelled to Parkview and Grange Grove in Johannesburg where he won (with scores of 76, 78 and 74).

The following year he again travelled to Johannesburg and again played a series of games with prominent amateurs winning them easily. His scores then included 72s and a 73. 'No one-course man!'

He was considered by many the most exceptional player in SA; and were it not for the 'colour' bar (because of the Colonial policies he was not allowed to participate in 'white-Open tournaments), there is little doubt that South Africa's golf history would have been materially different.

At the same time, he was a pioneer of black golf and founder member of the first black club in SA, the Durban Indian Club, together with his brother, R.L. Boodhun, who was the secretary, as well as being a committee member of the Indian Golf Association.

In 1929 as a return for his services, a subscription was opened for him to go overseas to compete in international tournaments.

By then the Indian Golf Association was well established, and Ramnath 'Bambata' Boodhun, the champion Indian golfer from Natal, was the first black golfer of quality to join Sid Brews (future runner-up to Henry Cotton in 1934) and play in the May 1929 British Open in Scotland, with Walter Hagen the defending champion.

When he arrived in England, Bambata had only five clubs, with no more than a mashie, and with no mashie-niblick. He found the English courses hard and fast greens with the closed texture of their fairways, compared to the soft ground of Durban, while the bunkers demanded a deeper-faced club. By the time he competed in the British Open he had nine clubs including a niblick (a normal set consists of 14 clubs).

The weather was bitterly cold with rain pouring continuously. Bambata said that his hands and feet were completely numbed with the cold, and his putting touch left him. He looked and felt cold. Added to these difficulties was the shadow which had covered his game. The ball slipped tantalisingly past the hole, as Bambata lost his confidence on the greens, and had to fight to keep his game from crumbling completely. All things considered, his score of 87 was a credible performance. The leading score at Muirfield was 74.

The following day, he played the second round at Gullane, scoring 82. Again the weather was as much responsible as anything for his poor score. He found it painful to swing a club, and the bitter cold and wet caused the skin of his hands to crack. His score of 169 was far too high to qualify. He also played in the 1929 German Open, and subsequently wrote instructional 'tips' for the Natal Advertiser (the articles were intended to aid his compatriots).

In 1939, the Durban Indian Sports Ground Association presented a cup to the Durban Golf Club, the 'Bambata' cup, to perpetuate the memory of Bambata. This is played for annually by the Royal Durban caddies on their championship day, and in 1968, 'Papwa' Sewgolum, the greatest Indian golfer, won the R.L. Bambata Boodhun Trophy over 36 holes.

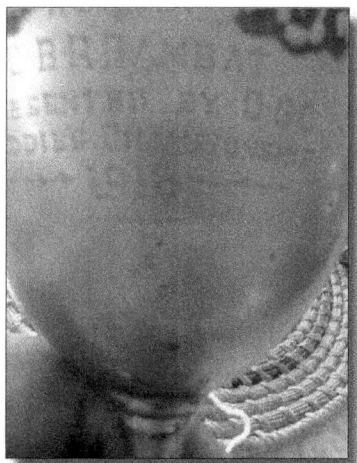

A most brilliant player. He was certainly the greatest little (7st) golfer Southern Africa has ever produced, and had he enjoyed the privileges which go with a white skin, there is scarcely room for doubt about his becoming an Open champion. — R. G. Fall (1953)

The Bambata Rebellion

In 1906, 'the Natal colonialist in the face of rising Zulu resentment against the imposition of a 'Poll Tax' unleashed one of the most brutal and bloody armed campaign to suppress and challenge the British colonial rule. The protest and subsequent armed rebellion against the tax was led by **Chief Bambatha kaMancinza**, head of the Zondi, a Zulu clan that lived in the Mpanza Valley in the Greytown district. Chief Bambatha, with the support of other chiefs in the area, refused to accept a new tax that was being implemented by the colonial administration. Together with a small group of supporters, he launched a series of attacks against the colonial forces, using the Nkandla Forest as a base. The campaign, later known as the Bambatha Rebellion, culminated in a pitched battle against the colonial forces at Mome Gorge, where Bambatha and his followers were finally defeated' and 3,000 to 4,000 killed. Bambatha was killed and beheaded during the battle. The B(h)ambatha Rebellion is regarded by many as the beginning of 'The Struggle against Apartheid' which culminated 88 years later almost to the day with the first Democratic Elections in South Africa on 27 April 1994.

—South African History Online

Frank AGG presents the Bambata Memorial Cup to "BANDY" winner of Royal Durban Caddies' Championship with a gross 77. Jack Brash (capt.) is standing on Frank's right. "Bandy," in a short speech after the presentation, thanked the secretary, committee and members for allowing the caddies the use of the course, and proudly pointed out that he is the first native to win the pot.

Second in the field with a non-European golf club and course was the Transvaal, where in 1930, the Payneville Golf Club (GC) was founded, and in the following year the Wynberg GC.

The president of this club was Mr J. Jass, and it was he who was so largely responsible for the formation of the Transvaal (Non-European) Golfing Union (T(N-E)GU) just before World War II. He presented the trophy at the commencement of the SA Non-European Championship in 1949, the 'J.M. Jass Floating trophy' in his name.

CHAPTER TWO

Spread of Black Golf

FAMOUS CADDY VICTORY

In 1937, the first black victory was seen when two Indian caddies, Jack Nathan and A. Seepersadh, playing sterling golf, astonishingly defeated the famous British Ryder Cup touring professionals Allan Dailey and Alf Padgham, the 1936 winner of The Open (also second and third) 2/1 at Beachwood Golf Club, which is now part of SA caddie folklore.

When you consider that these caddies were able to beat household names insofar as a Major winner and both Ryder Cup stars, it says a lot for the untapped talent waiting for an opportunity – an opportunity which sadly never happened due to the colonial and governing policies of the time. Were they good enough to compete overseas with the best? We will never know.

PRIMITIVE GOLF COURSES

In the 1930s, there was increasing interest among the many caddies working at the various clubs to take up golf as well as activity on the golfing front among the black communities generally.

Clearly, for the game to advance some sort of organisation needed to be put in place and proper, if somewhat rudimentary, courses provided.

Peter Louw had a passion for the game and the foresight to realise what had to be done. Without further ado, he started to put it all in place. Open areas of veld were turned into simple and very rough courses.

In 1937 or thereabouts, Peter Louw and his friends got hold of a bit of vacant ground off Ottery Road, Wynberg (near the present day Royal Cape GC), on which they worked to such a degree that they soon got a course going – the 'Sunningdale Park Golf Club of Ottery Road'. Kensington was the name of another course.

The 'Coloured Golfers Association of the Cape Peninsula' was formed that same year (1937) and almost immediately he had organised a tournament and most of the participants were caddies. As Peter said, 'Our ground is very rough, but we play really well over it, and at home we guarantee to beat the British Open champion, Alf Padgham, or anyone else who dares to face us on our own course!'

Well, that little piece appeared in 'South African Golf' and was read by one of the Indian golfers in Durban, and he got in touch with Peter. In his letter he said that he himself and 12 other men would come to play in the next championship if they were eligible.

Among the 12 would be the great R.T. Singh, who was regarded as unbeatable, and who had put up some truly phenomenal scores on all the courses he played on. Also in the 12 would be the two Indian caddies, Jack Nathan and

Seepersadh, who had defeated Alf Padgham and Allan Dailey over the Durban Country Club course.

Clearly the threat that Padgham or anyone else these Indian golfers ever met at Sunningdale Park would be beaten was no idle boast. If the British Open champion and a partner could be beaten over a championship course, what would have happened to them over the rough-and-ready affair is anyone's guess.

The following is a précis of a report in The Star dated 19 November 1938: Rand Natives are becoming good golfers. Regular club matches are played on eight Reef Courses in Johannesburg alone, including four native golf courses which, at the weekends, have scores of players out on them. The Bobby Jones Club is at the moment the crack club. The course of the Bobby Jones Club is situated at Western native Township and might pass muster for a wilderness at any time.

The other three are the Pimville Club (later Soweto GC), the St Andrews Club at Orlando, and the Wynberg Golf Club at Alexandra Township. The Wynberg Club is the only one which boasted an 18-hole course.

On the Reef outside Johannesburg were four more clubs; one at Benoni, one at Stirtonville outside Boksburg, one at Germiston, and one at Randfontein. There was also a course in Pretoria. Inter-club matches are played regularly with the seriousness of the best white clubs.

With more than a little ingenuity, members carved out nine-hole courses. Brickfields, ditches, drainage trenches and a marshy vlei formed natural hazards not normally found on a golf course. Greens were roughly smoothed patches covered with sand, called 'browns' because oil was mixed with the sand to make them smooth, and averaged three metres in diameter. It was easier to putt with a mashie than with an orthodox putter.

There is a spice of adventure about golf as the natives play it. They never know from one day to another whether they are going to find their course in the condition in which they left it. Someone may have dug some pot clay out of one of the greens. That is just too bad and they make another. Or a sewerage trench may have been dug across the course. That is equally bad luck. Their concern is that their courses may disappear altogether to make way for development. They play the game seriously and it would be a pity if they were deprived of their courses.

Carved out of the bush with no fences golf courses were full of hazards including dangerous animals.

An unofficial SA Non-European Open Championship was held each year. In 1938, it was played over the Wynberg course and won by J Dyasi with a 72-hole score of 332. Michael Swartz was the runner-up. Also, three Provincial Championships were played, the Transvaal Open, the Free State Open, and the Griqualand West Open.

In 1947 a new non-European golf course called the Bobby Jones Golf Club was officially opened at the old Newclare racecourse. The unofficial non-European champion, S. Swartz, was invited to drive the first ball. For at least the past six years, Swartz had been champion and played to a handicap of plus two. The Bobby Jones Club had apparently been forced to move from the site previously occupied in the pre-war years.

Meanwhile, J.M. Jass founded the 'South African Non-European Golf Association' and was elected the President, with the famous Sid Brews (who would go on to win eight SA Opens in four decades, the last just shy of his 53rd birthday) the patron. Peter Louw was similarly much involved in this formation with its headquarters in Bloemfontein, and as Vice-President, he played a significant role in the organisation of the SA Non-European Open Championship, which became a regular annual event from 1949 onwards under the control of the Association.

In 1948, as reported in the press, was the fact that Coloured golfers in Cape Town had formed their own 'Western Province Coloured Golfers Association'.

Golf on the Cape Flats - SA Golf:
May 1948: Despite the proximity of other Coloured sports pitches, houses, cows, horses, unsuitable ground, etc., the Coloured community, under the leadership of Peter Louw, has developed a golf course and a club (or association) at Crawford, Cape Flats. Over 200 members are now enrolled and monthly

(36-hole) competitions are held. The players are of an excellent type, and their competitions are models, well ordered, with a very fine appreciation of the rules of golf. The going is very rough; but if you lift, owing to any extraordinary bad lie anywhere, the penalty is one stroke. There is no free lifting and dropping. It is hoped that every effort will be made by European sportsmen to obtain for them a ground of their own, which they can fence that they may be able to enjoy the game much better than at present. Ex-caddies, of course, take the lead! There is even a clubhouse - their 'grand lady', Mrs Theys, permits the members to use her house for this purpose.

Accordingly, in the years before the unification, there were controlling bodies for golf among the black, coloured and Indian population, and tournaments of all kinds were a regular feature on the golfing calendar.

Golf clubs continued to abound, many consisting of small groups of enthusiasts playing on these rough and ready courses laid out on areas of the bare veld. 'That putting is difficult goes without saying. A small space was cleared and top-dressed with sand, but in spite of everything the ball weaved a very wobbly way towards the hole with most putts'.

From 1949 the official Non-European SA Open was hosted annually at Easter together with the General Meeting Association and the publication of an annual magazine.

1951 LOCAL RULES FOR BANTU GOLFERS

Grahamstown

Before republishing these rules, it is better to explain that Rules 6 and 7 have been included because, owing to the lack of putters and the roughness of the 'greens', the players have to putt either with the back of a club or with the back of the hand. The rules are definitely entertaining. Here they are:-

GRAHAMSTOWN TANTYI BANTU GOLF CLUB

All the official matches of this club will be played under the following rules.

RULES:

1. A ball lying in any ground under repair, must be lifted and dropped not near the hole, no penalty.
2. A ball lying in a hole made by an animal must be lifted and dropped within a club's length behind such a hole, no penalty.
3. A ball lying in a hazard must be played. If a player lifted that ball or dropped it out, stroke gone.
4. Before lifting any ball, a player must notify an opponent or a marker.
5. A ball on the putting green may be lifted and clean.
6. No player is allowed to use the front part of his club on the putting green. A penalty followed by a stroke gone to that player.
7. A player must not use a palm of his hand in a putting green. Doing so, that player will lose a stroke.
8. When the result of a hole has been determined, player must immediately leave the green. N.B: A player, while looking for a ball, must allow other matches coming up to pass them. After signalling the former should not continue playing until the latter is out of range.
9. Players must at all times play without undue delay.
10. A player using vulgar language on a course, the club is allowed to punish that player if the case is proved after discussion in their committee. N.B: It is the Committee that will punish that player.

OUT OF BOUNDS:
ALL GROUNDS ON THE OTHER SIDE OF THE NATIONAL ROAD, OUT OF BOUNDARY.

The Golfers' Annual published under the auspices of the T(N-E)GU appeared for the first time in 1953/54. The Chief Editor was Mr S. Mnisi, and other members of the Editorial Board were Mr A. Maqubela and Mr M.W.D. Bookholane. The Office Bearers of the T(N-E)GU were listed as:

Patrons	Hon Mr Justice O Schreiner
	Mr S F Brews
President	Mr A Maqubela
Vice-Presidents	Mr S Mnisi
	Mr D Masigo
Secretary	Mr M W D Bookholane
Ass. Secretary	Mr A W Selepe
Treasurer	Mr M Boice
Committee	Mr R A Ditsebe
	Mr P Tshoagong
	Mr L Kathidi

SPREAD OF GOLF CLUBS AND PROVINCIAL ASSOCIATIONS

The Viking Round Robin Tournament, formerly the Mike Round Robin Tournament, was introduced in 1952. Players entered as individuals and played 36 holes stroke-play to qualify. The top 16 going through to the match-play stages to play against the other 15. Points were determined by the number of holes won or lost against each opponent, with a floating trophy awarded to the winner, Ronnie Ditsebe (1949 first official SA Non-European Open champion) who won in both 1952 at Wynberg GC and in 1953 at Pimville GC.

The 'Bantu World' Tournament was one of the oldest sponsored by the T(N-E)GU and made possible by the donation of a floating trophy for the winning team by The Bantu News Publications. This was an inter-club event, the format also being teams of four medal play all four scores to count. In 1953, ten clubs entered, and the winners were the Wynberg GC on a total of 323, their team being S. Hlapo (77), A. Matsila (86), M. Ntsoseng (83) and J. Jass (77).

The Golfers' Annual also reported the death of Mr J. Jass, the foundation member of the Wynberg GC and one of the founders of the T(N-E)GU. 'His untimely death came as a shock to all of us, particularly to the golfers of Alexandra Township, an area which, through the influence of this great figure, can be regarded as the home of Non-European golf.'

Of particular interest where the Annual is concerned is the listing of all the golf clubs, 32 in all, affiliated to the T(N-E) GU with a total of over 600 members.

Bobbie Jones GC (1933)	Central GC (1934)
Homicide GC (1949)	Evaton GC (1952)
Payneville GC (1930)	Pimville GC
Round Robin GC	Royal Mid-Surrey GC
Sunningdale GC (1943)	Wynberg GC (1931)
Penfold GC (1949)	Alexandra GC
Alberton GC	Eligwa GC
Goodall GC	Humewood GC
Kliptown GC	Methodist GC
Pollak Park GC	Peter Thomson GC
Richmond GC	St Johnson GC
Sandridge Park GC	Stirtonville GC
Palmdale GC	Top Notch GC
Viceroy GC	Dunlop Sixty Four GC
Coombhill GC	Telford GC
Pinpointers GC	St Andrews GC

The annual also listed their aims and objectives:

Aims
- Foster interest in golf
- Improve standard play
- Inculcate spirit of sportsmanship
- Encourage inter-provincial competition

Objectives
- Organise annual SA Non-European Open
- Host annual General Meeting at the Open
- Publish annual magazine

Consisted of the following districts
- Eastern Cape
- Western Cape
- Transvaal
- Bantu GU
- Griqualand West
- Natal GU
- Basutoland GU

In 1954, the Johannesburg publication, The Post, reported that the Griqualand West Non-European Golf Open Championship would be played over the Versatile Golf Course in Kimberley. The entry fee was one guinea (R20) and board and lodging would be provided free of charge by the Griqualand West Union. 'It would be most interesting to test how some of the leaders of non-European golf would fare on a good course. The courses they play on are mere apologies.'

At this time there were no less than four non-European clubs under the jurisdiction of the Western Province (Coloured) Golf Association, all with courses on the Cape Flats.

THE EMERGENCE OF BLACK GOLFING CHAMPIONS

Against all odds, they did what they could, tied down by harsh restrictions .

By this stage a number of potential golf champions had started to emerge such as Simon 'Cox' Hlapo, Eddie Johnson-Sidebe, 'Papwa' Sewgolum, Ismail Chowglay, and shortly afterwards, Richard Mogoerane, Vincent Tshabalala, and later Joe Dlamini; all these players could hold themselves against any white opponents but had yet to make an impact.

But what is often lost in the record books is not only the daily discrimination and loss of opportunities forced upon them by the apartheid government, but the fact that the leading players well into their 30s, and in the prime of any golf professional, were only now starting to be allowed to compete on proper 'white' courses.

There is no way one can compare the courses they had to play on to even enable them to play in major non-European events, because of the so-called 'parallel but equal' apartheid policy where government and municipality funds were used only to build white courses.

This was even more evident insofar as caddies were allowed to play at the white course where they caddied, but only on a Monday when the course was closed. Meanwhile, white professionals practised daily on manicured top-class golf courses. Many of these professionals played fulltime, unlike their counterparts, who still caddied for a living. At best, they could rise to caddy master in their chosen profession. However, they were not allowed to engage in teaching or working in the professional's shop, despite the fact that they were more than qualified.

By 1957, there were five clubs in the Cape Peninsula and about 300 members, but when it came to the turn of the Western Province to be the 'host' club to a national championship golf tournament for non-European golfers, it certainly required something better than that which was offered, and accepted, at Thornhill. The host club did not even have a tent to offer their guests, never mind about a clubhouse.

The Coloured golfers of the Western Province deserve their chance of providing themselves with decent facilities, and they should get it. Who knows but they could be held up later on by Europeans as an example of what can be done in the way of providing cheaper golf than is available today. And the way they would do it would be to take their coats off and do something to help themselves.

But some clubs did assist in certain ways. The Westlake caddies received aid from the club's 'Welfare Fund', and permission was also given to the caddies to play on the bottom nine holes at certain hours. Far from damaging the course, the caddies acted as unpaid caretakers zealously safeguarding the club's welfare.

The Executive of the Western Province (Non-European) Golf Union (WP(N-E)GU) consisted of:

President	V Hendricks
Chairman	John Petersen
Vice Chairman	J Adriaanse
Secretary	B Adriaanse
Treasurer	R Brown

In 1958, it was reported that Mr F.L. Cannon, president of the Western Province Golf Union, presented a championship trophy. On the very rough courses, the greens were sandy and very bumpy, and as often as not putting had to be done with an iron. Meanwhile, there was a 'caddy strike' in Barkley East – over a demand for more pay.

In 1959, those township caddies denied the opportunity to compete on the 'white' SA Tour, set their sights on playing in 'The British Open' in the UK.

At this time all that the average white golfer knew about non-European golf was the annual caddy competition at his club. He knew, of course, that some of the caddies played very fine golf; he was made to realise it whenever he watched some of the lads swinging clubs, or apologies for clubs, either on the course or adjacent caddy enclosure. But it was not until the former Indian caddy, Sewsunker 'Papwa' Sewgolum, and the Transvaal African, Edward Johnson-Sedibe took part in the British Open, and Papwa won the Dutch Open with an excellent score that the average golfer realised how far blacks had advanced in the world of golf.

In 1960, it was the turn of Lawrence Buthelezi, a Beachwood Durban caddy, and later Howick caddy master to participate in The Open, in 1961 William Manie, and 1962 Ismail Chowglay, all without success. However, what is important was that they could compete, and that they aimed beyond the 'veld' courses they had to play on and attempts by the authorities to make them feel inferior.

Largely because of the higher numbers and willingness of municipalities and other authorities to permit the Africans to use certain sites for golf, but never with any security of tenure, the game among the non-Europeans in the Transvaal advanced far more rapidly than elsewhere in the Union.

By the early 1960s, there were over 64 golf clubs, mostly hued out of the rough veld, very primitive, but functional. Many of these were established by the tireless legendary administrator, Peter Louw. Unlike the 'supposed parallel' white tour, there was little distinction between amateurs and professionals. Of these, there were now well over 40 clubs affiliated to the T(N-E)GU.

Meanwhile, the first European president of the WP(N-E) GU was Mr R.K. Bromley. Sometime previously, he had presented a trophy to the Union, but it was only played for the first time in 1960.

At this time the office bearers of the Western Province Coloured Golf Union were as follows:

President	R K Bromley
Vice-President	D Hands
Chairman	A Whittles
	J D Joseph
Assistant Chairman	S J Samson
Secretary	Lionel Theys
Asst. Secretary	C Daniels
Treasurer	K Watson
M&R Secretary	B Adriaanse
Asst. M&R Sec.	A (Polly) November

Rex Walker and R.G. Fall (editor of SA Golf magazine from 1926) were elected the first life members of the Union. After that, it was recorded as R.K. Bromley, Vice-President and Mr J.D. Joseph as Chairman of the WP(N-E)GU.

Of the other centres which are affiliated to the South African Non-European Golf Association, WP may have been the first to be in the field with a club. However, it is more than possible that Griqualand West might have started before the Western Province, because the SA Championship was played at Kimberley in 1954, two years before it was held in the Cape.

One of their moves took them to Thornhill (Cape Flats). While there, Rex Walker, captain of the Westlake Golf Club at the time (1957), one of the patrons of black golf, issued an appeal for the support of an application by the Western Province (Non-European) Golf Union to the Cape Town City Council for help in establishing an 18-hole championship course for the use of Non-European golfers. 'A place in the golfing sun.' To have a 300-yard green belt round non-white locations being used for a golf course has everything to commend it. The Athlone Golf Course would eventually be the outcome

In 1960, at the annual meeting, the SA Non-European Golf Union officials were, with one exception, re-elected. There were now five provincial unions affiliated to the national body, with the promise of two more. Once again, this advance was due chiefly to Peter Louw.

President	Alfred Maqubela (Transvaal)
Vice-President	Peter Louw (Western Province)
Secretary	David Phala (OFS)
Assistant	Sam Mnisi (Transvaal)
Assistant Treasurer	D R Mashego (Transvaal)

After that many clubs were formed in the Orange Free State, Border, and the Eastern Province. The game advanced rapidly everywhere.

Not so in Natal as when the course at Curries Fountain was destroyed to make way for schools, and for several years there was no golf course for blacks until Springfield was opened in 1961. And that course did not have a clubhouse until 1980.

In 1962 tour players held card games and other fundraising efforts to send Ismail Chowglay, the Cape and SA champion to 'The Open', where the media confused him with representing Egypt (at least from East Africa) because 'there were supposedly no players of colour in South Africa'. At that stage, he was viewed as potentially a better player than Sewgolum.

By 1963, golf was not only popular in Cape Town and environs, but was also played by the coloured community in the smaller Boland Towns, such as Caledon.

The SA Non-European Open Championship was first played at Kimberley in 1949 after the formation of the SA Non-European Golf Association. 'Papwa' Sewgolum only appears for the first time in 1960, significantly he was already 31 years old.

This is perhaps surprising as by then Papwa was well known in Natal where he had won the Natal Non-European Championship numerous times and, more significantly, he was already the 1959 Dutch Open champion. There must be some reason for his not winning the national championship sooner than this. It was not until 1961 that the championship was held in Natal for the first time, and before that, except for Milnerton in 1960, it seems that Papwa was not willing to travel.

Papwa's dominance over his competitors was such that there was Papwa's level, then quite some distance Chowglay and later Tshabalala, then Hlope and Mogoerane, followed by the rest. He dominated the tournaments, and his positive golfing personality and confidence awed and crushed his opponents. An overview of his dominance substantiates this.

The important years for Papwa on the Non-European golf scene in SA were the 1960s and into the 1970s. Previously, he had won the Natal Non-European Championship in 1954, '55, '57, '58, and '59, but it was in 1959 that he made his first visit to Europe where he played in The Open Championship and hit the world headlines by winning the Dutch Open. In 1960, he launched his remarkable career on the golf courses of SA, and it was perhaps his victory in the SA Non-European Championship at Milnerton that marked the beginning.

In the 11 years from 1960 to 1970, he won the National Non-European title no less than nine times (out of ten attempts), and it was during this same period that he played and won provincial tournaments all over the country. In addition, he made history at East London in 1961 by being the first golfer of colour to play in the 'whites only' South African Open Championship. When his often busy schedule allowed, he did play in what might be considered the more important non-white provincial championships, and his record in these events in the years 1960 to 1970 speaks for itself

But it was not always one-sided. Walmer Country Club again made their course available for the Eastern Province (EP) Non-White Championships in 1963. This was won by Ismail Chowglay whose score of 309 was one shot better than Papwa Sewgolum making his first visit to Port Elizabeth. Papwa made a strong challenge for the title, scoring a record 71 in the last round, but it wasn't quite good enough. Chowglay was given a warm welcome by golfers in the Peninsula on his return to Cape Town.

The tables were turned in 1964 when he beat Chowglay by an easy ten shots, but in 1968, Chowglay again turned the tables on Papwa.

Kimberley was an important centre for black golfers in the 1960s, not least because of the support they were given by the Kimberley Golf Club, and Papwa was always ready to play in the Griqualand West Non-European Championship. In fact, he won four times in a row from 1961 to 1964, and then again in 1966 and '67.

His avoidance of the Free State would almost certainly have been because a local, provincial law prohibited Indians from remaining in the Province overnight. There are only two recorded instances of Papwa playing in the Orange Free State (OFS) Non-European Championship, and these were in Bloemfontein in 1966 where he won followed by Hlapo and Mogoerane, and in 1968, when he and Ismail Chowglay drove into the Free State for the day, and then left, returning the next day.

The Bloemfontein Golf Club had become the regular venue for the OFS Non-European Championship and hosted the 1968 event which was won by Richard Mogoerane (302) from Papwa (304) and Cox Hlapo (306). Papwa was leading Hlapo and Nkosi by one shot after 36 holes but failed to master the breezy conditions on the second day of the championship.

Also, making a name for himself at this time was Johannes Simenya who started his golf involvement as a small boy-caddy and was appointed assistant professional at Waterkloof Country Club. He finished fifth in the 1960 Transvaal Non-European Open, including rounds of 64 and 67.

The Transvaal was a hive of black golfing activity over all the years, and it was inevitable that sooner or later Papwa would make his first appearance there. He entered the 1964 Transvaal Non-European championship at the Benoni Country Club and went on to win it in fine style, stamping his authority on the tournament with an excellent 65 in the third round.

In 1964, Papwa sunk a 15-foot putt on the final hole for a birdie to complete a brilliant days performance, and win the 72-hole Transvaal Open championship at Benoni CC. Sewgolum had a four-round record aggregate of 284, 20 strokes better than his current rival, Eric Boorman, with the defending champion, Cox Hlapo slumping to the tenth position on 313. Sewgolum was in top form over the last 36 holes, the highlight of his dynamic play came in the third round where he set up a new course record with a 65. His purse was R100.

Papwa returned the following year and won at Glendower. He won again in 1966 and was runner-up in '67 to Richard Mogoerane, while Chowglay won in 1968, but he won again in 1969, and '70 when he beat Vincent Tshabalala, Solly Sepeng and Ronald Anooplal who all tied for second.

In 1972, Papwa (now 43) was beaten by two shots by Vincent Tshabalala for the title. Later that year in a tournament sponsored by Luyt Lager, Papwa tied with Cox Hlapo (now 46) only to lose the sudden-death playoff.

Papwa was not a regular visitor to the Cape but, when he did make the trip, he usually went home with the title although Ismail Chowglay did provide some opposition.

There were simply tournaments where Papwa was unstoppable. His first appearance in the Western Province Non-European Championship was in 1960 which he won, then in January 1964 at Royal Cape he demolished the competition, running further away from the field with every hole he played. Opening with an excellent 68, he was followed by Chowglay on 71.

That was the last time Chowglay saw Papwa as thanks to a brilliant 65 in round two, he went on to win by no less than 27 shots. And this was with champion golfer Ismail

Chowglay in the field! His total of 275 was the second-best score ever shot over 72-holes at Royal Cape, with only Gary Player shooting 271 in 1960.

Windy conditions upset most of the player's score-cards. However, a 4-under par first nine if the final round threatened more of round one fireworks, but he produced poor golf by his own standards over the second nine.

Wally Johannsen, overnight in second place after two rounds fell away, and Chowglay and Philip van Dieman came up into joint second place.

In 1968, he was second to Chowglay, and on his fourth visit in 1969, the championship was played on the new Athlone course and, true to form, Papwa came out on top, and in 1976 (now aged 47), he won again 'by the proverbial mile'.

In his home province of Natal, Papwa reigned supreme for many years. When he won the Natal Non-European Championship in 1960, it was the fourth time in a row he had done so, and his sixth victory in seven years. But he was not finished there. In 1961 he won at Umbogintwini once again by a mile going away, and again at Kloof CC in 1962, and then at Circle CC in 1963. His winning streak ended in 1964 when he was runner-up by one shot to Raydmuth Rajdaw at Kloof CC, but took off again with a win in 1965. The records also show a win for Papwa in 1966.

Also, in 1968, the golfing maestro provided some thrills for the big gallery which followed throughout the final round of the Natal Non-European Open played on a Tuesday. All black tournaments were played on a Monday and Tuesday (36-holes each day), unlike their counterpart white tournaments which were played daily from Thursday to Saturday (36-holes). Papwa clinched the title and prize money with scores of 71 76 69 70. He was followed home by J. Ranjith with 299. A field of 120 golfers from all over SA took part.

He won again in 1969, and '70.

In 1971 he lost the title to Vincent Tshabalala, who won the following year again, but won again in 1974, then lost to Ismail Chowglay in a three-hole sudden-death play-off in 1976. The last results on file were those for 1977 when he won for the last time.

At the same time, there were numerous tournaments for prize money, albeit very small, held around the country, with the first 'official' SA Non-European Open in 1949 won by Ronnie Ditsebe. In 1950 the winner was Jacob Gumbi, '51 and '52 Eddie Johnson-Sedibe, '53 Bob Nkuna, '54 L. Khatidi, '55 Simon Hlapo from Ismail Chowglay (as he emerged onto the scene), '56 'Polly' November, '57 Simon Hlapo, '58 David Motati, and '59 Simon Hlapo once again.

THE SEPERATE AMENTITIES ACT FORCED PEOPLE TO USE SEPARATE BUSES, TRAINS, PARKS, BENCHES,HOTELS, MOVIES, HOSPITAL, AMBULANCE, TOILETS, ECT

In those early days, there was no question of their being able to use a 'white' golf course, and the championships were played on the courses laid out by the golfers themselves on any areas of open veld with sufficient space to accommodate a course, usually only nine holes. These courses inevitably were very rough and ready, but they had to make do. Thus when the venue is given as being Kimberley or Bloemfontein, this refers to the 'make-do veld' courses in those towns. This was until 1960 at Milnerton.

The coloureds, driven off the only available course of their own at Thornhill, tried hard to construct an 18-hole golf course in two months at Wetton on the Cape Flats, on the ground that had been made available to them through the intervention of Messrs Rex Walker, Jack Bowie and Dick Hawke. They were in a real quandary. 'How could they invite their friends from the Transvaal, Natal, Griqualand West, Free State and EP to play over a scratch-about affair only two months in the building for the national title of best black golfer?'

Coming to their rescue was Mr F.L. Cannon, President of the Western Province Golf Union (WPGU), and 26-year-old Mr Anton (Tony) Buirski, Captain of Milnerton GC, an attorney, who agreed to make their course available. This was in the face of fierce opposition from the club's president, Sir de Villiers Graaff (leader of the opposition United Party) who was concerned that the club would be invaded by swarms of blacks (the De Villiers Graaff Trust owned the land) - the first time that such a thing had ever happened in the history of golf in South Africa. Her Worship, the Mayor of Cape Town, Mrs Joyce Newton Thompson consented to hold a mayoral reception in the Woodstock Town Hall and to present the prizes.

Thus history was made when the SA Non-European Championship was played for the first time on a 'white' course. This set a precedent and, except for in 1969, when the Championship was played over the Athlone course, it was after that only played on a 'white' course.

The question of European golf clubs lending their courses for significant black tournaments is important. Now blacks at least were competing on an equal playing field although they were not allowed to practice there before the event. Milnerton had set a sporting precedent. Never again would blacks play a major tournament on a 'scratch-about' course that did not provide a fair test.

This then became the norm as Kloof, and Royal Durban offered their courses for the 1961 SA Non-European Open. Everything was as it should be, and every assistance received from the Europeans both in the way the players were cared for and made to feel at home. Catering arrangements were everything that could be desired – huge tents and marquees were in use as well as many tables and chairs.

The tournament attracted a very considerable amount of attention. Many leading players, all the local professionals, and many golf administrators were among those who watched the play. African Consolidated Theatres were also there to take pictures for the cinemas

There were kind messages from everywhere including a cable from the New Zealand Golf Union and a beautiful shield from the Australian Golf Union.

One of the players was asked how the Natal courses compared with those in his own district. 'Sir,' was the courteous reply, 'that is indeed a difficult question to answer. You see, I have never been allowed to play on a European course previously'.

It was not all smooth sailing for the players. With the south-easter blowing harder than it has done for years – and that south-easterly wind can 'pump', Milnerton proved a real testing challenge to the best golfer – poor 'Bra Cox' Hlapo (winner of the championship three times during the previous six years) suffered more than the others. He was blown clean off his game. And whereas on his own artificial sand greens in the Transvaal he putted well, or even on rough grass greens on which he putted with an iron, he was altogether at sea on good grass greens, with a proper putter in his hand.

Hlapo's swing was as smooth as butter! Not one of the others hit the ball quite so far with such an effortless, graceful swing. In November 1959 at Kroonstad, he won the NE Free State Championship with two 68s. In winning the SA title in 1958 with 290, he had a second round of 66. He had an incredible record, but this was a different challenge as he was all at sea, leading to a huge score.

Nevertheless as R.G. Fall (Editor SA Golf) stated: 'If you had seen some of those non-European swings in that hurricane at Milnerton: seen some of those No. 2 iron shots straight as a bullet, "quail high" straight to the mark against the wind, you would, like I did, begin to wonder'.

Whereas Milnerton was the first European club to offer the non-Europeans their course for a big meeting and to have that kind offer accepted, gratefully, other European clubs subsequently made similar gestures. Maritzburg Country Club were hosts for the competitors in the Natal Midlands Non-European Open, which Papwa won after a tie with Lawrence Buthelezi, now the Howick caddy master, shooting record scores including 72s.

Mention of the 72 by two black golfers at Maritzburg Country Club leads one inevitably to the question: 'Just how good are these players? How would they compare with the best of the Europeans were they to be given a fair chance of getting accustomed to golf on championship courses?'

The West Bank GC, East London, also permitted blacks to hold an open event over their course once a year. The club was the first ever to do so. It is doubtful if any more clubs made similar gestures. At any rate, it was a start.

Elsewhere, an interesting letter to Walmer CC from Port

Elizabeth (Non-European Golf Union (PE(N-E)GU) signed Kenneth Gwaxula (secretary) and Reginald Schultz (President) thanking them for the use of their course for the N-E, EP and Border Open. 'We are not the prophets but we dare to predict that very soon, sport, and only sport will bring about mutual understanding to South Africa's different races.'

Meanwhile, in Rhodesia – 1963 was the year that non-racial golf arrived in the Federation, this being the Rhodesias, Southern and Northern, and Nyasaland. Golfers of any race could enter for the national championship which was run by the Central Africa Golf Union.

Sadly, it remained an all-white event because none of the affiliated clubs had any black members. Membership of an affiliated club was a prerequisite for entry in the contest.

What was described as the first non-racial match in Rhodesia had taken place a short while before this when a European police side played against an African team in Salisbury (now Harare). The Africans were members of the Gleneagles Club which had a membership of about 70 including three whites.

As in all the leading centres in SA, so too in Rhodesia the game flourished among the black community and 'bush' clubs were formed and courses built around the country no matter how difficult this might have been. In Bulawayo there was Tshabalala and Zenzele, in Gwelo there was Mukoba, Gordon Mapfungautse, and Chizema, while in QueQue it was Zisco, and in Umtali there was Dangamvura

'Top non-White golfers have to rely on the mercy of White clubs to allow them to play on Mondays when courses are generally closed.'

In 1964, the WP Coloured Championships from year to year typically involved professional golfers who were playing for prize money, small as that might be. For the first time on record a WP Coloured Amateur Championship was held, and the venue was the Milnerton golf course. It was played as a 72-hole stroke-play event, with an entry of 78, and was won by Michael Godfrey (310).

Golfers came from all over the country and were accommodated in private homes in the coloured township. Beds were put in the crèche for those who did not have accommodation with friends.

In 1965 the OFS Non-European Championship was won by Jacob Gumbi, a former SA and Transvaal champion who had been playing since 1936. In terms of the permit issued by the Department of Community Development, access to the premises was restricted to 'non-whites'. President of the Orange Free State Golf Union (OFSGU), L.H. Marquard was asked to give away the prizes but because of the terms of the permit, he declined to do so.

BLACK WOMEN GOLFERS

The first mention of an African woman golfer in the records is Lily Themba in the 1930s, but nothing else is known about her.

In 1952, Mary Mofokeng (26) from Harrismith, OFS, was described as a young woman golfer – the first and only African women golfer in the country. Unfortunately, she could not find another competitor among her sex.

African women felt that golf took too long, expensive, and was nothing compared to tennis for gaiety and social freedom. Because of the lack of female competition, Mary did not take part in the SA Non-European golf championships at Wynberg, Johannesburg. Instead, she decided to spend her holidays in Durban while the championships were in progress for fear of embarrassing the crowd by being the only female spectator at Wynberg and the only golfer without a handicap.

In 1958, the Transvaal Non-European Mixed Four-somes championship was held at Wynberg and won by Miss Langa and M. Boice on 78 from Mrs S. Tau and D.R. Mashigo on 79.

In 1961, Dr N. Moeti became the first women golfer to win the 'SA Non-European Ladies Championship' at Umgeni from a field of four, scoring 207 for the 36 holes; Ms D. Xaha (Tvl) was runner-up, 208. The course was not in good condition such that the scores do not reflect the ability of these two players. 'Dr Moeti is a medical practitioner at Springs and is the wife of Dr Moeti, well-known medico and golfer.' The fact that golf was now being played by women is significant.

Rhodah Muridzo

In 2005, Rhodah Muridzo (Lewis Chitengwa's sister) won the Zimbabwe National Match Play and Stroke Play, 2nd Kenya Ladies Open, represented Zimbabwe in regional tournaments, and turned professional in 2009, subsequently being appointed as the Zimbabwe National Lady's coach.

Nobuhle Dlamini

In 2013 Nobuhle Dlamini, who had won everything of significance in a highly impressive amateur career, broke into the world's top ten in 2012 and rose to an eventual high of 'world number two', and whose career was then capped by a successful defence of her Sanlam South African Women's Amateur Stroke Play title in April 2013 at the Pretoria Country Club, cementing her status as the South African number one. In 2018 Nobuhle won her first women professional tournament on the Sunshine Ladies Tour.

Letitia Moses

Mention should also be made of sisters Amelia and Letitia Moses who both went to study at Coronationville University. Letitia played for SA in the Ladies World Cup, and in 1995 she was the SA female amateur 'Athlete of the Year', being the youngest lady to win the SA Ladies Amateur and the SA Ladies Junior championship, and thereafter earned the medallist honours in 1997 at Coronationville before turning professional.

CHAPTER THREE

Characters

THE AMAZING PETER LOUW

Peter Louw, Vice-President of the SA Non-European Golf Association – 'prince of non-European golf
management' organised golf among his fraternity
from late 1920–1970s. In the Cape Province, he organised
clubs, and then later formed them into district associations.

Peter was a tireless worker for the development of the
game among the non-white community countrywide and
did more than anyone to spread the golfing gospel. He
made regular annual trips around the country, particularly
in the Cape Province, and also further abroad, giving advice
on the formation of clubs where there were none and on or-
ganisational matters where clubs had already been formed.

After the war, with Peter Louw firmly at the helm,
things moved on apace. Under his leadership, a course was
laid out at Crawford, and the Midlands GC was formed on
the Cape Flats. At one stage there were four courses in use.
Monthly medals were arranged under Peter's watchful eye.

In 1948, Peter was much involved in the formation of
the SA Non-European Golf Association with its headquarters in Bloemfontein and as vice-president played a major
role in the organisation of the SA Non-European Open
Championship which became a regular annual event from
1949 onwards under the control of the Association.

Some indication of the difficulties facing the black golfing community is evident from the report on the 1956 SA
Non-European Open which was played in Cape Town on a
rough and ready course of nine holes laid out on the Cape
Flats. The grass greens were described as being as 'unpre-

dictable as an April day in Britain'. The Championship was won by A. (Polly) November with the incredible score of 305. Simon Hlapo came down from the Transvaal and finished in sixth place.

The 1960 SA Open was again scheduled in Cape Town, and to this end, a new 18-hole course was laid out at Wettonville, close to the Wetton railway station. In a press preview of the event, the comment was 'the going will be rough, but it is wonderful what these enthusiastic golfers can achieve with a man like Peter Louw to guide them'.

The postscript to the Wettonville project is that the Milnerton Golf Club offered their course to the Association for the Championship, the first time a white club had ever done so. This marked a turning point. Never again was the Non-European Open Championship played on a make-shift course carved out of the open veld. The Wettonville project did not go to waste and later that year played host to the Western Province Open Championship.

Over 800 spectators, many of them Europeans, followed Papwa round the Milnerton course early in January during his last round, when he won the SA Non-European Championship with returns of 80 80 74 74 – a fantastic effort given the ferocious south-easter that threatened to bowl every player off his feet. And he only won by two strokes from one of the Western Province players, R.L. Brown, who also had a 74 on the second day, when par could be rated at 78. It could have been rated at 80 during some portions of the first day.

By now, Peter Louw, vice-president of the SA Non-European Golf Association had been organising golf among his fraternity for over 30 years. A truly amazing man. He seems to live for golf. There can be no doubt that he played an exceptional and vital role in the history of the game in SA, one which few people today know about.

Above: President of the South African Non-European Golf Association, Alfred Maqubela, on his left Peter Louw, vice-president of the Association. Right photo: Peter Louw.

BLACK GOLF CLUBS

1928 Durban Indian Golf Club	1949 Richmond GC
1930 Payneville GC	Sandridge Park GC
1931 Wynberg G.C.	Palmdale
Benoni	Viceroy
Stirtonville	Coombhill
Germiston	Pinpointers
Randfontein	Homicide GC
1933 Pretoria	1952 Evaton GC
Bobby Jones Club	1959 Umgeni
Primville Club	P E
1934 Central GC	1963 Mfola
1938 St Andrews Club	Beaufort West
Transvaal x4 courses	Kimberley
Alexandria	Wettonville
Eligwa	1965 Bloemfontein
Humewood	Umlazi (18)
Methodist	Crawford
Peter Thompson	Thornhill
St Johnson	Midlands
Stirtonville	Durban
Top Notch	1967 Athlone
Dunlop Sixty Four	Grahamstown
1943 Sunningdale GC	Tantyi Bantu
1949 Penfold GC	'Grahamstown
Alberton GC	1968 Tantyi Bantu
Goodall GC	
Kliptown GC	
Pollack Park GC	

SIMON 'COX' HLAPO

The record books may be incomplete, but one thing cannot be questioned: before the arrival of Papwa Sewgolum in 1960, there was one name that you always found in the top three, usually at number one, Simon 'Cox' Hlapo.

'Cox' proved beyond doubt that he was the most consistent African golfer in the country before the advent of Papwa Sewgolum in 1960, and there were repeated calls for the T(N-E)GU to do something to enable Cox to play in the British Open – 'he'll certainly not disgrace us'.

Barred from playing on white-golf courses, still playing on their bush pop-up courses, the challenge for black golfers was how to finance a trip abroad with the British Open, especially following Bobby Locke's successes, as their focal point.

'Bra Cox' or 'The Great Cox', as he was affectionately known, matriculated at Marian Hill High school in Kwa-Zulu Natal. His classmates and friends at the time were Archbishop Emeratis Desmond Tutu, the music maestro, Professor Mzilikazi Khumalo, and former Drum magazine editor, Stan Mutjuwadi.

The role played by Simon Hlapo is of particular importance given the context of where black golf was positioned at the time. His was a name that showed up on every leader board. He dominated the game of golf not only with his aggressive style of play but with his uncompromising personality. This was at a time when black golfers were forced by the political laws of the time to have separate tournaments.

1963 Transvaal Open, Benoni
Simon 'Cox' Hlapo and Dave Motati on the first tee

Born in Alexandra Township in 1924, he was a Putco bus driver working the morning shifts, so by 11am, he would be hitting golf balls at the Alexandra golf course. One thing in his favour at the depot was that his big boss, Uncle Sam Mnisi, was the president of the SA(N-E)GU, and uncle Mnisi was understanding of Bra Cox's passion for golf. 'On reaching home, I would take my clubs and run to the Mofolo golf course. Even if I hit 6 balls I was always very happy after such a practise. Evey ball I hit meant something to my game.'

He started playing in the 1940s at two open velds; one at Alexandra near Wynberg along the old Pretoria Road and the other in Sophiatown on the outskirts of Tobby Street between Sophiatown and Linden, and it was there where the tall strong and humble Bra Cox enjoyed his game.

In 1949 he joined the Wynberg GC, where he was taught by one of the greats of golf, J. Jass and Uncle Sam, and he dominated the 'black' golfing fraternity between

1955–1959, before being overshadowed by Papwa Sew-golum when black golfers were permitted to start using proper golf courses.

After only playing the game for little over five years, he won the highest honour in South Africa when he was 30 years old, his first SA Championship played over the New Year weekend, and to make it more memorable, his team won the huge Drum Golf Trophy.

Suddenly black golf had their new hero, and adverts featuring him and brylcream appeared in numerous magazine and newspaper advertisements

He was called the Maestro of the sand greens, mainly because of the unique way he hit the ball during his drives and chipping. 'When he had focused his playing form and rhythm, we all knew he was untouchable, we all knew we were in trouble.' (Richard 'Boikie' Mogoerane)

Bra Cox, although cool and icy on the golf course, was a bundle of fun off the course, frequently playing practical jokes on his friends. He won over 27 tournaments including the SA Non-European Open in 1955, '57, '59, runner-up in 1961, and as late as 1964, '67 and '68, then aged 44, he was still able to finish in the top five.

Following another generous sponsorship by Alf Mag-erman of 100 pounds at the 1959 Kroonstad Open tournament, Bra Cox won with a record breaking score of 68 68 (136) followed by David Motati (140), Ronnie Ditsebe (141) and D Harrison (141).

He captured the Orange Free State Open in 1953, '60, '61, '62 and '63, third in '68, the Transvaal Open in 1957, '59, '61, '62 and '63, and the Northern OFS Championship and the North Eastern Transvaal Open in 1959. Griqualand West second 1966, third '64 and '67.

His last major win was the Luyt Lager Tournament in 1972, aged 48, when most of his peers had given up competitive golf, and finally he won the 3M Classic at the Soweto Country Club in 1983.

Bra Cox became a role model to many black golfers. 'Every player wanted to play like him.' said John Mashego. Sadly he was too old when the doors opened for black golfers to compete in major tournaments.

Like so many other wonderfully talented golfers of the time, his career was undoubtedly curtailed due to political policies, but it didn't prevent him from playing both the game itself and a role in the administration of black golf affairs.

He died in 1986 aged 61, the towering father of black golf, pennyless, but his community, friends and family rallied and ensured he received a proper send-off.

In 2011 he was inducted into the Southern Africa Golf Hall of Fame, and in 2018, the Minister of Sport, Tokozile Xasa, awarded him the 'Andrew Mlangeni Green Jacket' award.

SIMON 'COX' HLAPO   (1924–1986)

- Leading black golfer in the Transvaal and OFS for many years, and probably South Africa before the advent of Papwa Sewgolum in 1960.

- His career was curtailed due to the Apartheid policies of the time, and he was not allowed to play in 'white' tournaments.

- 1980 elected Chairman of the Tournament Players Association – controlling body for black golf.

- 2011 inducted into the Southern Africa Golf Hall of Fame.

- 2018 Andrew Mlangeni Green Jacket award.

Disadvantaged by apartheid – prevented from playing the SAPGA 'white' tour.

Record

Non-European SA Tournament victories (28)
- South African Non-European Open (3), 2nd (1)
- Provincial Non-European Titles (10), 2nd (3)
- Lesser SA Tournaments (15)

- South African Non-European Open 1955, 57, 59
- South African Non-European Open 2nd 1961; 3rd 1968; 4th 1962, 67
- OFS Non-European Open 1953, 60, 61, 62, 63
- OFS Non-European Open 2nd 1966; 3rd 1968
- Transvaal Non-European Open 1957, 59, 61, 62, 63
- Transvaal Non-European Open 2nd 1958; 3rd 1953, 60 (low score of 63)
- Natal Non-European Open 3rd 1960, 64

- Griqualand West Non-European Open 2nd 1965; 3rd 1964, 67
- Transvaal Non-European Matchplay 1955, 61 – semi-finalist
- North Eastern Transvaal Non-European Open 1957, 2nd 1958
- Northern Free State Non-European Championship 1959
- Western Transvaal Non-European Open 2nd 1959
- Kroonstad Non-European Open 1959, 64
- Transvaal Non-European Invitation Tournament 1962
- OFS Non-European Open Special Strokeplay 1964
- Far North & Eastern Open 1966
- Bantu Team Championship 1953
- Litchfield-Bornman Tournament 1958
- Green Valley Open 1961
- Special 72-hole Non-European Tournament 1968
- Luyt Lager Tournament 1972
- 3M Classic 1983

* records incomplete

CHAPTER FOUR

Professional Tournaments

PROVINCIAL RIVALRY

W hat was important to note was that it was the prominent white golfers who inspired the black golfers, and gave them a benchmark to aim at, as could be seen by the colourful names attributed to them, such as Atrol 'Sid Brews' Mazibuko and David 'Bobby Locke' Motati, together with other interesting nicknames such as 'Otto' Lee, 'Goli-Goli' Mdeni, 'Baby-face boy' Chowglay, 'Bra Cox' Hlapo, 'Bambata' Boodhun, 'Boikie' Mogoerane, 'Star' Naidoo, 'Polly' November, J. 'Fiver' Mazibuko, 'FM' Paul, 'Doe' Khumou, 'Ram' Rajdaw, 'Eddia' Johnson-Sidebe, and 'Papwa' Sewgolum.

In 1954, Papwa (25) won his first Natal Non-European Open, and in 1955 Chowglay (22) won the WP Non-European Open. Likewise, Gary Player (19) earned his first provincial title in 1955 winning the East Rand Open, and then proceeded to win the SA Open the following year.

His rigorous practice regimen contributed to his success, and he was quoted as saying, 'The harder I practice, the luckier I get'. Their paths were yet to cross, although Papwa had already caddied for Player when he visited Durban.

Ismail Chowglay and Papwa Sewgolum, born four years apart, both disadvantaged by apartheid, were not permitted to play on the 'white' SA Tour until into their thirties. Between them they won at least 52 Non-European Provincial Open titles (probably more as the records are incomplete), Sewgolum 38 (second nine times) and Chowglay 14 (second eight times), and 12 SA Non-European Open tiles, with Sewgolum winning 10 (second once) and Chowglay 2 (second three times).

Even though there are gaps in the results of a number of provincial and national Non-European tournaments, it is interesting to review how the dominant golfers, Hlapo, Sewgolum, Chowglay, Tshabalala, and Mogoerane fared when competing against each other. This is not to take away from the fact that many of Papwa's victories were often by the proverbial mile, sometimes by 10, 20, and as high as 27 shots ahead when in 1964 Papwa beat Chowglay and van Dieman for the WP Non-European Open title, this was especially so during the 1960s. But every now and then his rivals rose to challenge him until eventually, Vincent Tshabalala took over his mantle.

Papwa dominated black provincial golf in Natal, but it is interesting to examine their records in other centres, especially the Cape where Chowglay prevailed, (similarly 'Cox' Hlapo dominated early on in the Transvaal as well as the OFS before Richard Mogoerane).

Played over the brand new 18-hole course at Wetton-ville, another of the Cape Flats courses, the 1961 WP Open Non-European Championship was won by P. van Dieman. With scores of 72 74 77 70 (293), he finished two shots better than his protégé Chowglay. It was a close thing. Van Dieman holed out from 70 yards at the last hole.

For some years, Ismail Chowglay was regarded as the best non-white golfer in the Western Province; he won the 1967 Western Province Non-European Championship at King David CC with a score of 77 77 77 75 (306). He was the only player to break 80 in all four rounds. Runner-up was Wally Lewis, including the best round of the tournament, a 72. David Motati, the winner of the 1966 SA Non-White title, was leading with nine holes to go, but he found plenty of trouble in the King David rough and took 87 for his final round for a total of 314.

Papwa Sewgolum, Ismail Chowglay, David Motati

King David CC closed the clubhouse for the duration
of the tournament, and no European members or spectators were allowed on the course, much as they might have
wished to see the play.

Papwa demolished the field at Royal Cape in January
1964. The 1968 Western Province Non-European Championship was played on the newly-opened Athlone course for
the first time and was won by the holder, Chowglay with
a score of 297. Papwa was runner-up on 305. Chowglay
played steady golf throughout while Sewgolum got off to a
poor start with 83 in the first round and could never recov-
er from this setback.

Papwa did not play in the WP Championship every year,
but when he did make the trip to Cape Town, he was always
a significant threat. So, in 1969, it was at the relatively new
Athlone course when he came back to Cape Town as the SA
Non-European Champion and won the WP Non-European

Championship as well. His four round total was 74 74 76 72 (296) with Vincent Tshabalala runner-up on 298. Papwa had to wait for the last round before he obtained the lead, but his brilliant 72 was too good for the opposition.

Ismail Chowglay, the former champion, had a great victory in the 1971 Western Province Championship held at the Athlone GC. With scores of 79 76 72 75 (302) he beat defending champion Abe van Rooyen (306) into second place. His prize money was R200.

The 1973 WP Non-European Championship was again won by Ismail Chowglay played on the Athlone course. He was at that time still the leading player in the Western Province.

It was Papwa Sewgolum (now 47) again, in a canter, winning the 1976 Western Province Non-European Championship by six shots from Johnson Chetty. His scores were 78 70 76 77 (301). Papwa and Noel Maart were level after 45 holes, but then Papwa started to forge ahead. This was to be his final victory outside his home of Natal.

SOUTH AFRICAN NON-EUROPEAN OPENS

In 1960, when it all changed and for the first time, the Non-European Championship was played on a 'white' course. The Milnerton Golf Club made their course available to the SA Golf Association for their championship and, perhaps because of this, Papwa did make the trip to Cape Town and ended up winning his first SA title. It was not to be the last.

Shrewd judges of golf who saw Papwa battling his way through a near galeforce Cape south-easter to a brilliant victory reached a unanimous conclusion; Here is a golfer who is on the way to becoming great.

The SA Non-European Open was always scheduled for New Year's Day and the following day, that was 36 holes per day (the Natal provincial open was played on Christmas and Boxing Day) as these were the only times available for black golfers to play a tournament at A-listed courses, but they had to make the most of an unfair arrangement.

Just like the domination of the SA 'White' Open by Bobby Locke in winning nine Opens in nine attempts, and Player winning it thirteen times, so to having broken the ice, there was no stopping him, and Papwa completely dominated the championship right through the 1960s. In the 11 years up to and including 1970, he won the title eight times and shared it once. This was with Vincent Tshabalala at Alexander GC in East London in 1965.

Having won again in 1961 (where Mr Cannon became the first European sponsor for the SA Non-European Association), the following year at Kimberley, Papwa was not at his best – 1962 was not a good year generally for Papwa – and he finished in eighth place behind Ismail Chowglay, with Hlapo also only finishing fifth.

The SA Non-European Golf Association were hoping to play their championship over the Bloemfontein Golf Club's course but the permit from the Government for non-Europeans to play over a course occupied by European golfers was not granted due to the Free State statute which forbade any Indian from staying overnight in the Province. Instead, it was played at the Kimberley Golf Club.

Meanwhile, Alf Magerman, a leading coloured Free State sportsman, gave R100 to the SA Non-European Golf Association. Shortly before this, he had given R300 prize money in promoting the Green Valley Open championship at Kroonstad, won by Hlapo.

Besides these administrators, the most energetic and able organiser of the tournament was again Peter Louw, vice-President of the SA Non-European Golf Association, to whom much of the credit for the successful event was due.

As ever, many people gathered round to give support to the tournament. There was a civic reception at which the

Mayor of Kimberley, Mr G.J. Hugo, presented the winner, Ismail Chowglay, the Western Cape champion, and possibly the finest left-hand golfer in the country (except for Bob Charles, winner of The Open, who married Verity, a SA girl, and when not competing abroad spent much of his time living in Johannesburg), with his prize after scores of 72 74 74 77 (297). The tournament prize money was R300. Chowglay had every reason to feel optimistic about the future of his career.

Suddenly Ismail was now the flavour of the month and was even approached by sponsors, for instance, he featured in advertisements for 'Wilson Three-X Mints'

Following his victory, a resolution was taken by the South African (Non-European) Golf Association (SA(N-E) GA) to send him on an overseas campaign that included the British Open. A levy was placed on each of the nine affiliates to the association to assist with Ismail's trip. Papwa hoped to raise enough money to join Ismail in his campaign.

However in The Open, Ismail failed to progress beyond the qualifying round after opening with a reasonable 75, he then blew up with an 83 and missed the cut.

The SA Non-European Golf Association was non-racial such that their clubs and their unions determined that there shall be no differentiation between Coloured, Indian and African golfers.

Also in 1962, the government gave R3,000 'as tangible proof of the government's desire to support the establishment of separate sports facilities for non-whites'. It was suggested that this was the policy the government was holding out as justification for banning the previous week's non-white golf tournament at the white-Irene golf course. Their decision stated that competitors would be 'insulted by being disallowed clubhouse facilities'. Furthermore, if they allowed the Open to take place, this would pave the way for mixed sport as the field included black, coloured, and Indian golfers, including Chowglay and Sewgolum. As such it was described as 'an apartheid grant', and many prominent members of the coloured community were by no means happy with this. Another donor to the fund was Gary Player who gave R60.

The 1963 SA(N-E)GA was played at Walmer CC, and anticipation was rife. Would Chowglay once again dethrone the iconic Sewgolum? The tournament committee consisted of Messrs Peter Louw (vice-president), D.R. Phala (secretary/treasurer), Louis Nelson (assistant secretary and now Papwa's manager), and Samson Mnisi (assistant treasurer).

At the end of round one, Chowglay the defending champion was one ahead of Papwa equalling the course record and maintained this lead after round two. But this changed and after round three, Papwa found himself three shots ahead of Chowglay thanks to his deadly putting, and as Chowglay's game fell apart, Papwa simply ran away with the championship

A 75 in the third round gave him a lead by three strokes over Chowglay, while a 74 in the last round added another nine strokes to his lead as Papwa went on to win by 13 strokes, Chowglay still being the challenger though that is perhaps not the right word

It is true that the ball was not running well for Chowglay in the last two rounds, time and again the putts were just slipping past, but there was no doubt who was the better man on the day. Papwa was out in 34 in the last round, but neither he nor Chowglay shone in the last nine holes, played in a continuous heavy drizzle.

Throughout the tournament Papwa's chipping was deadly, and most of the time so was his putting. But it was the approaches and chips that made the putting-count so small. Accordingly, Papwa won back his national title from the previous year's winner Ismail Chowglay with scores of 75 77 75 74 (301).

Papwa received the J.M. Jass Floating Trophy; named after the founder of the SA(N-E)GA in 1947, who died in 1953, and with it a professional purse of R500, donated by Gordon's Dry Gin Co.

Other trophies included the Drum Trophy for the Inter-provincial Teams Championship and Cannon Trophy for the Inter-Club Championship. In addition, there was the UTC trophy for the inaugural competition for the Seniors Championship, age limit 55. What was so remarkable about the play of the two leaders was their grip. Papwa, a right-hander, gripped the club with the left hand under the right on the shaft: Chowglay, a left-hander, gripped with the right hand under the left. Call it the wrong grip or the reverse grip – what you will – but it worked with these two golfers.

Everything possible was done to make the tournament a success: food, refreshments and equipment were on hand when required, and a record attendance was most capably catered for. As ever, the ladies of the golf section did much to add to the success of the meeting.

The Mayor of Port Elizabeth, Mr Monty van der Vyver, arranged a civic reception in Port Elizabeth mayoral reception in the Feather Market Hall. Among the speakers were Messrs F. Erasmus, executive member, EP(N-E)GA; Alfred Maqubela, president, SA(N-E)GA; D. Durow, representing Gordon's Gin Co., who sponsored the tournament; R.

Simpson, vice-president, EPGU; and champion amateur golfer Ben Ryan, captain of the golf section.

Several speakers paid tribute to Peter Louw, vice-president of the SA(N-E)GA, for the admirable manner in which he had organised the tournament.

1963 Sewsunker Sewgolum is seen teeing off in the final round of the SA Non-European Open at Walmer Country Club, Port Elizabeth. He won by 13 strokes from Ismail Chowglay (holder, on the left). S Dondashe is in the middle. Papwa's left-hand-under-right-hand grip is plainly visible. It is two handed, not overlapping (Photograph by A Doulman, Weimar).

In 1964, Sewsunker 'Papwa' Sewgolum was once again the winner at Glendower GC with scores of 71 72 70 75 (288), followed by a huge gallery. He received the first prize of R200 plus R12.50 for each of the first three rounds for the leading score of the day. Stylish Edward 'Otto' Lee and Johannes Semenya tied for second on 300, with 'baby-face' Ismail Chowglay fourth, followed by Simon 'Cox' Hlapo and David 'Bobby Locke' Motati.

Prizes were presented including the J. Jass trophy to Papwa by Mrs I.W. Pitman at a civic reception in the Coronationville Hall at which the Mayor of Johannesburg, M.J.F. Oberholzer, M.P.C. and the Mayoress were present.

The R500 tournament was played over three days under the banner of the SA(N-E)GA and attracted an entry of 190 players, with the result that there was a pre-qualifying event with 40 golfers going into the championship proper.

Clearly, Papwa's victories were having an effect on the explosion of black players at the non-white golf courses. Meanwhile, top black golfers had to rely on the mercy of white clubs to allow them to play on Mondays when courses were generally closed.

PROVINCIAL RESULT COMPARISON

Chowglay – Hlapo – Sewgolum – Mogoerane - Tshabalala

Transvaal Non-European Open

YEAR	FIRST	SECOND	THIRD
1953			S Hlapo
Pre-1957			
1957	S Hlapo		
1958		S Hlapo	
1959	S Hlapo		
1960			S Hlapo
1961	S Hlapo 68 70 67 69 (274)		
1962	S Hlapo (274)		
1963	S Hlapo *65 course record		
1964	S Sewgolum (284) *65 course record		
1965	S Sewgolum 70 70 71 71 (282)		
1966	S Sewgolum 69 70 70 73 (282)	S Hlapo	R Mogoerane
1967	R Mogoerane (302)	S Sewgolum	S Hlapo
1968	I Chowglay 73 69 73 73 (287)		
1969	S Sewgolum	I Chowglay	
1970	S Sewgolum	V Tshabalala	
1971			
1972	V Tshabalala (295)	S Sewgolum (297)	
1973-79			
1980			
1982			
1983	I Chowglay		

O.F.S. Non-European Open

YEAR	FIRST	SECOND	THIRD
1960	S Hlapo (272)		
1961	S Hlapo (268)		
1962	S Hlapo 67 74 68 72 (281)		
1963	S Hlapo 76 76 77 75 (304)		
1964	I Chowglay		
1965			
1966	S Sewgolum 69,70,70,73 (282)	S Hlapo 69 76 75 71 (291)	R Mogoerane 73 75 75 76 (299)
1968	R Mogoerane (302)	S Sewgolum (304)	S Hlapo (306)
1969	S Sewgolum		
1973	R Mogoerane		
1974	R Mogoerane		
1975	R Mogoerane		
1976	R Mogoerane		
1977	R Mogoerane		
1978	R Mogoerane		
1979	R Mogoerane		
1980	R Mogoerane		
1981	R Mogoerane		

Natal Non-European Open

YEAR	FIRST	SECOND	THIRD
1954	S Sewgolum		
1955	S Sewgolum		
1956		S Sewgolum *lost playoff	
1957	S Sewgolum		
1958	S Sewgolum		

YEAR	FIRST	SECOND	THIRD
1959	S Sewgolum		
1960	S Sewgolum 74 72 75 73 (294)		S Hlapo
1961	S Sewgolum 73 73 71 73 (290)		
1962	S Sewgolum		
1963	S Sewgolum		
1964		S Sewgolum (294)	S Hlapo (297)
1965	S Sewgolum 72 71 73 75 (291)		
1966	S Sewgolum 70 71 73 74 (288)		V Tshabalala
1967	S Sewgolum		
1968	S Sewgolum (286) *63 3rd round		
1969	S Sewgolum *by 21 shots		
1970	S Sewgolum		
1971	V Tshabalala	S Sewgolum	
1972	V Tshabalala 73 69 69 71 (282)		
1973			
1974	S Sewgolum		
1975	S Sewgolum 73 73 77 71 (294)	I Chowglay (303)	
1976	I Chowglay *play-off	S Sewgolum	
1977	S Sewgolum		
1983		R Mogoerane	

Western Province Non-European Open

YEAR	FIRST	SECOND	THIRD
1956	I Chowglay		
1957			
1958			
1960	S Sewgolum		
1961		I Chowglay	
1962			
1963	I Chowglay		
1964	S Sewgolum 68 65 72 70 (275)	I Chowglay (302)	
1965	I Chowglay		
1966	I Chowglay		
1967	I Chowglay		
1968	I Chowglay (297)	S Sewgolum (305)	
1969	S Sewgolum 74 74 76 72 (296)	V Tshabalala (298)	
1970		R Mogoerane	
1971	I Chowglay 79 76 72 75 (302)		
1973	I Chowglay		
1974			
1975			
1976	S Sewgolum 78 70 76 77 (301)		

Eastern Province Non-European Open

YEAR	FIRST	SECOND	THIRD
1963	I Chowglay (309) *course record	S Sewgolum (310)	
1964	S Sewgolum	I Chowglay	
1965-67			
1968	I Chowglay	S Sewgolum	

Griqualand West Non-European Open

YEAR	FIRST	SECOND	THIRD
1960	S Sewgolum 69 72 72 72 (285)		
1961	S Sewgolum 75 68 69 73 (285) *68 course record		
1963	S Sewgolum (285)	I Chowglay (293)	
1964	S Sewgolum 77 72 74 72 (295)	I Chowglay 75 75 73 78 (301)	S Hlapo 80 76 77 77 (310)
1965	S Sewgolum 71 69 70 71 (281)	S Hlapo 75 69 71 71 (286)	
1966		S Hlapo	
1967	S Sewgolum (300)		S Hlapo 78 79 74 76 (307)
1969	S Sewgolum 78 78 75 69 (300)		

Chapter Five

Challenge to Apartheid – The Long Road to Non-Racial Golf

'Two roads diverged in a wood, and I – I took the one less travelled by, and that has made the difference'.

Robert Frost

THE 'PAPWA' STORY – AGAINST ALL ODDS

Papwa Sewgolum was able to change the individual focused sport of golf, and prove that blacks can become the face of change.

Golf is a game generally associated with the wealthy. One has to pay considerable tuition fees to learn the game, purchase expensive golf clubs, balls, clothing, special shoes – and then pay up to R500 or more to play 18 holes.

Above all, one needs time to play golf. While South Africa's black nouveau riche are now found frequenting the golf courses in our democratic dispensation, the majority of black golfers in past years were working-class citizens who learnt the game while caddying for whites, and were usually allowed to play on white courses on Mondays. In the whole of Durban, for example, there was just one golf course for blacks, Curries Fountain.

But ultimately no memorial, no biography, no written account or account of any other nature will be able to reflect the ignominy, hurt and shame that the crippling racial laws inflicted on the emotions of the majority of South Africans. They were restricted from participating in the broadest possible opportunities – such as to play golf when they wanted to, loved it, and were good at it.

Due to an almost total lack of proper equipment or anything resembling an actual golf facility, and the endemic poverty affecting the majority of black person in SA when compared to the white population, and despite the obvious talent, the standard of play was lower than that of the affluent white golf scene.

Talented black golfers of the past include names like Ramnath Boodhun, R.T. Singh, Vincent Tshabalala, Jacob Gumbi, Ronnie Ditsebe, Bob Nkuna, L Khatidi, Johannes Simenya, Eddie Johnson-Sedibe, David Motati, Richard Mogoerane, Ismail Chowglay, Simon Hlapo, Johnson Chetty, Daddy Naidoo, and many others.

The most celebrated black golfer, however, was Sewsunker Sewgolum.

Sewsunker[3] 'Papwa' Sewgolum was a SA professional golfer of ethnic Indian origin, who carved a niche for himself in golfing folklore when he became the first golfer of colour to win a provincial 'white' open in SA. He became an international symbol of the sports boycott movement and hated race laws when pictures of him appeared receiving his trophy outside in the rain were published across the world, because due to apartheid, he was not allowed to enter the 'whites-only' clubhouse.

He is regarded as 'the greatest black golfer produced in this country', and one who would certainly have been among the country's best ever golfers of all races were it not for apartheid. His story exposes and highlights the poor sportsmen of the world with the wealthy, and directly; as a result, a life of triumphs and tragedies.

Papwa was famous for both his unorthodox method of holding the club, with a back-handed grip, hands positioned the opposite way to the traditional grip, as much as he was for his 'short game' - pitching, chipping, putting and bunker shots within 100m of the hole.

He was always a drawcard with an enthusiastic gallery, 'Papwa's army' or the 'Indian army', and he used to get around the golf course faster than most. He would walk quickly up to his ball, take a few practice swings, and even if in a bunker, blast out without further ado. He also putted with his unorthodox grip, but as a spectator muttered, 'who cares – he still sinks 'em doesn't he?' His long irons were punched crisply, and around the greens' his approach shots were deadly.

---

3   Correct spelling is Sewshanker 'Papwa' Sewgolum — not Sewsunker 'Papwa' Sewgolum as it appears in many articles and books. However due to the passing of time, I have spelt his first name as 'Sewsunker' so as not to create confusion

As a teenager, he began shooting sub-par rounds as well as several unofficial 62s – well below the Beachwood course record of 64. Analysts said he was able to draw on his deep spirituality as a practising Hindu to release any physical and psychological tension in his body – on and off the course.

Papwa had already won the Natal Indian Amateur in 1946 at the nine-hole Curries Fountain course with borrowed clubs and shoes, aged 16, and the Natal Non-European Open Championship in 1954, '55, '57 and '58 (second in '56).

He was keen to play professionally but did not have the funds to do so.

For the first time in the history of the South African Open Championship, or of any other championship held under the control of the South African Golf Union (SAGU) and its affiliated provincial unions, a non-European golfer, Sewsunker 'Papwa' Sewgolum, was a competitor.

These historic words were reported on the SA Open Championship held at the East London Golf Club in March 1961.

However, as often happened, the tension of not knowing whether he could play or not until the last minute, not to mention that he was given no opportunity to practice over the course before the tournament took the edge off his game.

Nevertheless, Sewsunker 'Papwa' Sewgolum was one of the most promising names in early SA golf, before his struggle with inequality reduced his legacy to a mere 'could-have-been' story etched in local history.

HUMBLE BEGINNINGS

But for apartheid, South Africa could have had another world-beating golfer at the same time as Gary Player.

Sewgolum's grandparents had come to SA in 1860 along with many other indentured Indians from Calcutta and Madras to work in the sugarcane plantations on the Natal North coast. They hoped to make a new life in the land of milk and honey, and prosper, and to get away from their grinding poverty and punishing colonial taxes (which would eventually lead to Gandhi's march to the sea against the salt tax) much like Bambata's grandparents. His father had already told Papwa stories about the great Mahatma Gandhi, one of two black lawyers in SA previously living up the road in Pietermaritzburg, who subsequently returned to India to confront the British Colonial government. If only someone would do this for the SA Indians.

The first group of 342 indentured Indian labourers to work the sugarcane plantations arrived in the Natal Colony in 1860 speaking Tamil, Telugu, and Hindi, and embarked from the 'Tarulo' from Madras, a goods ship, followed by the 'Belvedere' from Calcutta, having secured a three-year contract paying 30 shillings a month to cut sugarcane.

They came because the colonial authorities found that local black Africans were economically self-sufficient and thus unwilling to subject themselves to employment by colonial farmers, while other colonial powers believed that the 'hunting and warrior' African culture of the time was incompatible with a sudden shift to employed labour.

Over the next 50 years, more than 150,000 Indian labourers arrived in Durban, and many stayed on after the expiration of their contract. This led to a further influx of wealthier established Indian tradesmen and businessmen paying their own fares and travelling as British subjects, whose numbers now started to cause concern in government circles.

Papwa, meaning 'small' or 'darling child' as he was known, of Indian descent, was designated as 'coloured' in the country's prismatic social structure. He was born in December 1928 to a blind mother in a tin shanty in Riverside, in a part of the world with a history of oppression.

This was about two kilometres from the all-white Beachwood Golf Club, and three years after the opening of the first black golf club, the Durban Indian Golf Club at Curries Fountain. It was in Natal that Southern Africans experienced their first taste of systematic segregation, under the British colonial 'Shepstone system'.

Riverside was situated in Durban North with unparalleled views across a magnificent green belt, stretching from the Umgeni River mouth with its abundant bird life on the Umgeni Estuary, across the Indian Ocean, and towards the beachfront beyond. A mere 12 minutes walk to the beach, set one kilometre from the banks of the Umgeni River, yet close to the city centre of Durban.

Pounding surf crashed on the shore not far from the little shack which he called home. The tropical air was humid as Papwa and his father left for their late afternoon fishing along the Umgeni River to supplement his meagre wages.

Papwa held the greaseproof paper with their bait, dough made from flour and water, and his father explained that by placing some dough in a bottle in the water, it would attract smaller fish to swim into the bottle and these could be used as bait for the bigger fish.

Just then they heard a shout of 'fore' as a white ball crashed into the colourful bougainvillea bush close by. His dad retrieved the ball, only to be accosted by an elderly red-faced man holding a stick as he came crashing through the bush wanting to know whether the 'coolie' was stealing his golf ball.

Such was his introduction to the game of golf and it peaked Papwa's interest. When the man was told that the ball had nearly hit his little boy, he gave a half-hearted apology and gave his father a tickey as a reward for finding the ball.

While fishing, and in the quiet moments, his father explained the game of golf to young Papwa, and how the great Ramnath 'Bambata' Boodhun, a Hindu man like them, who started out as a caddy-boy, and lived just down the road, had gone to play in the white man's British Open at Muirfield, the greatest tournament in the world. Also, when he was a bit bigger, he too could go and carry the white man's bag of golf sticks and earn some money

Papwa immediately told his father that he would be as great as Bambata, even greater and that he too would go and play in The Open. His father looked down at his little 'laaitjie' boy, and smiled, proud to have his son tagging along for company. 'Little boys are like dogs', he thought, 'they got to be taught', as he started to whittle away a small syringa tree branch.

Finding a pebble, his father demonstrated how to hit the 'ball', and how to putt. Papwa was intrigued. Later, they made their way back home and his father pointed out the Durban golf course, and the strange white men, as they hit the white ball into the bush, retrieved it, and then hit it back into another bush.

To Papwa it seemed funny, and excitedly he described the scene to his mother. The strange men with canvas bags, and what looked like thin bamboo shoots, hitting this little white ball trying to get it into a small hole with a flag, on what appeared to be a freshly-mown lawn, clapping each other on the back, while Indian boys carrying bags watched and exchanged money amongst themselves at the end of the hole.

Young Papwa Sewgolum had witnessed this unique sport which was sweeping the colony, a game that had commenced in SA with the first member golf club in 1886 (or possibly earlier at Cronstadt in 1878). This was the Cape Golf Club (later Royal Cape GC) at Cape Town, although prior to this there had already been 3-hole golf courses constructed at military bases in Port Elizabeth and Natal by British soldiers to keep themselves occupied.

It may have been a world away for a poor Indian boy, but Papwa was fascinated, and the seed was planted. He too would one day stride those fairways followed by hordes of supporters with the sole aim of getting the white ball into the hole. His mother smiled at his babbling, then prepared their small spiced fish supper and it was time for bed.

While his father played football for the local Indian team, Papwa would sneak away, squirming his way through the Beachwood Golf Club's fence and watch these strange white men at play, waiting for the opportunity to 'find' a golf ball for his own use. He had his father whittle him a syringa stick putter, and after placing tin cups in the sandy ground at home, he challenged his father and little brother to a 'game of golf'.

Every night he putted over his 'green', placing balls

around the cup, first from 2-feet, and when he had holed these, he would place them once again around the cup, but this time a foot further away, until he had sunk these putts before extending further back.

Like other Indian boys, he also fashioned golf clubs from branches and rolled iron, and taught himself to swing with what was to become his famed cross-handed grip (hands positioned the opposite way to the traditional grip) to get the ball quickly into the air due to the light weight of his 'clubs'.

This grip had become popular with the other caddy boys throughout the country for the same reason, and was called the 'caddy grip'. Papwa's future provincial rival, Ismail Chowglay would also use this grip with much success in Cape Town, and later Vincent Tshabalala, who was destined to win the French Open, with his long irons.

As he did not go to school, he sometimes played 'golf' with his friends after a midday swim in the Umgeni River. By now, their clubs were mid-ribs of palm leaves and their golf balls palm nuts. Three sticks were set up around the river bank, indicating where the holes were:

> *But it was their mannerisms — obviously modelled on their pet 'Bwana' — their power drives, the wrist play, the disgust after a bad shot, the putting stances. Everything, and even after all the practice swings, mimicry, etc., they cracked the old palm nut as to the manner born, with perfect timing, as far as any man born of woman could hit a palm nut with a palm-leaf mid-rib, on river-sand, in the same set of circumstances.*

As his hands were still tiny, Papwa's hands were separated with no overlapping or interlocking of fingers to assist the wrist in holding the club. He swung the 'club' back past parallel almost bouncing off his right shoulder, with his hip fully turned, and then with his trademark dip, as he bent his knees to get to it, he swung downwards as hard as possible, often falling back onto his right foot, which later became a part of his style, and whipped his right hip through the swing to generate the clubhead speed.

His putting style was interesting with his left foot leading his right, helping to counteract the wind and steady himself. Given his grip, he would 'pop' the ball putting down into the stroke .

His grip was an unorthodox way of holding the club with a back-handed hold, hands left-to-right, an unconventional hold sometimes found in geniuses (many top golfers today use Papwa's cross-handed grip for putting, even chipping, but virtually no one uses it today for all shots). 'I believe a man should swing a club the best way he knows how', Papwa told Golf Digest in 1964.

Before long Papwa had found an old rusted club in the bush alongside the fairway, which his father cut down for him as it was far too long and heavy, and with the few balls he had found, Papwa began playing whenever he went to watch his dad fishing. Much like the famous Seve Ballesteros starting out as a caddy with one club, with which he would one day learn to play.

And he would watch the great Bobby Locke (already the SA Open winner – who would go on to win four British Opens and nine SA Opens – that is every time he entered, until he virtually lost the sight of his eye in a train-crossing accident), the greatest putter in the world, sneaking onto the course whenever he came to play.

Locke would pace around the hole as if he was in a bull-fight. First, he would look behind the hole, then from side to side, and finally from behind his ball to make sure of all the twists and turns, knowing the ball would also move away from any mountain or koppie and towards water. He would approach the hole examining the way the grass was leaning; if it were leaning towards the hole, it would be a fast putt, and a slow putt if it was away from the hole. Finally, he looked at the position of the cup in the hole, as if the hole was more upright at the back, he could hit the putt just a little firmer.

He would crouch down on his haunches behind the ball, twirling his famous wooden-shafted blade putter until he could actually visualise and see the path along which he needed to putt the ball. Now standing over the ball with his right foot behind the left, he took the blade back in a curve following the line of his feet, a closed face, pressing forward brought it down onto the ball, minimising the bounce as the blade made contact and conveying the spin onto the ball. Magically, the ball hooked from right to left as it made its way towards the hole.

He gave the impression, and the false hope to many an opponent that he would hook the ball offline, but he always hit it in the middle of the putter in the right direction, and amazingly, it would make its way into the hole. Nobody, no one ever hooked their putts, yet Locke was the greatest putter the world had seen, and he viewed the putt as having three opportunities to go into the hole, from the left side, the right side, or directly into the hole. And so Papwa learnt, and his confidence and concentration grew.

Then suddenly his father, his role model, passed away in 1938 when he was just 11, leaving Papwa as a breadwinner. His sister helped around the house, but Indian women did not go out to work, so he had no alternative but to go out and try and earn some money to support his blind mother, sister, and younger brother.

Eventually, he found work as a thread-cutter in a garment factory in Prince Edward Street in Durban. But three years later, to make ends meet he was earning money caddying at the Beachwood Country Club – caddies were also allowed to play on Monday when the course was 'closed'. It was here that Papwa learnt the art of golf.

I had no love for the game of golf when first I started. I was 13, and my father had died leaving me to help my mother and younger brother. My stomach was my introduction to golf, and at seven shillings a week I wasn't able to fill it often.

So Papwa had learnt to play, first by knocking pebbles along the beach shore with a stick, and later by caddying for and watching the rich white folk hack around the golf course. Sometimes giving advice but usually having to remain quiet when they admonished him for their poor shot-making.

There were times when he brought home as little as 7/6d (R14.50) per week (he was paid one shilling and six-pence plus a possible tip per round) and the family often went hungry. But he was becoming involved with the game of golf and practised whenever he could. He would start out every morning with a rusty 5-iron and two old golf balls and hit these balls two kilometres, all the way to the golf club, including over the river. On his return at 4pm, after carrying two bags during the day, once again he would hit the golf balls on his way back home.

There were sand dunes on both sides of his home, and a stream between them, and each evening, he would hit golf balls from one end to the other.

All caddies were allowed to play at Beachwood on a Monday (likewise at other clubs) from 5–9am. So in the early morning hours around 04:30 they would catch the bus to steal a round on those hallowed grounds, just as long as they could play 18 holes before the club members started to arrive at 08:30.

If they missed this time, they had to wait another week

before they could play. Of course, people of colour were not allowed to be members of golf clubs at this time.

Allowing caddies to play on Mondays encouraged them to have a chance at the game of golf, and on the other hand, for them to show responsibility insofar as filling in divots and learning the etiquette.

Eventually, he started to enter local tournaments and became more interested in the game when he won a minor Indian competition where the prize was a case of cool-drinks. Soon his golfing prowess was good enough for him to win the highest competitions in the non-white golfing world.

When I played caddy matches there was a bunch of my mates jeering at my grip and once in a fit of temper I broke a club. But never again. That club cost me six months wages. Much has been made about my unorthodox grip, but it works for me and that is all that matters.

In 1946, Papwa, now aged 16, won the Natal Indian Amateur championship at the Curries Fountain course, his first big tournament victory. This was a phenomenal achievement, and pressure was placed on the organisers as they were reluctant to give him the trophy because of his youth.

Soon he had shot an unofficial 64 beating the Beachwood par-73 course record of 66 set by Sandy Guthrie, and then later shot a 59, but because it was a 'caddy tournament' and he was not a member of the SAGU, this course record score was not officially recognised. This was only the second recorded sub-60, the other shot by Louis Crozet at Queenstown GC in 1925.

At that time, Curries Fountain golf course consisted of nine indifferent holes repeated from different tee-boxes masquerading as an 18-hole course. Scattered about the course were the wrecks of old cars and trams, and during the round, the players' traversed two soccer fields, a car race track, and a tennis court. There were no greens to speak of, and the holes were set into uneven sand that was not regularly rolled.

He won in grand style, stunning spectators with his powerful grip which allowed him on his backswing to get the club up quickly with plenty of time to get his hips through ahead of the club on the downswing, but that year would be remembered for another reason

The Indian government requested that the discriminatory treatment of Indians in SA be included on the agenda of the very first session of the General Assembly at the newly formed United Nations (UN). This after the government of General Jan Smuts had enacted the notorious 'Asiatic Land Tenure and Indian Representation Act', the so-called 'Ghetto Act', in the face of an outraged Indian population and the strongest of protests from the Indian Government, in that this legislation sought to limit Indian political representation, and define where they could live, own land, and trade.

Outraged, India immediately imposed trade sanctions and withdrew their High Commissioner. Mahatma Gandhi gave the Durban community his blessing to launch a two-year passive resistance struggle but to no avail.

Meanwhile, Jan Smuts addressed the UN Assembly arguing the right of the country to defend its policies and that the UN was not the right forum for discussing this matter, which was rejected. The requisite two-thirds majority demanded that the government conform with the basic principles of the newly-formed UN Charter in its treatment of the Indian population. Smuts did not comply. Worse was to come as the National Party was to take over from Smuts and impose their form of 'apartheid' on all people of colour.

In 1951, Papwa married Suminthra, in an arranged low-keyed Hindu traditional marriage. They were both

22-years-old. The couple would have five children: Dinesh, Rajen, Sewnarain, Romilla, and Deepraj.

Although an individual sport, golf managed to hammer one of the first nails into the apartheid sport's coffin, as the simple, poor, illiterate Natal-born Indian, Sewsunker 'Papwa' Sewgolum began to make waves on both the local and international fairways.

Self-taught, Papwa would be an immediate success, but this brightness was tarnished and blackened by the humiliation heaped on him in his own country.

At this time, Gary Player won his first international tournament in Cairo – in 1955, the Egyptian Open – and went out the same afternoon and practised until it was dark. Brian Wilkes, a fellow pro who was with the group making the trip was flabbergasted.

'What the hell do you think you're doing, Gary?'

'Brian,' replied Player, 'In four years I am going to win the British Open.' It took him exactly four.

These were the early years for Gary when he needed somebody to snap at, and his dad, Harry 'Whisky' Player was there for him – 'Geddy, that's the finest golf shot you ever made,' and, 'Geddy, if you live to be a thousand you will never hit it any better'.

'Whisky Player' got his name as a young man of action at a downtown Johannesburg hotel. He had led a delegation of miners into the hotel to celebrate the impending marriage of one of their number, and when refused anything appropriate with which to celebrate, he clambered up on the table and shouted, 'We want whisky!'

'All of us Players were high-strung,' he said as he stood watching his son practice. 'That's the fantastic thing about Geddy, the way he has mastered himself. I would have flapped. I would have had my chips under all that pressure. Not him. Oh, when it was just the two of us out there, we bloody well had our fights, all right. He'd tell me he couldn't make it, and I'd tell him he was talking rot. I'd tell him he was falling back off his shots, and he'd say, "I don't want to hear it," and I'd say, "well, the hell with you," and then later he'd put his arm around me and kiss me and say, "I'm sorry, Dad, I just got to explode sometime, and you are the only one who can take it".'

When Player would come to Durban to play, Papwa would occasionally caddy for him. These on-course encounters between the two would start to shift towards competitive instances when funded by Oil of Olay founder, Graham Wulff, Papwa joined Player to play in the 1959 British Open at Muirfield.

The year 1956 also saw the removal of coloureds from the voting roll; it was the year after the writing up of the Freedom Charter, followed by the Treason Trial. Prime Minister J.G. Strijdom, followed by H.F. Verwoerd, saw the Nationalist Party enshrine its policy of race absolutism.

"Blacks should never be shown the greener pastures of education,
they should know that their station in life is to be
hewers of wood and drawers of water"

Hendrik Frensch Verwoerd was prime minister of South Africa from 1958 until his assassination in 1966. He is regarded as the mastermind behind socially engineering and implementing the racial policies of apartheid, the system of legal racial classification and forced racial segregation that existed in South Africa from 1948 to 1994, and he has been dubbed the *Architect of Apartheid*, a policy which led South Africa into the wilderness and international pariah standing.

During his time in office Verwoerd rigidly enforced apartheid policies through further introducing oppressive laws, which diminished the rights of South Africans who were not white.

Verwoerd was prime minister during the establishment of the Republic of South Africa in 1961, thereby fulfilling the Afrikaner dream of an independent republic for South Africans. During his tenure as prime minister, anti-apartheid movements such as the African National Congress (ANC) and the Pan Africanist Congress (PAC) were banned, and the Rivonia Trial, which prosecuted ANC leaders, was held. His term ended with his assassination on 6 September 1966 by Dimitri Tsafendas.

Nelson Mandela in his autobiography 'Long Walk to Freedom', states 'Verwoerd was the chief theorist and master builder of grand apartheid'; a man who 'thought Africans were lower than animals'.

— South African History Online

DISCOVERED

When you are just surviving, you cannot dream.

By now others were taking notice of the quiet Indian. Reg Sweet, sports editor for the Sunday Tribune and Daily News wrote in his 1957 article; 'Papwa really does play to a plus one handicap. In fact, he is the only plus Indian golfer in Natal, and in the matter of golf at the top level, he compares with the best of them', and went on to urge; 'there are good reasons why golfers as good as this should be given every encouragement'.

Although he was a better golfer than the men for whom he caddied, the racial laws of apartheid SA prevented him from demonstrating his prowess. He would regularly shoot in the 60s and had already made a hole-in-one on Beachwood's par-4 16th hole. He was soon winning local tournaments for 'non-whites,' often by more than 20 shots, and routinely setting course records.

Papwa's break came one afternoon in 1957 when he was caddying for heavyweight businessman Graham Wulff. Wulff, a chemist who had recently invented the now global 'Oil of Olay' brand, and a member of Beachwood Golf Club, who was playing a round of golf with two of his colleagues, Jack Lowe and Edmund Anderson, with another Beachwood member, David Andrews making up the four-ball. On the fifth hole, the volatile Andrews hit a weak drive and asked the barefoot caddy for advice on the club selection for his second shot.

With 146m remaining and playing into the lightest of breezes, Papwa drew a 6-iron from the bag and handed it to him. The man took his advice but played a poor shot taking his frustration out on his caddy's selection.

Papwa didn't take kindly to the abuse, and with tempers frayed, he placed the bag on the ground and turned and walked away. Wulff, who regarded Papwa as 'very timid and respectful', was silenced by the reaction, then whistled and called him back.

'Hey, caddy, where do you think you are going?'

'To the clubhouse, Sir', Papwa replied quietly, 'to fetch a first-class caddy'.

Wulff looked at him quizzically. 'So what made you so sure a 6-iron was the club for that shot?'

Papwa hung his head for a few moments. Then said: 'I play a bit, Sir'. Wulff, dropping a ball in exactly the same spot, asked Papwa whether he would demonstrate using the same iron to reach the green.

There were stifled smirks and exchanged glances as Papwa, with his awkward grip, addressed the ball and had a practice swing. But the swing was supple, the rock and roll motion, with a snap in the wrist at the top of the swing, and the ball soared high, then dropped, momentarily landing and biting 4m beyond the flag, then spinning backwards to within a mere one foot from the pin.

Andrews and the rest of the four-ball were suitably impressed, particularly when Freddy Govender, the caddy on Wulff's bag revealed that Papwa was a plus-one golfer and that although he was not allowed to play in the white-only Natal Open, he had secured a string of victories in local non-white tournaments.

After witnessing his extraordinary skill, Wulff decided to take Papwa under his wing, encouraging him to consider a career in golf. Papwa was given a permanent job at his cosmetic factory to support his wife and child, and time off to practice the sport. Actually, he spent more time at the golf course than working.

Papwa was a natural golfer, and it was just as well no attempt was made to mould him into more orthodox, but for him, less effective lines. But Papwa was not allowed to play in the white-professional tournaments.

To break this stranglehold, Wulff and his business partner, Jack Lowe came up with the idea of getting Papwa to tour Australia. They arranged for a film to be made of Papwa demonstrating his reverse grip with Athlone professional, Phil Ritson (the future world-famous coach inducted into the Southern Africa Golf Hall of Fame in 2010).

It was sent to the Australian PGA, and shown to the appropriate authorities, but they would not grant him a visa to go there. Clearly, the Australian authorities did not encourage dark skins. 'The Australian darkie colour bar is as effective as ours', said Wulff with some bitterness.

This was 1958 when Papwa, now 29, was no longer a youngster. He had already shown his potential by winning the Natal Non-European Open four times in the last five years (his only loss was in a play-off for the title).

Wulff also bought Papwa a decent set of clubs and his family a comfortable single-storey house nearby. However, Suminthra, deeply superstitious, vetoed the idea of relocating and Wulff was forced to sell the property.

SA Open
G Player 1956, '60
D Hutchinson 1959
H Henning 1957

Papwa dominated the non-European tournaments, yet it seemed that he, like his fellow black golfers, would never get the opportunity measure himself against the likes of Bobby Locke, Harold Henning, Retief Waltman, and the jewel in South Africa's golfing crown, Gary Player.

These heroes of the public had lifted South Africa's already rich golfing heritage to among the top of the world and were regularly winning top tournaments against the very best in Europe, America and Australia.

To compete in this stratosphere, Papwa would need to get accreditation from the PGA. Although SA hosted several so-called 'Open' tournaments that were part of the PGA circuit, Papwa was barred from entry as these were classified by the government as 'white-only' events.

Wulff then encouraged him to enter The Open Championship to be played at Muirfield, and so Wulff and his partners raised the money and took Papwa to play in the British and Dutch Opens in 1959. His promise to his dad was becoming a reality.

However, Papwa, being illiterate encountered obstacles with things as simple as getting a passport and receiving permission to leave the country, and even when he obtained those, he hit another barrier. When Wulff tried to buy tickets for the flight to London, they were told that South African Airways (SAA) didn't carry black passengers.

It wasn't feasible to have non-white sections, and although they did carry the odd black passenger, the check-in agents made sure to keep seats vacant around these blacks. There were no facilities for black passengers to check in or go through security, wait for their plane or collect their bags because the economic toll of apartheid and its consequences ensured that these facilities were not required. The fact that 'non-whites' were not allowed on SAA was purely political in line with the ideology of 'separate but equal'. If any more than a tiny minority of white passengers had ever had to sit beside or even near black passengers, there would have been angry scenes.

Undaunted, Wulff drew on his own savings to buy a light aircraft and stated that he would fly him out of Africa in his new tiny Piper Comanche 250 ZS-DRT four-seater to have a crack at the greatest title of all, the British Open at Muirfield. Together with his wife, Mavis, they flew with Papwa to Europe, paying for all the costs that came along with this trip.

At this time, Wulff was well on his way to becoming a giant of the international cosmetics industry following his successful invention in 1952 of one of the leading skin-care cosmetic, 'Oil of Olay'. Within five years of setting up 'Adams National Industries' to produce and market Olay, his product enjoyed phenomenal success in South Africa because he had struck an important chord with women – 'to look good and feel good were inseparable'. In 1959, Wulff felt it was time to introduce Olay to the world (today it accounts for well over $3 billion of Proctor & Gamble's annual revenue).

There was also excitement among the local black golfers as the Natal Indian golf champion would get his big chance when he teed off at the British Open in Scotland, and as the first black golfer since Bambata Boodhun he was showing the world that there were black golfers of quality from Africa. He represented them, so that they would be in their glory if Papwa made it through the qualifying rounds into The Open proper.

THE LEADER, MARCH 13, 1959

By the late 1950s, the National Party government was battling to deal with the complex race issues, and a groundswell of antagonism from countries around the world, especially those in Africa and Asia, in addition to pressures faced at home. The sweeping race laws in this deeply divid-

Indian Golfer for Overseas

This is the great Bambata, the grand-daddy of our golfers. Will the sensational Papwa go further than this grand golfer?

The outstanding golfer, Papwa, who learnt his golf through caddying for White golfers on Durban's magnificent golf courses will soon be leaving for England.

ed country were also proving a challenge for sports administrators as there was uncertainty concerning its implemen-
tation and substantial penalties for non-compliance. Could
people of colour compete, and if so, where, and who could
attend, and could each race group mix with the other?

So, in 1959, Papwa's entry for The Open at Muirfield
was accepted but, as Wulff recalled, that was the easy part:
'He had no papers whatsoever, so we had to guess a date of
birth for him, get him a passport, and teach him to write
his name simply by copying one I had written out for him.'

At this time, Papwa had never set foot outside Durban,
let alone flown in an aeroplane. Wulff was proposing that
they fly through Africa in this tiny four-seater single-engine
aeroplane; it had a retractable undercarriage and was only
capable of flying up to 1,000km at a time, meaning they
had to plan to find multiple airports even in bad weather.

'A good friend of mine, Wolfie du Plooy, who was an
airline captain with Rhodesian Airways and had recently
flown a light aircraft to Europe from Durban, gave me lots
of good tips, and I planned the trip very carefully before
setting off,' recalled Wulff years later. 'As the Comanche
did not have an autopilot, I would have to fly and navigate
myself, so I planned to fly only in the mornings, leaving
the afternoon free to do some business where possible and
some sightseeing.'

On 27 May 1959, friends, family, and supporters arrived
at Durban's Stanford Hill airport to bid farewell to their hero,
a caddy of 16 years, sometimes earning as little as seven shillings and sixpence a week, who was off on the adventure of a
lifetime, which would change the world he lived in.

The Durban Indian Golf Club presented him with their
club blazer which he wore proudly and whose pockets were
stuffed with loose cash which they had collected. There
were no so such things as travellers cheques.

*I learned from my mother's death the most valuable lesson about life
– and – curiously enough, about golf itself. It had happened and there
was nothing I could do to change it. The ball just had to be played
as it lay. There was no point in protesting about bad luck or cursing
misfortune by demanding why it had happened to me. The only task
was to make the best of what was left and to get on with it.*

Gary Player

Waving goodbye, the aircraft lifted into the air, and suddenly the full horror of what Papwa was doing scared the living daylights out of him, he gripped the seat tightly, scarcely able to breath, as the plane banked over the sea – there was no ground below him, while the wings were gently buffeted by the breeze as the plane peeled away rising higher and higher into the air. He squeezed his eyes shut and prayed. Then they turned again and headed back towards the land, for Johannesburg and the customs.

Would he ever see Suminthra and his children? Why had he agreed to come?

From Johannesburg, they flew to Beira, Mozambique's second largest city, which is located on the banks of the Pungue River near the beautiful palm-tree lined beaches of Pemba, already a diving mecca known only to the locals.

They stayed at the Grand Hotel – a palace of unlimited luxury where glamorous Hollywood starlet Kim Novak had recently been a guest. At that time, it was the 'pride of the nation' but fell into decay later serving as a Frelimo military headquarters and jail, and then as a refugee centre during the Mozambiquan Civil War from 1977 to 1992. At present, it is occupied by over a thousand squatters who use the famous Olympic swimming pool overlooking the Indian Ocean to wash their clothes.

The exterior of the Grande Hotel was done in the Art Deco style that was popular in Portugal during the 1930s and '40s, while the interior had an eclectic style with the use of modern materials. Of course, Papwa had never stayed in a hotel – the room seemed huge – and Wulff recalled how he entered Papwa's luxurious room 'Papwa had a huge double bed to himself, and when I went to see him, he was chipping across it.'

Back then it was spectacular, red earthen floors, an overhead fan in each room to circulate the tropical air, and where dining included mangoes and other exotic fruits, while the waiters hovered with big smiles and white gloves.

Dinner that evening was another eye-opener. 'He was quite bewildered with everything, especially the meals, and did not know why we each had knives and forks to use when we could use our hands'.

Next stop Dar-es-Salam, Tanzania's former slave trade stopping-off point, with palm-clad beaches and rolling surf, staying again at another beachfront hotel. Then past the Ngorongoro crater to Kenya, and the Rift Valley, soaring over the herds of elephants and wildebeest, swaying giraffe and antelope. They flew past the snow-capped Mount Kilimanjaro, the first time Papwa had seen snow.

By now he was getting quite used to flying and excited by everything, it was wonderful. 'The whole flight was a tremendous thrill, especially as it was at a comparatively low altitude level, and we were at the best advantage, as we were able to see all the features along the route,' said Wulff.

Then a night in Nairobi where Karen Blixen's farm (Out of Africa, 'I have a farm in Afrika' – Robert Redford and Meryl Streep) was already the premier Karen Golf Club, and on to Entebbe on the Lake Victoria peninsula, as the Royal Mail Ship MS Victoria steamed towards the port laden with passengers for a further fuel stop.

This was where in 1976 Idi 'Dada' Amin would hold the Palestinian-hijacked Israeli aircraft hostage until Israel flew a daring Mossad commando raid, 'Operation Thunderbolt', and freed 102 hostages with only one elderly hostage (Dora Bloch) taken to hospital, and later killed, as the world watched and held their breath. There was only one Israeli casualty, their commander Lt. Col. Yonatan Netanyahu. He was the older brother of Benjamin Netanyahu, the current Prime Minister of Israel

There were further stops at Juba, a river port of 35,000 people on the banks of the Nile in Southern Sudan, a strategic location and focus for much of the fighting during the first Sudanese Civil war, then 1,200km to Khartoum. Khartoum, at the confluence of the White and Blue Niles, had also been a slave trading hub where in 1884 the British army led by General Charles Gordon, was wiped out by the forces led by the Mahdi. Then over the deadly Sahara Desert and nothing, just shifting sand and more sand dunes, and every now and then a few herders with their 'ships of the desert', a few camels.

Wulff often let Mavis fly so he could rest his eyes and have a short sleep. One afternoon he was woken with a start due to the turbulence over the desert. A bolt of lightning followed by the crash of thunder. With a shout of alarm, he grabbed the joystick and pulled it down, dropping the aircraft to a low altitude so that the plane could fly out of danger. Lightning flashed continuously about them as rain battered the light plane.

Mavis was white with shock and Papwa had his eyes closed tightly, praying, hoping that the danger would pass. After 20 traumatic minutes, which seemed like forever, and during which the plane was buffeted from side to side, Wulff saw a break in the dark clouds and headed for safety.

Now the challenge was how to navigate without instruments which had been knocked out by the lightening? 'Look for the Nile,' he instructed, 'it will be our only guide for the route north.'

Anxious moments passed before they spotted the river. With a sigh of relief, they followed it across the parched landscape, the best navigation beacon of all, all the way to

Cairo, where the Roman Emperor, Julius Caesar had taken Cleopatra, the Queen of the Nile, as his bride.

Here they spent a week visiting the pyramids, and viewing the recently discovered god statue of the boy king, Tutankhamen, and posed for photographs sitting on camels in front of the Egyptian pyramids. Another exciting first for Papwa.

The final leg of their epic journey took them to Benghazi, and then Tripoli in Libya, where 18 years earlier most of the SA Infantry Division had faced General Rommel's Panza tanks at Tobruk and Benghazi, and where many SA soldiers were taken prisoner, and marched across the Sahara Desert to prison of war camps.

Despite the losses, General Montgomery regrouped, and in 1942 secured a key victory at El Alamein, and by May 1943 the entire North African region had been cleared of German and Italian troops, causing Hitler to order Rommel to take his own life.

Many of the Italian prisoners-of-war were brought back to camps in SA, including Cape Town, where they were put to work building Chapmans Peak in Hout Bay.

After crossing the Mediterranean, there were further stops in Tunis and Rome before heading to London, shortly to be regarded by young people as the music capital of the world with the advent of 'Beatlemania' in 1963. They had navigated across Africa and Europe, that was the easy part, but now in the mist, they could not find Gatwick Airport.

'I crossed the coastline at what I thought was Brighton after flying north from France over the Channel. We should have been at Gatwick in nine minutes. There are no real landmarks in that area, with numerous towns, railway lines, roads and rivers all looking the same. By this time Papwa was really panicking and shouting that we were all going to die, which did not help my nerves and Mavis told him to shut up. I could not spot the airport, and then I found we were approaching London, so I called 'Mayday' on the emergency frequency, and the RAF station answered. Suddenly I saw a huge aerodrome below, and as my fuel was running low, I decided to land and radioed Gatwick accordingly.'

The aerodrome turned out to be the Royal Air Force (RAF) fighter base Biggin Hill, the famous fighter airfield that defended London and won the Battle of Britain in 1940 by shooting down over 1400 enemy planes. Also, this was where the famous World War II ace, Douglas Bader, had been posted to command as Squadron Leader in the WW2 Battle of Britain despite having lost the use of both legs: 'and we received a wonderful reception.'

Bader was currently playing golf off a scratch handicap despite his artificial legs. He had just returned from Cape Town, where after climbing the stairs up onto the stage, with whispers circulating around the hall, he turned to the young SACS Junior School boys, and with a smile said: 'I bet you thought I was going to fall.'

'After taking on some fuel, we went on to Gatwick, where we again had a wonderful reception from air traffic controller, customs, and immigration, especially when we told them we had flown all the way from SA to play in The Open', which at that time was a South African domain with Bobby Locke winning in 1949, '50, '52, and '57. 'From there we caught a train to Victoria Station, and we were on our way.'

The city was alive with reconstruction work following the war, and tourists were pouring through Piccadilly Circus. Their accommodation at 30 Craven Road, near Paddington Station was basic but interesting as there was a brothel across the road.

The first thing they did was go to the West End, Prince's Theatre, where 'The original production of King Kong, uniting audiences of all races in SA had opened – a direct challenge to apartheid – it was billed at the time as an 'all-African jazz opera'. The musical King Kong portrayed the life and times of a heavyweight boxer, Ezekiel Dlamini, known as 'King Kong' or the 'The Spice Smasher' because of his size and strength. After a meteoric boxing rise, fighting out of the Bantu Men's Social Centre – a den for the hard hitters, he won the SA Non-European Heavyweight title in 1956 with a victory over Joe 'Foxy' Mtambo.

King Kong loved the attention and was often seen doing his roadwork carrying dumbbells and wearing weighted boots and shadowboxing in the busy Marshall Street in the Johannesburg city center. Crowds would run behind and alongside him ala 'Rocky' and chant his name.

An icon to millions of blacks, a year later his life degenerated into drunkenness and gang violence. He knifed his girlfriend, asked for the death sentence during his trial and instead was sentenced to 14 years' hard labour. He committed suicide at Leeukop Correctional Prison where he drowned in a dam, and a legend was born. He was 36.

The song 'Sad Times, Bad Times' was considered a reference at the time to the infamous SA Treason Trial in Pretoria in 1956, which lasted for more than four years before it collapsed with all the accused acquitted. Among the defendants were Albert Luthuli (African National Congress president), secretary Walter Sisulu, Oliver Tambo, and Nelson Mandela.

'King Kong' launched the international career of Miriam Makeba, who played the shebeen queen of the 'Back of the Moon', a popular shebeen of the time in Sophiatown, as well as Hugh Masekela who led the brass section.

Everything was new to Papwa, and he had to catch himself greeting everyone as 'master'. People walked on the same side of the street as he did and engaged with him as if he were one of them and not a person of colour. It felt so different not shrinking back when a friendly police 'Bobby' passed him by, and the shops, so rich and full of everything.

Wulff then flew his 'bewildered' passenger to Edinburgh and made arrangements for Papwa to practise golf at Gullane, North Berwick, and Muirfield, where the British Open was to be played, despite him not being a member. Gary Player was also in Papwa's corner at the tournament and lobbied for him to be able to practice on the course before the championship started.

He couldn't sign his name on the entry form, which he now wrote hesitantly regarding it more as a picture than a signature, but he had arrived on the international stage, reverse grip and all, and from then on would never look back.

One of the highlights of the week building up to The Open was that he was able to practice with Gary Player, who took a liking to Papwa. Player was beaten twice by Papwa in their practice rounds, although in essence Player was preparing for The Open and not competing with Papwa.

Player approached The Open with his customary determination. He minutely studied each hole, and the possible wind conditions, so that he would deliberately play short to some greens to prepare for a change of wind during the championship proper.

Papwa Sewgolum together with Gary Player after their practice round on the Gullane Course in Scotland. Player went on to win the British Open, while Papwa got through the qualifying rounds, into the Open proper but then failed to qualify for the final two rounds.

When the tournament actually started it was a different story altogether. Meanwhile, Papwa who shot a 65 in practice now knew he could compete against top-flight white-golfers.

Golf courses did not have yardage or metre indicating the distance to the front or middle of the green from the fairway, at best they had a white, yellow and red stake signifying 200, 150, and 100 metres or yards to the green, and Papwa had one big advantage over the field, he was a caddy. His depth perception was excellent, and he had learnt to estimate the exact distance to the hole, and although players were given booklets showing distances from various trees and bunkers to the green, he did not need this additional information.

Papwa also received his share of attention as he was the talk of the town early in the week; 'Papwa Sewsunker Sewgolum, the Indian-born man playing out of Durban, SA, who shot a 71 in the qualifying rounds using a cross-handed grip.'

Henry Longhurst wrote in Sports Illustrated: 'Papwa, like Sam Snead, reckons he plays his best in bare feet. He holds the club with his left hand below his right and in the first qualifying round went round in 71 in a downpour. So much for those of us who write books on how to play golf.'

And they referred to the irony of Papwa, the SA Non-European Open champion, being able to play in international tournaments, while his own country denied him the right to play in their decreed white-only tournaments.

With his sub-standard golfer clubs – other professionals had their clubs fitted for them – no previous practice on SA white courses, no coaching, nor the ability to read coaching manuals, his scores in The Open under the circumstances was none too bad. In the qualifying rounds, he breathed a huge sigh of relief when he sank a long putt for a birdie 3 at the 18th at Gullane for a second-round total of 147 (71 76) to be on the cut mark for the championship proper with 59 others.

Scores of enthusiasts following his progress congratulated him. 'I am so happy now. I will not be able to sleep tonight. The other caddies back home would never have forgiven me if I had not qualified'.

A really talented South African golfer, Edward Johnson-Sedibe who started out as a caddie (often caddying for Otway Hayes), and won the 1951 and '52 SA Non-European Open championships also tried to qualify to play at Muirfield, but missed the cut shooting 88 80 – 168.

Johnson-Sedibe didn't give himself any chance at all, as he only arrived the night before the championship, and then borrowed strange clubs, which were either too heavy or too light for him. Nevertheless, he was the first indigenous African ever to have taken part in The Open championship.

Edward Johnson never gave himself a chance in the "Open," says Player, who finds Johnson a great personality.

With his borrowed clubs, he turned in a score of 88 in the qualifying, and told anyone who listened that he liked being there so much that he planned on sticking around, especially if someone would give him a ride to London.

The journey from SA to Edinburgh was certainly more daunting and expensive than a trip to the same destination from New York. If Johnson-Sedibe, a player who didn't even have his own clubs, understood what just having a chance to compete in The Open should mean to anyone who loved the game, why were America's best players dismissing The Open?

Round One proper, Papwa was among the last to tee off in the lingering hours of the afternoon. The conditions were terrible – in the sleet, wind, and biting cold – and he was to struggle not relishing the strong west wind as heavy rain lashed the course and had many big names in trouble. Papwa, used to the Durban tropical heat, opened with a 79.

Round Two, wind and rain whipped the par-72 Muirfield course, an incredibly strong wind howled over the course for the early starters and then died bringing heavy rain and Papwa shot a creditable 73 (one-over par), but with a score of 79 73 – 152, he failed by four shots to make the cut for the final two rounds.

After 36-holes, Peter Thompson was the leader by two over Gary Player, 137 to 139, but Player went on to win the 'Claret Jug', his first Major victory. This was not quite what Papwa had hoped for, but it was a start.

Papwa's and Johnson-Sedibe's participation was to inspire a number of black golfers to try and compete in The Open, just like Bambata Boodhun had inspired Papwa.

Papwa was proud and happy for Player. He would not forget how Gary helped him navigate the Edinburgh transport system, often arriving at his hotel so the two could travel through the damp and mist to their practice sessions together.

The 23-year-old Player was equally impressed with Papwa. 'I practised with him on Gullane where the qualifying rounds were played, and he had a 30 for the first nine holes, returning in 38. Any player who can do a 30 on Gullane must be very good.' He went on, 'Neither Johnson-Sedibe or Papwa were likely to do well on a course like Muirfield without being experienced on courses like that. You only find this type of course, a real seaside course in Britain. Also given that it was cold, neither of them was acclimatised coming from Africa such that the course requires at least ten practice rounds because of the conditions caused by the varying winds.'

VICTORY

The Open was a stepping stone to other tournaments in the UK and on the Continent, and it was here that Papwa did not disappoint.

Wulff conceded that the expectations back in SA must have been 'a tremendous strain' on Papwa's nerves, but at the same time, he believed the experience had been invaluable and that it would surely be a launch pad for other victories.

The South African-born Indian was subsequently entered for further tournaments including the French and German Opens and performed 'reasonably well', but it was at the Dutch Open at the Haagsche Golf and Country Club in The Hague, one of the loveliest courses in Europe with switchback fairways and mature trees, where he made his mark.

However, on their way to the French Open, Papwa was harassed by the SA Secret Police wanting to know why he was in the UK. This caused a delay such that they arrived late in Paris and missed the French Open that had anyway taken place a day earlier than anticipated, but they reached the Hague Golf Club well in time for the Dutch Open commencing 16 August.

This dream landscape for golf with man pitted against nature on a grand scale set on rolling sand dunes was designed in 1938 by the famous golf course architect Harry Croft (who dominated golf in the Netherlands) and C.H. Alison – the latter's influence could be seen with the slightly longer bunkers. The course is still counted as one of the finest Colt designed courses in Europe.

The design of the course made use of the naturally un-dulating dune landscape. Each hole offered a completely different view and new surprising challenge. Driving was both challenging and adventurous, iron play demanding, and all sorts of shot-making were necessary to conquer the green complexes. A roller coaster fairway ride, up and down, from side to side, dips and valleys, leaving the golfer with breathless wonderment.

Thick, lush high seaside foliage flanked the fairway on both sides and no other hole was visible. The ground provided the challenge, so not many man-made hazards or bunkers, with only one fairway and 23 greenside bunkers, playing golf through rousing sand dunes. Finally tee-off on the 18th with the green in full view and the impressive clubhouse as the background.

Entrants included players from England, Scotland, Wales, Ireland, Australia, Belgium, France, Italy, Germany, Portugal, Spain, the Netherlands, and SA.

Papwa stood on the tee as the excitement mounted, crowds congregated around the tee-box, and his name was called out representing the Union of South Africa. Heart beating rapidly he gazed out over the course, much like Durban Country Club, with the first hole, a 3-shotter par-5 descending from one of the course high points to a very low one, and then straight back up the hill, with the green tucked away behind the dunes, and where a poorly struck ball was shed away.

Round One, displaying nerves of steel with an excep-tional temperament, he opened with an outward half of 35, and then five threes in an inward half of 32, coming home for a 67, a new course record, to take the lead.

He followed with an equally impressive 69 in the sec-ond round and, with a three-shot lead over Dutch champion Gerard de Wit (three-time runner-up), the Durbanite was in the driving seat. Those who witnessed his upside-down grip marvelled at his accuracy.

From off the green where most golfers were playing it safe with a putter, Papwa used his trusty deep-faced pitching wedge, spinning it as it hung in the air, trying to hole the shot as it dropped. All about 'feel' and making sure he did not decelerate.

A wobble in the third round saw him shoot a 74. He began the fourth and final round with a two-stroke lead over De Wit, and by the fourth hole, he had extended this lead to five strokes. At this stage, Papwa felt comfortable reverting to safety first golf, sensible, but he would soon regret his decision, as the Dutchman rallied to wipe out the deficit scoring an eagle at the 5th, a par-5, 448m hole, followed by four successive birdies from the 6th to the 9th hole, and go one stroke ahead at the turn with nine to play.

The crowds were cheering every shot De Wit played, and the scoreboards revealed the bad news to Papwa. He realised he was starting to panic as his caddy kept reminding him of his diminishing position.

Playing safe had not paid off, and so Papwa changed his tactics and went on the attack. On the 11th, a par-4, 377m dog-leg to the right, with a small green, he recorded a birdie, but De Wit matched that score with a long curling putt from the edge of the green.

The 12th is played from high point to high point across a shallow valley, while the green epitomises the requirement posed at Haagsche for crisp, accurate iron play. Past the lone front right deep bunker is an eight-foot swale with the largest green on the course. The green is the high point of its surrounds and its pronounced back to front left tilt made a recovery from any shot missed right particularly problematic.

Then De Wit's charge faltered when he hooked his tee shot at the short par-3, 153m 12th, one of the easiest holes on the course, and he was bunkered, dropping a shot. A turning point!

The predominantly Dutch crowd was stunned into silence as Papwa birdied the par-4, 378m 13th, and the par-4, 389m 14th hole to retake the lead. They matched each other in par for the next three holes.

Now he held a slender two-shot lead over De Wit with one hole to play, a hole some critics nominate as the best closing hole in continental Europe.

Papwa's uncanny temperament seemed to be carrying him to victory when more experienced players would have wilted away. The strain of knowing what one has to do is something that often twists the nerves of the stomach into painful sensitiveness and swings burn out as players lunge desperately at the ball. Nothing of the sort was happening to Papwa.

The 18th is a par-5, 499m. First, the golfer actually sees the clubhouse as it acts as a backdrop for the entire hole. Second, lined with trees left and right all along the narrow fairway, with out-of-bounds down the right, it is both more enclosed and sheltered than the previous 17 holes. Third, this is the flattest fairway on the course, and the golfer may finally enjoy a level stance on back to back fairway shots, and the green is protected with two bunkers in the front right with another bunker just short of the green to the left.

He looked down the length of the fairway that was alive with 5,000 spectators, and calmly considered how he would squeeze out a par-5.

Then, for the first time, with his stomach churning and his heart beating faster, he stumbled, as the wind changed direction blowing strongly across the fairway from left to right just as he was about to tee off. He pulled his drive into the rough on the left-hand side, while De Wit's effort was rhythmic and 216m straight down the fairway.

With 220m left to the hole, and the ball lying perched high up on a tuft of grass, Papwa pondered for a while discussing the options with his caddy, his hand moving over clubs as he changed his mind. Eventually he chose his favourite club, a brassie (3 wood), but felt himself tighten on the backswing, his hips came through too fast for his hands, which lagged behind, as he snatched and blocked it, fading long and left onto an adjacent fairway behind a row of trees which blocked his path to the green. De Wit's second landed safely on the green to cheers from the local gallery.

His third shot presented even greater difficulties as he now had to judge the distance and still clear the trees, then stop the ball on the green. With the wind shifting constantly, he changed his club repeatedly. He settled on a pitching wedge – leaving the face wide open – he cleared the trees but overshot the green settling in the rough again beneath a tree with low-hanging branches.

For his pitch, he opened the deep face wedge – a dangerous shot if there is any hesitation or body movement, as the spectators held their breath, many visualising themselves stabbing the ground and duffing the shot.

His fourth shot never left the pin and plummeted down safely five-feet short, checked, then rolled on another foot. Papwa lifted his cap to acknowledge the applause. His punchy putt was perfect, and the ball disappeared down the centre of the cup. He had beaten the Dutch star Gerard de Wit by one shot scoring 67 69 74 73 (283) (the fourth time De Wit had finished runner-up, and five times in all – never to win the Dutch Open), third was the well-known Belgian star, Donald Swaelens on 287.

The world returned, and he blinked back tears, hugged his caddy, and took off his cap. Papwa amazingly made history by winning the Dutch Open and a cheque for 200 pounds, the first time that a golfer of colour had won a major national tournament in Europe.

De Wit grasped his hand warmly, and the television cameras focused on his smiling face, while media cameras clicked, with images beamed across the world including

Durban. South Africans of colour rejoiced, especially the Indian population – he had shown whites that those of a darker hue could compete on equal terms and win!

'I am so happy to have won a championship here that I can hardly think straight,' Papwa told an interviewer. 'I'm only sorry that I did not have better scores on the final round, but my putting went off.' In response, the chairman of the organising committee responded, 'We enjoyed your golf, and we hope to see you back here to defend the title.'

'Tell the folks back in Durban that this is the greatest day of my life. I am proud to have won this championship, not only for myself, but for SA.' Across the Indian Ocean in SA, Papwa's victory was banner-headlined in the Indian and black newspapers, and less auspiciously and more as an oddity, reported in the white papers.

So Papwa, who had never had a golf lesson, had become the first man of colour, an Indian, designated a SA black, and the only player ever with a cross-handed grip to win a significant overseas national tournament in Europe, and the third South African after Sid Brews (1934 and 1935) and Bobby Locke (1939) to win this tournament. He attributed his success to his rusty putter. 'I would not change it,' he said.

'To win a tournament in the first year on tour is phenomenal,' stated Ryder Cup player Tommy Horton.

His name made the headlines in the press across the world and, like all great figures in sports, he attracted controversy wherever he went. As the Cape Times of July 19, 1959, trumpeted: 'Indian ex-caddy from Durban wins the Dutch Open'. The Dutch Open had attracted a first-class field and to beat the seasoned De Wit on his home ground took a great deal of doing.

Gary Player when asked for comment replied: 'Papwa has done very well. He is not only a fine man but also a fine golfer.'

1959	Sewsunker Sewgolum	South Africa	Haagsche	283	1 stroke	Gerard de Wit

For good measure, Papwa finished strongly at three under par in the German Open opening with a 76 and closed with a 68 for a score of 285.

On his return to SA, he cradled his replica of the Dutch Open trophy – too precious to be stowed away as cargo. As 'Zonk' newspaper headline screamed: 'Hero comes home – Former Durban caddy puts non-white golf on the world map'.

He was met by wildly cheering crowds, mainly Indians, at both Johannesburg, and an estimated 2,000 at Durban, where he was welcomed with garlands and flowers, and carried shoulder-high from the tarmac so that Papwa was almost overwhelmed by the excitement as he also placed a garland over Graham Wulff. Papwa was now a 'role model', and his win had made people proud to be Indians.

The white press, though, totally ignored his achievement. Papwa would make it harder for them the following year. South African golf would never be the same!

Lining the streets to see their hero.

From the National Party government, however, there was a steely silence as it tried to fathom the significance of the feat. 'The Leader' newspaper noted that the racial barriers the nationalist government had implemented in sport were backfiring badly: 'Papwa's success in his home country of the original Voortrekker, the birthplace of Dr Verwoerd, makes the embarrassment even more unbearable for the apostles of apartheid'.

And the 'Golden City Post' noted the irony in that Sewgolum's own government didn't recognise him as a full South African, and that 'back home, the winner of the Dutch Open wouldn't be allowed to take part in a white tournament except in a menial capacity'.

Papwa received a hero's welcome to the port city as his motorcade made its way from the airport. He was escorted by a cavalcade of cars, as the convoy accompanied by well-wishers drove towards his small wood-and-iron shack where he lived with his blind mother and family. Along the route thousands of cheering supporters went wild, while many jumped on his car and tried to shake his hand as he was greeted by crowds estimated to be 100,000 in number.

The streets were a splash of colour with thousands of saris, and the air was thick with the fragrances of incense and spices of India, and the roar of the crowds, the roar as if the 'heavens opened up' mixed with the exotic tunes of another continent.

The plan was that the tired sportsman should return home as soon as the aircraft touched down. But this was not to be. A cavalcade of cars and buses followed his car after he had been chaired shoulder-high from the tarmac airstrip. At Clairwood, the motor convoy was mobbed by residents. Many onlookers clung to his car, stood on the sides and even held on to the roof as it crawled along.

— The Daily News

So, this celebrated Indian sports hero returned home after winning the Dutch Open and qualifying for the British Open to a welcome which he never dreamed possible in the days when he was learning golf as a caddy in Durban. First at Jan Smuts Airport and then at the Louis Botha Airport, Durban, as thousands mobbed the man who had overnight become a golfer of world class.

From being escorted home by a convoy of cars to being the guest of honour, as he kicked off an inter-racial soccer match at Curries Fountain between the Natal Indian XI and Coloured XI watched by 17,000 spectators, which the Indians won 5-1, and saw him also hit four autographed golf balls from the centre of the field to the spectators.

Papwa was full of praise for his employers who had sponsored his trip overseas and made his triumph possible. He said that while playing in overseas tournaments, great crowds had followed him to see his unorthodox grip. Further, that he would like to become a fulltime professional, but his most important question to his friends was to know if the fish were biting.

For white South Africans who were relishing the successes of Bobby Locke and Gary Player at home and abroad, Papwa, with that upside-down grip, remained something of an enigma. However, for the hundreds of thousands of Indians (SA has the largest population of Indians outside of India), he was a giant, a homespun sporting hero. Like Tiger Woods decades later, he was responsible for taking what was almost an exclusively whites-only sport to a much bigger audience. And every youngster now wanted to hold his club like Papwa.

Nevertheless, once the euphoria died down, the Dutch Open champion found himself back at the Oil of Olay factory placing caps on the endless line of bottles. The fact that he was barred from competing in 'white' tournaments meant that the victories he continued to notch up didn't pay the bills.

Papwa's golfing potential and subsequent success on his maiden tour of Europe in 1959 was all due to the generosity of Wulff and his partners.

On their return, Wulff was frequently asked why they had helped Papwa: 'People are constantly asking us what we are getting out of this. The answer is - nothing. We simply felt that anyone with great skill, regardless of colour, deserves a chance. Wulff's generosity was to support an underprivileged, competent black golfer in a time when this was unheard of.

Other local golfers who went on to win the Dutch Open include Bobby Locke (1939); Brian Wilkes (1961); Retief Waltman (1963); Hugh Baiocchi (1975); and Harold Henning in 1981. Sid Brews was the only player who won the contest twice – in 1934 and 1935. Papwa was to win it three times and be runner-up.

Papwa's win in the Dutch Open increased his self-belief, and he was continually improving, even though he had little competition and had to put up with abysmal facilities. Meanwhile, he was snapped up to promote 'Success Cigarettes'.

Following his return home, he had further success, setting a new Beachwood course record with a record score of 65, winning the Natal Midlands Non-European Open, and succeeding Basil D'Oliviera as the Golden City Post's 'Sportsman of the Year'.

Within a few months, the Sharpeville massacre, on 21 March 1960, left 69 unarmed protestors dead, serving notice that there were grave problems with the country's race laws, and international antagonism towards apartheid regime continued to gather momentum. This double triumph once again shifted the spotlight onto his troubled homeland.

Sharpeville Massacre

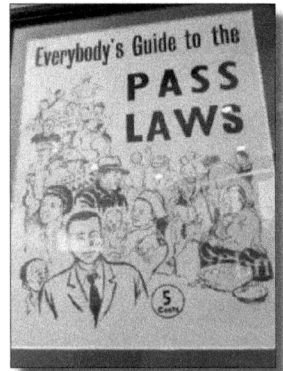

The Sharpeville massacre was an event which occurred on 21 March 1960, at the police station in the SA township of Sharpeville in Transvaal (today part of Gauteng). Leading up to the Sharpeville massacre, the National Party administration under the leadership of Dr Hendrik Verwoerd used the passbook laws to enforce greater racial segregation and in 1959–1960, extended them to include women. The Pan-Africanist Congress (PAC), a splinter group of the African National Congress (ANC) created in 1959, and led by Robert Sobukwe, organised a countrywide demonstration for March 21, 1960, for the abolition of South Africa's pass laws.

After a day of demonstrations against pass laws, a crowd of about 5,000 to 7,000 protesters went to the police station. The South African Police opened fire on the crowd, killing 69 people. The crowd had been hurling stones at the police, and the shooting started when the crowd started advancing toward the fence around the police station. There were 289 casualties in total, including 29 children. It was one of the first and most violent demonstrations against apartheid in SA. A state of emergency was declared, and more than 11,000 people were detained, while the PAC and ANC were outlawed. Reports of the incident helped focus international criticism on South Africa's apartheid policy.

—Accessed online Wikipedia

But Papwa might have been seen in the way that the Nazi Government saw Jesse Owens, a successful black athlete who took the honours in four events, winning gold medals at the 1936 Olympic Games in Berlin. This was not what the white followers wanted to see, neither, at the time, in Germany nor in the Afrikaner National Party racist-led government in South Africa.

His country's political landscape was not a pretty one for blacks, even more so after Harold Macmillan's warning about change to come in Africa (1960) followed by the events at Sharpeville (1960).

Wind of Change

The 'Wind of Change' speech was a historically significant address made by the UK Prime Minister **Harold Macmillan** to the Parliament of South Africa, on 3 February 1960 in Cape Town.

Macmillan said: 'The wind of change is blowing through this continent. Whether we like it or not, this growth of national consciousness is a political fact.' Macmillan's Cape Town speech also made it clear that Macmillan included South Africa in his comments and indicated a shift in British policy in regard to apartheid.

—Accessed online Wikipedia

At this time, SA's racial profile abroad had been severely tarnished. A sequence of demonstrations in Australia and New Zealand had ensued, and the issue around cricketer Basil D'Oliviera formerly denied the opportunity to play without restriction in the county of his birth, gained great publicity. It was a time of severe pressure on the National Party government, and the White Football Association was suspended from Fédération Internationale de Football Association (FIFA) in 1961.

Now playing on golf courses reserved for whites, Papwa's magnificent game escalated and gained 'white' support – not the kind of thing the apartheid government enjoyed. And his success at the game showed there was another way to generate income.

However, not even the close relationship with the in-fluential Graham Wulff would see Papwa participating and competing in white tournaments. The times were reminiscent of the Ghetto Act which reduced Indians to menial labour. Now added to this were the Separate Amenities Act, the Group Areas Act, and so many more heinous laws that took away opportunities for blacks.

They said Papwa couldn't handle a golf club 'right', but he kept collecting the titles. Now (1960) he added his first SA Non-European Open to his list.

Recognising that Papwa had little or no opportunity to compete on the SA professional circuit after his application for membership of the South African Professional Golf Association (SAPGA) was rejected on the basis of race, the British Professional Golf Association offered him membership and opened the way for him to play in all tournaments in the UK, Europe and beyond.

For Papwa the problem was being able to afford to get there. To raise money, the Trust published the 'Dutch Open Champion' book at two shillings and sixpence (R4,50) – as critics agreed that he was capable of beating the best in the world.

Back home Verwoerdian ideology excluded blacks in every sector of society, not least sport. While in Europe, Papwa played alongside the greats such as Bobby Locke and Gary Player, playing with them in tournaments in Britain, France and Germany, and with fans from all over following his career including SA whites, while the race laws in SA were intensified.

Funding remained a problem, and Louis Nelson, a former caddy and now a trade union leader in the Liquor and Catering union, took over and managed the rising star as Wulff was simply too busy following his dream setting up his worldwide business, to set up the 'Papwa Sewgolum Trust Fund' with the aim of raising funds for international travel.

The 'Papwa Trust Fund' was formed under the chairmanship of Louis Nelson, the committee comprising Louis Nelson (chairman), R.S. Govender (secretary/treasurer), E.I. Haffejee, G. 'Pumpy' Naidoo and T. Lutchman were confident of a generous response being made by the public. A cheque for 25 pounds had been received from Papwa's employers.

Money was raised by various means with a target of 1,000 pounds. It was a bit of a battle, but finally, the goal was reached after a few months and in 1960 Papwa was able to make his second trip to the UK and Europe, albeit using a more conventional flight.

Once again he played in the centenary Open Championship at St Andrews (won by Australian Kel Nagle). It proved to be a repeat of the previous year. Papwa opened with a 70, followed by a 74 (144), but he again failed to make the cut, with Gary Player leading the qualifiers on 137–67, 66.

This time 'native' Johnson-Sedibe opened with a 77 together with Brian Wilkes, followed by a 75 for 152, a much better effort than the previous year, but he too failed to make the cut for the championship proper. He would try the following year again starting with a 76 but would not qualify.

Then on to the Dutch Open as the defending champion, whose main point of interest to people outside SA was that he played cross-handed – the left hand below the right.

Papwa's movements were being carefully monitored by a pair of Special Branch operatives who trailed him wherever he went, ever concerned that he would bring SA into disrepute. Papwa was not a political man and had never been one for pronouncements, but the fact that he was competing on an international stage, and won tournaments, did not sit well with apartheid leaders.

'The Leader' headline shouted out: 'A nerve-wracked despondent Papwa does it again'.

Suffering from 'serious neurosis' and having lost 9kg in weight after his failure in the Daks Tournament, and his disastrous British Open, Papwa became very despondent and kept repeating that he had let everyone down in SA.

Papwa had come to the notice of the world when he won the Dutch Open in 1959. Now gathering newly-found courage from his rudely shattered hopes and dreams, and proving that his 1959 feat was no lucky streak, he once again found his touch to repeat the achievement of the previous year, as success came his way on the Continent when he successfully defended the Dutch Open Championship played at Eindhoven.

The Eindhovensche golf course was ranked in the top 20 of the world's leading Continental Europe Courses. Designed on heathland near the town of Valkenswaard by Harry Colt in 1928, the two 9-hole huge clockwise loops each return to the lovely thatched-roof clubhouse, and consist of excellently crafted holes with each hole individually routed through the tranquility of this large and impressive woodland area. Blessed with sandy soil, it has one of the most beguiling starts thanks to the deft and deceptive mounding Colt employed to the left on the short par-4 2nd and right of the green on the par-3 3rd.

The fairways were wide, some flat, others more undulating, and the greens well guarded by large and deep bunkers. The most demanding holes were the 3rd, 7th, 10th, 13th, and overlooking four holes the historical natural 'swimming pool', a large pond, which especially came into play on the 10th and 17th holes.

Staying out of the trees and hitting the putting surface in regulation was the key to Papwa scoring well. Nicely elevated tee-boxes on several holes provided him with an excellent view of the challenge ahead.

Several golfers had won the Dutch Open more than once but to win it twice in succession is a feat accomplished only by golf's immortals. What stood against Papwa doing the trick? Well, when he stepped on to the first tee and wound up that long swing of his and was under the whip from the start. He was the champion and in the eyes of the rest of the field became the pacemaker. Above all, he was fighting against the thought that in the last 23 years since Flory Van Donck (others were Sid Brews 1935, and Henry Burrows 1921) no champion had retained his title. They said that to win the Dutch Open was difficult, but to defend the title successfully was well-nigh impossible.

Determined to retain his title and to justify the faith everyone had in him, Papwa could still hear his father's words 'reach for the stars Papwa'. He opened with a beautiful first round 69 and took a three-stroke lead from Belgian Arthur Devulde. He had another good round of 71 but found himself in joint leadership with Devulde who went round in 69.

In the third round, after a 71 he was back out in front, two strokes ahead of Brian Huggett and Denis Hutchinson (1959 SA Open champion), and with a final round of 69 and with scores of 69 71 71 69 (280) he romped home beating fellow South African Denis Hutchinson 72 71 70 70 (283) into second place, followed by Ryder Cup star Bernard Huggett and Gerard de Wit, for a three-shot victory.

1960	Sewsunker Sewgolum (2)	South Africa	Eindhovensche	280	3 strokes	Denis Hutchinson

Prijswinnaars in het Internationaal Open kampioenschap op de Vinjkuesse Golf Club: e.l.n.r. G. de Wit, B. Shelton, M. Crafter, A. Devulder, B. Huggett, D. Hutchinson (runner-up), & Sewgolum, met de kampioene-beker, die hij opnieuw won; zittend A. F. Knipscer, eerste amateur

Edward 'Eddia' Johnson-Sedibe

Carrying his relatively good form in The Open qualifying, and eight years after winning the 1952 South African Non-European Open (and the year before), 'Eddia' Johnson-Sedibe headed for the famous Wentworth golf course (home of the 1953 Ryder Cup and 1956 World Cup), and the Ballentine Bigger Ball tournament.

This was the first tournament in Europe where the American 1,68 inch (42,67 mm) and not the smaller British 1,62-inch golf ball, which had always been in use, was now compulsory.

Why? A 0.06-inch difference in golf ball diameter doesn't sound like much. But the smaller ball provided around ten per cent more distance and was more workable in the wind. However, it didn't sit up quite so well on the grass and was, therefore, slightly harder to hit well, while the larger ball made putting easier and had more weight to fall into the hole.

Eddia opened with an astounding 65 to take the first round lead at the East course. He certainly had no reason for complaint as he beamed over his card, which was easily his best effort so far in a British tournament. He had a good homeward half of 32 including twos at the 10th and the 12th. Bobby Locke opened with a 69 and Harold Henning a 70.

Here was Eddia leading the best of Europe, only allowed to play with his friends on their pick-up golf course in the bush, not allowed to play on a white course back home, denied membership of golf clubs or the ability to play in a white tournament.

What would Simon 'bra Cox' Hlope (now 36) and already the winner of the SA Non-European Open titles in 1955, '57, and '59, have achieved if he had been let loose on the European fairways? Meanwhile, Edward Johnson-Sedibe had arrived.

And England, Europe, and the World thought we had no black golfers, let alone quality players. Certainly, those playing in Europe had no idea there were black golfers in

Africa, as Eddia became the first African to take the lead in a major tournament in Britain.

After Round Two, Bernard Hunt had taken the lead on 132, followed by Christy O'Connor on 135 (69, 66), then came R.M. Jacobs 136, John Panton 138, all Ryder Cup players, and then Eddia after a 74, but still in the hunt, together with Peter Thompson (five-time British Open champion), and Eric Brown (Ryder Cup player)

The tournament was eventually won by Irishman Christy O'Conner Snr on 277 by two-strokes over John Patton. Sadly Eddia fell away with an 84 and 78 (301), but this gave him the encouragement to stay and persevere, eventually becoming the leading golf coach in Germany. In SA, he would not have been allowed to coach or enter a clubhouse. What talent had apartheid SA driven from its shore!

Eddia also finished twenty-sixth in the 1960 Italian Open, and thirtieth in the Portuguese Open; and in 1961 he finished twenty-sixth in the Spanish Open. He also won some minor tournaments in Portugal and England.

In 1962, Eddia had his first employment as the assistant professional to the Royal Winchester Golf Club Golf, and in 1965 he was the professional at Hamburg-Ahrensburg GC in Germany, which at the time consisted mostly of beginners, and where he formed a pop band, and taught golf for 20 years.

Meanwhile, Papwa played in a number of tournaments with varying success, his best finish being fifth on 281 in the Yorkshire Evening News Tournament seven shots behind the winner Peter Thompson (Eddia with 84 76 failed to qualify for the last two rounds), and twelfth in the French Open.

Papwa had carved a niche for himself in golfing folklore when he won the Dutch Open in 1959 and 1960 which caused the government to reconsider their ban as they deliberated allowing him to play in some white tournaments. He was already aged 32, an age when many golfers reach their peak.

Against high calibre opposition, Papwa was accorded the respect and courtesy befitting a top-class sportsman wherever he played abroad. But when he came back to the country of his birth, he had to revert to a sporting life of second-class status and needed official permission to compete each week against white golfers for who he was more than a match because multiracial contests were forbidden by law – such that he was judged by standards other than skill whenever he came home in triumph.

When the Natal Golf Union received Sewgolum's application to compete in the whites-only Natal Open Championship in 1960, it became a political hot potato. The issue was referred to the SAGU – the country's governing body – but the request was turned down because the entry of non-Europeans into national and provisional championships 'would be a departure from the customs'.

The South African Non-Racial Olympic Committee (SANROC), headed by Denis Brutus took up the cudgels and urged the British Professional Golfers Association to reprimand the SAGU.

Dennis Brutus was a co-founder of the South African Non-Racial Olympic Committee (SANROC), an organisation that would be heavily influential in the banning of apartheid-era South Africa and the Olympics in 1964. In 1961, Brutus was banned for his political activities as part of SANROC, arrested and sent to Robben Island for 16 months, five in solitary. He was in the cell next to Nelson Mandela.

—Accessed online Wikipedia

CHAPTER SIX

Playing in White Tournaments

A LOOPHOLE

The golfing establishment regarded Papwa with amusement and mild embarrassment, while to the apartheid officials he was a black troublemaker who should not have aspired to play golf professionally. For years, Papwa had been forced to pursue his game only in 'non-European' tournaments.

He applied for permission to enter numerous 'white' tournaments, and the government turned each one down.

But there was ambiguity in the law: Was it really illegal for a 'non-white' to 'occupy' a white area if that area was, say, a cinema, or a golf course? The Olympia bioscope in Kalk Bay, Cape Town, for instance had coloured folk sitting upstairs while the whites sat downstairs, and where for fun, those upstairs would throw water-bombs at those below them.

Meanwhile, Papwa was watched continuously – and sometimes directly threatened — by the secret security police. He lived in two worlds, the have not and the have for 18-holes.

Papwa applied to compete in the SA Open in March 1961 (Nelson: 'We have to keep on challenging them, or accept that we can't change a thing.'), and the SAGU approached the government for authorisation. In terms of the Group Areas Act – one of the cornerstones of apartheid – different 'races' were required to live in separate areas.

Nevertheless, there was a senior advocate's legal opinion, a loophole in the law that was open to interpretation. If, for example, a golf tournament that permitted all races was held in a so-called white-only area, then 'non-whites' would be allowed to compete – with restrictions.

The next hurdle was to circumvent the Group Areas Act by securing a permit enabling Papwa to travel from Natal to East London in the Eastern Cape, where the tournament would be staged. On the eve of Dr Hendrick Verwoerd's departure to a Commonwealth Prime Ministers' Conference, where SA was to withdraw and set up a Republic – a permit was granted under the Group Areas Act signed by the Minister of the Interior, Jan de Klerk, but he was not allowed to use the changing rooms.

This loophole enabled Papwa to gain permission to play in a few white tournaments, starting with the 1961 SA Open, but in the convoluted logic of the day of placing a round peg into a square hole, he would be allowed to 'occupy' only the golf course, not any of the facilities, including the clubhouse, and the permit was just for the days of the tournament – no practice rounds were possible. Such permits were very rarely granted, usually at the last minute, and always came with significant restrictions.

The fact that no practice round was allowed was to become a feature of all future permits, as not only would permission sometimes be granted at the last minute, but he was always at a huge disadvantage as he would have to play the course 'blind', so that he was participating 'cold', while the other competitors had time to formulate their strategy.

The day before the tournament, Papwa slammed his hand in a door gashing a finger. He was using the car as a change room and was treated by a doctor. That morning the hand was still throbbing and bandaged. He could only hope the hand would not affect his grip and swing, and he could play through the pain.

Barred from entering the clubhouse, he ate his vegetarian sandwiches lovingly prepared by Suminthra, with a flask of tea and some painkillers while sitting in his car, but it did not do the trick. Meanwhile, the other competitors entered the clubhouse for their sit-down meal.

That year another first-time winner came to the fore at East London in the SA Open, 22-year-old Retief Waltman (289). He won by eight shots from Free State amateur Barry Franklin (297), aged only 17 years, with Bobby Locke (298) a further shot back in third place.

Papwa was given every support by the East London GC, its members and fellow competitors, but the tension of not knowing whether he could play or not until the last minute for every tournament affected Papwa's game and left him emotionally exhausted, taking the edge off his game.

Papwa failed to mount any challenge during the tournament, his hand was hurting, and he finished way down the field (76 77 75 79 (307) in sixteenth place. He failed to get into the money but lost nothing of his reputation. He departed feeling disappointed that he had let down his army of fans, friends, and the caddies at Beachwood, but more important than his score was the fact that he was able to play at all.

1961 South Africa becomes a Republic

Meanwhile, at the Commonwealth Heads of Nation Conference, the Afro-Asian countries were especially critical of apartheid, with Nkrumah and Nehru leading the discussion. Canada also criticized South Africa openly, and the call was for South Africa to abandon her racial policy. Verwoerd refused and felt that nobody should have the right to dictate to South Africa what actions should be followed. Verwoerd decided it would be best to leave the Commonwealth before South Africa was expelled. On 31 May South Africa became a republic, with her membership of the Commonwealth simultaneously expiring.

Nelson Mandela described this as 'the unwanted republic'. He wrote: 'The adoption of this part of the resolution did not mean that the Commonwealth conference
preferred a monarchy to a republican form of government. Such considerations were unimportant and irrel-
evant. The point at issue, and which was emphasised
over and over again by delegates, was that a minority
Government had decided to proclaim a White Republic
under which the living conditions of the African people
would continue to deteriorate'.

The ANC called for a National Convention and the organising of mass demonstrations. A three-day general strike was called in protest at the declaration of a
republic, leading to the arrest of thousands in black
townships, although Mandela, by now head of the underground movement, managed to escape arrest.

— Accessed online Wikipedia

Quitters are not winners, and winners are not quitters.
Jackie Mercer.

Money was always a problem, and the Papwa Trust
Fund did not have enough in the kitty to send Papwa back
to Europe in 1961, and he was, therefore, not able to defend
his Dutch Open and win the title for the third time.

By July there were murmurings concerning the Trust
Fund's lack of accounts. Nelson replied with the docu-
ments as evidence, but contributors were not satisfied, and
suspicion continued. Papwa, of course, could not read and
became the victim of rumour mongering.

Meanwhile William Manie, an East London caddy
worked his passage to take part in the British Open at Birkdale, but alas, he too did not make the qualifying cut.

Papwa was then invited to play in India as part of a famous television series entitled 'The Shell Wonderful World of Golf' where he was to join 21 other leading players to compete for a winner's purse of R2,140 and a guarantee of R1,200 plus all expenses.

With a population of 439 million, Papwa had become a hero to the masses in India, and there was much speculation as to how their new Indian hero would perform against the best in the world.

However, after signing the contract, he was informed that India had been eliminated from the competition and accordingly his selection had been cancelled. Gary Player nonetheless was featured playing against Peter Thompson in Australia.

Sharpville was a thing of the past, a 'mistake', and South Africa was now a republic, and the Commonwealth could no longer dictate policy to the nationalist government, and this included the Indian golfer and his horde of unruly Indian fans.

Meanwhile, the Springfield Golf Course was opened on 16 December 1961, this being the new 'Home' course of the future Durban GC. At Springfield, the Durban Corporation agreed to level the land, turf and drain the grounds with the necessary amenities to be undertaken by the members, a gigantic task. Once again the course consisted of nine holes with no clubhouse facilities. Players and officials conducted their own affairs from their vehicles.

Papwa Sewgolum, Censer Skakarie, Fred 'FM' Paul and R.T. Singh were the very first four-ball to tee off on the new course. A temporary Clubhouse was officially opened by Papwa on 30 August 1969.

Past President, Hassan Mall, in 1975 wrote: 'Given that the Durban City Council spent little or no resources on the Springfield Flats Golf Course, the course was maintained by members of the Durban Golf Club. Broken tractors, burst water mains, weeds, collapsing grass mowers and blunt green cutters were a few of the nightmares experienced, but the Club managed each week to turn out a golf course of pride.'

The year 1962 was a disappointing one as the tide started turning against Papwa as far as participation in tournaments in SA were concerned. Limiting his chances to play restricted the family's income. Not even the support from the top ranks in the golfing world could persuade the authorities to allow Papwa to enter national tournaments, yet his performance in the non-European competitions was riveting.

After a long break due to a family tragedy following his young son's death after a short illness in November 1962, he won the Natal Non-European tournament for the fifth time smashing Harold Henning's course record with a five-under-par 67 which was recognised now that he was a member of the British PGA. A title he successfully defended the following year.

Papwa once again entered the Natal Open and was accepted, but this time it was turned down by the Minister of Community Development.

PERMISSION

The most important quality in a champion golfer is your mind, and the power to remain positive.
Gary Player

The 1963 Natal Open with R2,000 in prize money staged at the Durban Country Club was the tournament that would put 'Papwa' on the map for various reasons. Like many other exclusive clubs around the country, it selected its members by race and religion, so, at various times, different ethnic groups, such as Afrikaners and Jews were excluded.

Finally, in 1963, and now at the age of 34, he was given permission to compete in a number of events including the Natal Open, a tournament that had previously refused his presence because of the colour of his skin. For the first time, Papwa's application to play in the Natal Open was accepted.

When Durban Country Club course was constructed by Laurie Waters (inducted into the Southern Africa Golf Hall of Fame) in the early 1920s, with a combination of lush vegetation, sand dunes, and stunning views of the Indian Ocean, the art of architecture as we know it today had not seeped into the consciousness of golfers. His adventurous layout instinctively followed good basic principles such as very little interference with nature's works, and the player was not shown everything at a glance but was given a thrill of anticipation and uncertainty.

The holes fell into one of two categories: those that played in and out, and over the dunes, such as holes 1–5, 8–13, and 18, and those that were farther removed from the dunes and ocean. The remaining seven holes, 6, 7, 10 and 11, and 14–16 played across the flat land where the high to low point was less than seven foot. The dunes and holes were full of allure given how distinctive the landforms were and how they were captured within the holes.

One could point, for example to No. 18, only 253m, as being technically weak – too short for a four. But this hole had character and 'personality', a teasing hole with its own 'Valley of Sin' (like St. Andrews) off the front of the green, snaring either tee balls or approach shots that were a shade too weak, sending them well back onto the fairway. While a tee ball that faded down the left of the fairway took the left-to-right fairway slope, bounding past the depression at the front right and onto the green.

A great finishing hole of real risk-reward, where anything could happen, eagles or double-drops if the golfer decided to go for the green with his tee-shot, while the bushy vegetation masking the seaside road gave a feeling of isolation from the outside world. It had a spice of danger and was memorable – Sam Snead once asked, 'Where is the other half of the fairway?' The right side favoured the tee-shot as the fairway sloped left to right towards the green if you have a go at the green with your drive. But for the over-cautious or fearful, flinching from the out-of-bounds, and blocked too far left, left the player unsighted from a hanging lie, and the hollow in front of the green backed by a massive dune.

Papwa had once again applied to play in the Natal Open, and after procrastinating on the matter for several years, the SA government together with the Natal Golf Union, and the local Durban Country Club executives buckled to international pressure, eventually allowing Papwa to compete locally in the 1963 Natal Open after having been satisfied that apartheid laws would not be broken. 'Suitable arrangements' were made for Papwa to use a combi as a change room and eat his meals with the caddies, while white golfers ate food prepared and served, ironically, by Indians in the luxurious clubhouse.

The 'whites-only' club attracted some of the most affluent and successful businessmen and other personalities of the time, where they were served by Indian staff. Indian doormen would welcome them, Indian chauffeurs parked their cars, and Indian waiters served them food and drinks, and the caddies were Indians.

The favourite was Harold Henning, and he was no pushover – he won more than 50 tournaments worldwide in his professional career, including victories in the US and Europe, and teamed up with Gary Player to win the Canada (World) Cup in 1965.

Papwa Sewgolum was very popular with the Indian community and everyone came out in droves to watch him.

Harold Henning opened with 68 at the end of the first round. Henning seemed to have a liking for the Durban Country Club, particularly in damp conditions. Two years previously, he had won the Natal Open in a play-off against Alan Brookes after a devastating last round in the pouring rain. It was not raining but the course was still saturated, and the greens slow after 36 hours of continuous rain. Hugh Inggs also joined him on 68 which included four 3s while his card showed seven birdies (3rd, 6th, 7th, 8th, 10th, 16th, 18th) and two dropped shots, as they took the lead.

They were three strokes ahead of Mike Finney and Phil Ritson (the future great golf coach in America). Close behind in third place were Denis Hutchinson and Springbok amateurs, Barry Franklin and Murray Grindrod.

Durban Indian golfer, Papwa was on evenpar-73, a modest start in eighth position, together with defending champion Stewart Davies, Cobie le Grange, Terry Westbrook, Peter Leighton, and Taff Evans the Natal Amateur, then followed Retief Waltman, Bobby Locke, and Cedric Amm.

Papwa was just a little unlucky in the round, but he took it all on the chin and remained quite unpeturbed outwardly. He had, however, made up his mind that no one would ever see him play like that again during the tournament. He was proud to still be in the running in spite of everything.

Eagles were on the cards at the signature 468m par-5 3rd hole, rated the third-best hole in the world. An elevated tee gave the golfer an extended carry from the tee and a windless day brought the green in reach in two. However, the fairway took on the appearance of a narrow ribbon winding its way past thick vegetation along the entire length on both sides, and a well-placed bunker on the left-hand side cut into the dunes, made it tricky but reachable.

Papwa had one of the biggest galleries of the day made up mostly of Indian caddies as well as those that didn't even know golf, and he did not disappoint. In charge of both his golf and the crowd – he rebuked them sternly if their whispered chatter interrupted his concentration – he played solid golf to gain birdies at the possible eagle 3rd hole, the 12th, and 18th, but short putted the 4th, 11th and 17th to lose the advantage.

His best shot and the one that drew most applause was at the 18th green, a 45-yard nine-iron chip that landed 15cm short of an eagle 2.

After opening with a lacklustre 73, he 'bared his teeth' in the second round with a brilliant 70, which saw Papwa tied with Barry Franklin, just a shot behind the leader Cobie le Grange (later ranked 15th in the world and destined to win the 1964 British Masters). His best shot was on the long 8th where he slammed a wood off the fairway to only 8-foot from the pin and then sunk the putt.

Nobody could read the green like a caddy. Papwa played golf as in a complete world of his own. Nothing ruffled him. He could play in the wind and believed everything followed the sun. Putting with a bent shafted putter (like

Tommy Bolt), he brushed the grass with his putter to see which way it lay. In the morning he putted lighter, and in the afternoon, he putted harder. He said the grass followed the sun.

On Saturday, the last day, the car park with dilapidated cars and even some horse-drawn carts was bursting at the seams, paired with Cobie le Grange, Papwa was the crowd favourite. It was one of the most extraordinary scenes in SA sport.

After the third round, he still shared second place with Bruce Keyter, both 217, Hugh Inggs (68) having taken the lead. The leaders after the third round: Hugh Inggs 215, followed by Papwa, Bruce Keyter 217, next came Denis Hutchinson 218, and Cobie Le Grange on 219.

Papwa went into the last round in the driving rain that fell in the late afternoon, two strokes behind Hugh Inggs after a morning round of 74, one-over par,

Papwa, drenched by rain, was forced to eat in his car because only whites were allowed into the Durban Country Club

and when all those in with a chance crashed about him over the 18th, he dealt with the conditions much better than his nearest rivals playing steady golf. 'We were wet, our grips were wet, and we could hardly stand up, but he played like there were no problems', said Cobie le Grange.

Such was his gallery that the only way individuals got a chance of seeing him was by putting their heads down and rushing from one vantage point to another.

Miracle shot at 15th! Once again, as in the earlier rounds, it was his immaculate work around the greens that set the seal on a grand victory. His chipping was near perfection, and few of the gallery of over a thousand Indians and Europeans would forget his masterful chip at the short 15th, only 177m, but playing a little longer than expected.

This shot could well have won him the tournament for the bush telegraph tom-tommed news informed him that he had to par the next four holes to beat Bobby Verwey who was already in the clubhouse.

Verwey's performance was magnificent, but it was only an excuse for Papwa to produce a further display of his brilliance allowing him to prove once again that he had control over every club in the bag and his own temperament. He knew what he must do and proceeded to do it, and this showed once again why his Indian army of supporters believed that there was some old black African magic in his swing. His tee-shot drifted to the right of the green and landed in a water-filled bunker. Taking a free drop out of the bunker, the ball settled on to one of the dew patches, as smiling, he asked for his sandwedge and proceeded to explode with water spraying into the air while at the same time imparting a reverse spin on the ball.

Today it is normal to see backspin, but in those days with those golf balls, it was unusual. The ball pitched about five foot past the pin, stopped momentarily, and then to almost everyone's amazement spun back as though bewitched, finishing eight inches from the hole, and giving him a most-needed par-3 at a time when he had dropped three shots and reports had filtered back that he needed a final round of 76 to win. It was such a romance!

In his final two rounds, Papwa made only two birdies; that was in the morning when he got a three at the 338m 7th, and at the 453m 14th. For the rest he played 29 holes in regulation figures, dropping shots at only five holes. It was remarkable golf under any circumstances, and more so considering the wind and driving rain in the late afternoon as he took control of the elements as if it was a clear day filled with sunshine.

And while Papwa was working towards his victory, there was high drama among the remaining professionals who, in their own words, did not play good enough golf to win.

Hugh Inggs was one player who twice had the tournament in his grip. He had two rounds of 68, in the first and third rounds, and sandwiched in between them was a 79 and an 80. The tall, handsome Harold Henning found the touch that had deserted him for so many months when he opened with a 68 but then blew up with a 78.

Then Bobby Verwey almost stole the title from under the noses of the leaders as he posted a brilliant 70 that included six birdies including the 5th, 8th, 13th, 14th, and 18th. Cobie le Grange started 73 69, and as the overnight leader, he was drawn with Papwa over the final 36 holes but found the tension just that too much for him as he blew out with 77 78 to finish on 297.

Watched by a surging legion of Indian supporters shocking the conservative white bastion Country Club members, and with squalls of tropical rain passing through, Papwa kept his game on track and found himself on the par-4 18th. He needed just a par to beat Bobby Verwey (Gary Player's brother-in-law following Gary's marriage to his champion golfer sister Vivienne) and Denis Hutchinson (both later to be inducted in the Southern Africa Golf Hall of Fame).

The 18th has a steep bank to the right. Marshalls struggled to hold the gallery at bay as many wanted to touch Papwa to inspire him. Papwa nailed a solid drive, but it caught the breeze and ended up deep on the right-hand side, below the fairway green.

Down the steep slope, Papwa could not see the flag. Back up the bank he strode and took a fix on the east side of the clubhouse. Drawing out his club, he opened the face, had a practice swing, addressed the ball, and without much hesitation planted the clubface into the ground with a thud, crisply connecting with a full pitching wedge, dislodging the turf, as the ball rose to land on the edge of the plateau green. The crowd gave him no chance to see where the ball had finished.

His first putt, delightfully struck, just drifted narrowly missing the hole, and he tapped in the winner for par, a one-shot victory, and the purse of R800.

Pandemonium broke out as cheering ecstatic followers swarmed across the green and chaired blue-jerseyed Papwa shoulder-high off the green – a new icon for any person of colour in this land of apartheid. Every caddy, waiter and labourer in Durban stood a little taller that day.

History was thus made at Durban Country Club when with scores of 73 70 74 76 (293), Papwa had finished one shot ahead of Denis Hutchinson and Bobby Verwey. Playing the game with his characteristic serenity and a strange upside-down grip, the man they called 'Papwa', had overcome some of the best SA professionals of the day to win the tournament, and in so doing became the first person of colour to win a professional golf championship previously set apart only for Europeans in SA (the 1937 caddy victory by Nathan/Seepersadh over British professionals Padgham/Dailey 2/1 was not a championship).

It was an astonishing victory which made not only golfing history but sporting history. To the large Indian community in Durban and to observers around the world,

Papwa was a revelation, a homespun hero, a dark-skinned 'David' in a world of white golfing 'Goliaths'.

That Papwa deserved his victory cannot be denied. He played well with every club, but, as ever, his chipping was again his strongest point, and it may be that his 'reverse' grip had something to do with his success in this department. That left-hand-under-the-right on the grip kept the club on the line long after impact compared to the normal grip.

Mobbed by supporters, he walked to the car to change. Papwa had done the seemingly impossible; he had beaten 103 white golfers including the favourite Harold Henning, as well as Hutchinson and Verwey, and won the 'white' open tournament.

This was the first time a provincial championship, previously reserved as the right of whites only, had been won by a golfer of colour.

FIRESTORM

But with Papwa's first local victory came the first backlash in what was to be a series of injustices that would tarnish his short-lived career.

A closing ceremony that turned into an internationally publicised event caused Papwa to be thrown into the limelight in a very harsh and degrading manner.

The event gained notoriety and is perhaps most often remembered as the championship where Papwa was presented with the trophy on the 18th green in the rain, with the other white golfers looking on from inside the clubhouse.

The legend of the ensuing prize-giving has been handed down through the decades like folklore. Papwa surrounded by hordes of Indian supporters who were clamouring to touch him and shake his hand, made his way back to the car park where he changed in his manager's car and combed his hair, the rain was falling.

What followed went down as one of the most shameful incidents in South Africa's sporting history. As the rain swept across the course, the laws of the land kicked in, and the white competitors, their supporters and club members made their way to the clubhouse. The planned outdoor ceremonies would have to be moved inside, into the clubhouse.

Papwa remained waiting outside the clubhouse because he was a man 'of colour' and, therefore, under apartheid laws, prohibited from entering the building for fear of the club losing its liquor license. And it was raining.

And so it was, in a game of fair play and integrity, Papwa was barred from attending his own prize-giving. Instead, in a downpour, he was quickly presented with the trophy beside the 18th green. The evening was lit up by smiling Indian faces, by photographers' flashbulbs, and, as if in benediction, by forks of lightning in the sky that highlighted that moment – the rain, sweat, and tears on his face as he received his cheque for R800 under an umbrella. 'A fierce wind suddenly blew and the sky blackened ... then came the rain in pounding tropical torrents'.

Then as the whites sought refuge in the clubhouse, where the celebrations got underway, with the remainder of the prizes presented half-an-hour later in the lounge, Papwa and his fans made their way home.

It was not the choice of either the Durban Country Club or the Natal Golf Union that this differentiation was made. Just because there was a risk that under the Group Areas Act, it was possible that if Papwa had gone into the clubhouse he might have been guilty of a crime under this act, and the club may have lost their liquor licence.

Incredibly, and against all the odds, Papwa had caused a stir in 1963 apartheid as although non-political he inadvertently became the reluctant symbol of the anti-Apartheid sports boycott movement when pictures of him receiving his trophy outdoors in the rain, with the white players looking on from within the clubhouse, were published across the world.

Whatever the truth of the conflicting details of the prize-giving, the incident was just one of countless apartheid assaults that Papwa endured. But as a potent symbol of exclusion, it turned into a firestorm, starting with press commentary at home and abroad. 'In any normal land the treatment of this fine player would be considered an insult to him and an acute embarrassment to everyone else,' said the defiant Rand Daily Mail the day after the event.

'Papwa wins the Natal Open', and the 'GLORY and the SHAME' screamed The Post newspaper headline, and none of the players spoke out!

27 January 1963: Natal Open at Durban CC. Papwa finishing the 72nd hole in a light shower.

27 January 1963: Durban Country Club, Papwa receives his R800 Natal Open cheque and the trophy as it gently starts to rain from Mr. RA Bell (Gilbey's). Behind the microphone is Louis du Plessis, President of the Natal GU, and on the far right Felix Fielding, chairman of the Durban CC

The local and international media devoured the story. Images of the prize-giving were flashed around the world and played a significant role in cementing the sporting boycott against SA. The headline of The Daily News: 'South Africa is a land of perpetual mid-summer ideology madness'. And the London's Daily Mirror smirked: 'Here's a story to warm the cockles of your heart – that is if you are bigoted, prejudiced and vicious racialist'. While the SA state broadcaster, the South African Broadcasting Corporation's (SABC) planned airing of the tournament was suddenly cancelled for the final round at the last minute, and they failed to announce the result.

The SABC said no coverage was given to the Natal Open won by the Indian, Papwa Sewgolum, in terms of policy laid down by their board of governors, namely; 'We do not broadcast multiracial sport. We have separate programmes for Bantu, Indians and Coloureds in which we cater for the broadcasting of sporting events of the various race groups. On the English and Afrikaans service coverage is given to sport in which whites compete.' An official confirmed that results of the Natal Open were not included in the Monday morning national news bulletins.

Reg Taylor (SA's all-time leading amateur) praised Papwa's victory insofar as it would keep SA golf free of the expected onslaught by the outside world when golfers plied their trade overseas. Prophetic words for the future boycotts and demonstrations yet to be unleashed on SA white sportsmen competing abroad.

Allan Henning, who won the 1964 SA Open (played in 1963) and who played against Papwa on many occasions, stated, 'it was an absolute crime. I could cry about it.' Henning went on to say: 'The guy was a phenomenon and he had a massive support base. When he played in Durban, the place would swarm with his supporters. It was an unbelievable experience.'

The incident further highlighted Papwa's potential and, at the same time, marked a new low point in the failed experiment of racial segregation. The issue was addressed in parliament when Helen Susman, the lone parliamentiary representative of the opposition Progressive Party noted: 'Papwa receiving his trophy in the rain will do more to establish our true image abroad than all the glossy sunny SA pamphlets issued by the State Information sports department.'

The Minister of the Interior, Frank 'Bunty' Waring, conceded that the incident had caused the country considerable harm, but blamed the opposition parties and the media for fuelling the flames. The question now, was could they turn down his request to play in the SA Open?

Papwa's low-keyed response to the saga was: 'There would have been no fuss if it hadn't rained'. He remained silent about the snub — and about all the indignities to which he was subjected.

'I've read so many stories about what happened, and nobody's ever got it right,' says Bobby Verwey, who finished tied second in the tournament that day. 'Papwa was a friend of mine, the loveliest guy you'd ever know. In those days they gave out prizes to the top-five finishers. And the five of us got together and decided to have the prize-giving outside because Papwa wasn't allowed inside. It wasn't just Papwa – we all got our prizes outside. There was no prize-giving inside. And it was barely even raining. I don't think we even had an umbrella.'

However, in the photo below, it would appear that Bobby Verwey received his prize indoors, and probably in the lounge as not only is there a woman in attendance, but she is seated, and there is a bottle of beer on the table. Further, Colonel D.W. Geddie is now presenting the prize, whilst

Colonel D.W. Geddie, secretary Natal Golf Union, presenting Bobby Verwey with his prize as joint runner-up in the Natal Open.

Papwa received his prize from Mr R.A. Bell.

E.S. Reddy, a former director of the UN Centre Against Apartheid, wrote in 1998: 'The photograph of 'Papwa' receiving his trophy in heavy rain outside appeared in many newspapers around the world and greatly helped the boycott of apartheid sport.'

Papwa had unintentionally become the figurehead of the anti-apartheid sport movement, and the government, already under scrutiny, received even more criticism, and this gave impetus to the international movement to boycott apartheid sport, as a number of countries reacted by imposing sports sanctions on SA.

This is the story of South Africans such as Papwa forced to be second-class citizens in their country of birth. For inadvertently putting the bigoted state policy under the international spotlight, he now became a target of official harassment and underhand scheming.

Had Papwa had access to the clubhouse and been treated as an equal, things would have been different during the ceremony and tournament, and certainly for Papwa's golfing career.

The images of him being presented with the Natal Open trophy under leaden skies were flashed around the world, serving notice that something had to be done to address SA. A year after this infamous ceremony, SA was barred from the Tokyo Olympics (following a proposal by India) and, within a decade, the country was formally expelled from the International Olympic Committee.

Clearly, Papwa was now a catalyst for the movement that brought about bannings from international sport.

Although he did not participate in this Natal Open, Gary Player's career was now intertwined with that of Durban-born Indian 'Papwa' Sewgolum, now a worldwide symbol of the country's hated race laws.

APARTHEID THORN

Papwa put the government in a spot. The administration was in a dilemma over the Indian golfer. It didn't want him to play in multiracial golf tournaments – but he was apparently not committing an offence by doing so.

Nor was the government keen to introduce legislation to stop him doing so. This would shatter the international image it had been cultivating of trying to create an image of being flexible and reasonable. 'The situation was plain crazy'.

Meanwhile, the general feeling was that nothing was more calculated to bring SA's name into disrepute among influential circles overseas than the Papwa incident. Golf had become the aristocrat of games played by men of high positions all over the world – men like Britain's Premier Harold Macmillan and American President General Dwight Eisenhower.

To these people, it would bring home the meanness of apartheid more than anything else. It would make a particularly bad impression in the US where golf was a game played by the influential and the rich.

Clearly with continued practice over good courses, a player like Papwa was definitely bound for the top places.

Then history was very nearly made at the SA Open Championship at the Durban Country Club, having been given permission to play at the last minute. The tournament was the next day, and around midnight Louis Nelson got a call to say Papwa could play the following day as the permit to play had now been issued. The entry of another non-white player, William Manie who had previously played in the British Open Championships was refused.

A statement issued by the SAGU stated that entries for the 1963 Open had closed and two entries from non-Europeans were received. A decision was reached to the effect that, with regard to their respective records, the extraordinary qualifications of Sewsunker Sewgolum were such that he should be permitted to play. Similar considerations were lacking in the other entry which was refused.

This was to motivate William Manie to emigrate, and he became the assistant professional at the Royal Winchester GC, and later the club professional at Richmond (UK).

In the light of the statement made by the Minister of the Interior that, if the SAGU accepted Papwa's entry, the government would consider legislation to prevent racial mixing on the sports field, and they requested that the SAGU reconsider the conditions of entry for future championships.

The SA Open Championship is one of the oldest national open golf championships in the world. In 1903, the first formal event was organised following a series of exhibition matches held over the preceding ten years. The championship was initially contested over just 36 holes until 1908 when it was extended to become a 72-hole tournament.

The Indian gallery had one hope to represent them, and despite not being allowed to play any practice rounds, Papwa took the lead after the first round, opening with a 70, one-shot ahead of Bruce Keyter and George Farmer, followed by Harold Henning and Stewart Davies a further shot back.

After round two, and a 71, Papwa was still leading on 141 followed by Farmer a shot back. Three-shots behind on 144 was Keyter, with Retief Waltman lurking a further shot back.

Round three, and moving day, saw Waltman shoot a magnificent 67 climbing the leaderboard to share first place with Papwa who shot another 71 – 'Papwa dipped his knees and chipped the ball into the hole at the 18th' – both on 212. They were leading from a group of players, Keyter, Farmer, and John Hayes the amateur (Dale's brother) who shot an excellent 69, all on 216. Denis Hutchinson also shot a wonderful 67, but he was too far back.

Papwa was aiming to become the first person of colour

to win the SA Open Championship as he and Retief Waltman battled it out all the way playing together in the final round.

By the 14th, many people were running to get to the next tee-box after Papwa had putted out, and Waltman had to request that they halt to allow him to putt out. Papwa needed a 5m putt on the last green to tie. It just slid by the hole, and he was eventually beaten by a single shot, (70 71 71 70) 282, to Waltman's (74 71 67 69) 281, but it could not dim the brilliance of his fighting display. Papwa was the only player to score under par in all four rounds.

Retief was 24, Papwa 34, a new generation of youngsters were now coming through, yet Papwa had only been allowed to play his first 'white' tournament in SA aged 32, and then only sporadically.

The leading scores were:

R Waltman	74 71 67 69 — 281
S Sewgolum	70 71 71 70 — 282
S Davies	72 75 70 70 — 287
J Fourie*	78 73 70 67 — 288 (Freddie Tait Cup)

B Keyter	71 73 72 73 — 289
G A Farmer	71 71 74 75 — 291
D Hutchinson	75 76 68 73 — 292
A D Locke	76 71 74 72 — 293
P Oosthuizen	76 74 72 73 — 295
H R Henning	72 75 74 74 — 295
J Hayes*	73 74 69 79 — 295

Papwa's second-place finish to the brilliant Retief Waltman by one-shot needs to be put into perspective.

By then, Waltman was 24 and had already won the SA Open twice. The whole world lay before him. He was a potential superstar. Consider that Bobby Locke and Gary Player won the SA Open ten times between them from 1950–1969, and at the age of 24, Waltman had already won twice in that era.

He was a hero at home. A good five years after Waltman had handed in his golf shoes, a boy from Pietersburg was named in his honour. The young Goosen was christened Retief.

At this time, Retief Waltman was the brilliant young heir apparent to Gary Player having won the SA Open in 1961 and 1963, for which he believed in his own case, he received 'divine help and guidance'. For him the meaning of life lay in the Bible and not birdies.

In the 1964, Waltman narrowly missed the cut in his first Masters after rounds of 72 and 78. And that, he decided, was enough. "I wanted a purpose for my life. I was devoting my whole life to a game. Being so involved in golf limited me. Man is his own biggest enemy".

Consequently, shortly thereafter he just packed up his bags, gave his clubs away, said goodbye to the circus, and walked out on the game, found 'God' and engaged in missionary work retreating from the world of news and celebrity, and occasionally holding church services for black golfers prior to their events.

Meanwhile, Papwa took back his title when he won the 1963 SA Non-European Championship by 13 strokes at Walmer CC over the defending champion, Ismail Chowglay. Now a seasoned traveller, he finally returned to Europe, but on this occasion in 1963 with somewhat mixed success.

Further validation of Papwa's golfing prowess came when he finished thirteenth in the British Open played at Royal Lytham & St. Anne's Golf Club in England, won by Bob Charles (the most successful left-handed golfer that century winning more than 70 worldwide titles) with a score of 277 (-7) in a playoff with Phil Rodgers, with Jack Nicklaus a stroke behind.

In the first round of that championship, Papwa was tied tenth on the leaderboard with a score of 71, together with the greatest player of all time, Jack Nicklaus!

The Dutch Open played at The Hague was also won by SA Retief Waltman on 279. Papwa finished down the field on 289. Next came the German Open where Papwa was disqualified for being late on the tee. In truth, he was not well and only too happy to return home. Later in that year, the decision was taken to dissolve the 'Papwa Trust Fund'. The thought was that it had served its purpose. However, from a management point of view, Louis Nelson had failed Papwa.

A manager is supposed to source sponsorship and place a management team around his man to allow him to concentrate on his golf, and not only apply to participate in tournaments and travel arrangements (it appears as if that was all he did). All Papwa had to show insofar as sponsorship were golf balls from Dunlop and a set of clubs every five years.

At the same time, he should have either invested some of Papwa's winnings or at least mentored and instructed Papwa insofar as to the management of money and ensured there were funds for further escapades abroad. Instead, Papwa would continue to generously spend the majority of his winnings and bring home only a minor portion.

By this time trade union leader, Nelson was becoming politically vocal and tried unsuccessfully to also persuade Papwa to speak out against the apartheid regime. This irked Nelson. But it was Papwa's living and Papwa's neck, not Nelson's which would be on the line. It was obvious that Nelson was now too busy to manage Papwa's affairs.

I Have a Dream

August 1963: Martin Luther King Jnr

'I have a dream that my four little children will one day live in a nation where they will not be judged by the colour of their skin, but by the content of their character. I have a dream today!'

While there was always the veiled threat that Papwa's participation in open competition was contrary to government policy, nevertheless permits to play were mostly granted and the summer of 1963/64 was a busy one for Papwa.

A series of three Grand Prix sponsored tournaments was on the schedule to be held in Durban, Cape Town and, finally, Johannesburg. Papwa played in all three, and in November 1963, he won the prestigious Grand Prix tournament at Royal Durban CC with scores of 71 72 73 70 (286). Once again, he received his trophy in the rain, but this time – the runner-up likewise received his outside.

Papwa was proving to be a thorn in the side of the National Party and the invincibility of white sportsmen, but they still had their white champion, as he was runner-up in the Richelieu Grand Prix to Gary Player, at King David, Cape Town.

He had opened with a 72, which placed him two strokes behind Player, and he had the second largest mixed-race gallery of 2,000 following him. They drew reverberating applause when he recovered from behind the tree for a par-4 at the 17th after his drive, instead of drawing continued straight down the left side of the fairway into the rough. His curious upside-down grip continued to fascinate the gallery, and his courtly manners made an excellent impression.

He finished twelfth in the third leg at Kensington GC, and tied for eighth place on 289 in the 'Open 5000' sponsored tournament held at Kensington GC.

A few days later he was told that his application to play, along with that of Ismail Chowglay (now 31 and playing in his first SA 'white' tournament), in the 1964 SA Open had been accepted, but no practising, and only for the four-day duration of the tournament – this time in Bloemfontein in the OFS, where Indians had been barred since the 1890s. (It would take until 1972 before an African was allowed to play)

The event in Bloemfontein presented fresh challenges for the two players of colour and the National Party government. In terms of the laws of the Free State province at that time, Indians were not permitted to spend more than 24 hours at a time inside its borders. As a result, the two Indian golfers were forced to commute from Kimberley every day. At the tournament, they were provided with a standing-room tent, pitched a few metres from the clubhouse in which to change.

The evening before the commencement of the tournament, Papwa and Chowglay were barred from the golfer's reception for the visiting 300 golfers playing in the SA Amateur and Open championships as municipal regulations did not allow social fraternisation with non-whites.

Meanwhile, during round one, the foreign television crew focused their camera on the tent provided, and their coming and going, and then panning back to the luxurious clubhouse with the white players entering, thereby causing the organisers much embarrassment, so that the following day they replaced the tent with a caravan. Supporters of both players were now entertained, but still separated from the white players and their supporters.

Papwa opened with an eventful 69 round one, only one shot behind the maestro Bobby Locke and Bruce Keyter who both shot 68s, and one shot ahead of Retief Waltman and Allan Henning.

Round two, Papwa found himself tied for fourth place on 140 (70, 70) together with Keyter, five behind the leader, left-hander Bob Charles who had shot a brilliant 66, and one behind second-placed Trevor Wilkes and Bobby Locke.

Chowglay failed to make the cut, and it would be a number of years before he was again allowed to play in a 'white' tournament.

After the third round having shot 71, he was right in the mix on 211, now only four shots behind Charles and young Allan Henning who shot an outstanding 67, and one shot behind third-placed Keyter and Trevor Wilkes. With Graham Henning on 212, followed by Player, Locke, and Waltman on 213. All to play for.

Another first-time winner of the SA Open emerged when no one was able to mount a challenge, although Gary Player shot an excellent 68, as 19-year old Allan Henning with a 71 for a total of 278 won the title. He was followed by Bruce Keyter on 280 and, tied for third place on 281, S. Sewgolum, G. Player, and New Zealand star Bob Charles, followed by the maestro Bobby Locke.

Bob Charles had a four-shot lead after two rounds and was tied with Allan Henning after the third round, but he finished weakly with 74. Three Henning brothers were in the field, Allan, Harold and Graham. Papwa was again under par in all four rounds.

One of the few photographs of the Henning brothers taken together. L. to R. Alan, Harold, Brian and Graham.

Leading scores were:

A Henning	70 70 67 71 — 278
B Keyter	68 72 70 70 — 280
S Sewgolum	69 71 71 70 — 281
R Charles (NZ)	69 66 72 74 — 281
G Player	74 71 68 68 — 281
A D Locke	68 71 74 69 — 282
T Wilkes	72 67 71 73 — 283
G Henning	71 69 73 71 — 284
R Waltman	70 75 68 71 — 284

Papwa was then back overseas campaigning, playing in a number of tournaments in Britain, including the Open Championship, then a fifteenth place in the German Open, and returning to Holland where amazingly, for the third time, he won a magnificent 3-stroke victory in the Dutch Open, once again over a top field of international golfers. This was again played at Eindhoven, and his scores were 67 71 66 71 (275), giving him a three-shot victory over Australian Ted Ball.

Papwa was lying second at the end of the first round two shots behind Harold Henning. But he took a two-stroke lead the following day, and almost made sure of winning with a 66. At this stage, he was five strokes ahead of Ball. In the final round, Papwa carded a 71 while the Australian returned a credible 69 to reduce the final deficit to three strokes, with Hutchinson fourth and Henning fifth. Papwa's win gave SA their fifth success in the championship in the previous six years.

1964	Sewsunker Sewgolum (3)	South Africa	Eindhovensche	275	3 strokes	Ted Ball

This victory, his third in the Dutch Open, received less publicity in Durban than his previous two triumphs in Holland as he was now an established name in world golf.

'The record books don't lie, three Dutch Opens, I repeat, three Dutch Opens in four attempts in six years.' said Ken Schofield, Executive Director European Tour

To put this into perspective, in the modern area, the only other players who won the Dutch Open three times were Seve Ballesteros, Bernhard Langer, and Simon Dyson.

Papwa often had problems with his health and, in spite of 'enjoying the best of my four trips overseas', this 1964 tour had to be curtailed when his struggle with jaundice proved too much.

He was once again mobbed by thousands of supporters at Durban airport, and it clearly shook the government.

But Papwa was denied entry for the Dunlop Masters, the Natal Open, the Transvaal Open, and the Western Province Open. 'The door was not permanently open'.

Both Sid Brews (eight-time SA Open champion and British Open runner-up) and Reg Taylor (inducted into the Southern Africa Golf Hall of Fame) came out in support of Papwa stating that an 'Open' is to allow the best players, irrespective of race, colour, nationality, religion, and any other affiliation, to compete and that Papwa had proven himself.

However, he was denied entry to the WP Open, forced to withdraw from the Transvaal Open, and initially refused entry to both the SA Open and Natal Open. He finished eleventh in both the PGA Championship at Germiston CC and the SA Masters at Zwartkops CC. The SAGU now instructed him to apply directly for his own permit.

Left-handed Ismail Chowglay playing with the reverse grip together with Papwa Sewgolum (right)

Similarly in 1964, it must have been difficult for Ismail 'Boy' Chowglay, the 1962 SA Non-European Open Champion, and caddymaster at Clovelly Country Club, now in his prime at the age of 31, to just watch Retief Waltman win the WP Open with a record breaking last round of 65 from Gary Player, followed by Harold Henning and Bobby Locke, at his home Clovelly course, where he would regularly shoot sub 70s. With his local knowledge, he would have been one of the favourites had he been allowed to compete. Permission still denied!

Of some interest were the measures that had to be taken to accommodate Papwa during the playing of the 'white' tournaments. At Houghton, he had a special flatlet at the back of the clubhouse with bed-sitting room and separate shower and toilet, and to allow the gallery to be mixed, a special permit was obtained

Insofar as the other tournaments where he could participate, he won the Cock 'o North Tournament in Ndola in Zambia against a strong 'white' field.

Papwa mesmerised the black SA opposition, and when he moved on to defend his SA Open title there were few who looked further than him for the winner.

He duly won the 1964 SA Non-European title at Glendower with a margin of 21 strokes when he retained the title, winning R200, with scores of 71 72 70 75 for 288, a new record for the Open and cemented his position at the top of the golf ladder (his 27-stroke win in the Western Province N-E Open merely confirmed this).

Ed 'Otto' Lee and Johannes Semenya on 309 were second sharing R150, Chowglay fourth and Hlapo fifth. Colourful Otto Lee playing with Papwa, entertained the gallery with his antics after hitting the ball as he twisted and swerved his body as if piloting the ball in flight.

There was Cox Hlapo, the Transvaal champion with his characteristic, enormous beard wearing a multi-coloured woollen headgear that looked like a beret, and then 'Goli-Goli' Mdeni, another fancied player.

On the whole, participants were more accustomed to the grass-veld courses in the townships and were somewhat disadvantaged when it came to the greens, as they simply 'cracked' when facing the pin. And that's where Papwa, now seasoned in playing on proper courses, capitalised.

1964 SA Non-European Championship, Glendower. Mrs F W. Pitman handing the trophy to the winner, 'Papwa' Sewgolum

Had Papwa any real opposition among the non-white golfers in the country? The answer was simple – he was unbeatable at this stage, and it would be many years before he would be ousted from that top position. Once again, Papwa was honoured as The Leader newspaper's Pepsi Cola 'Non-European Sportsman of the Year'.

History in the making: The Rivonia Trial

In 1963, Nelson Mandela was arrested for conspiring to overthrow the state and sentenced to life imprisonment in June 1964 in the Rivonia Trial. Mandela served 27 years in prison, split between Robben Island, Pollsmoor Prison, and Victor Verster Prison.

For the next 17 years, while Papwa challenged white sports superiority, Mandela and his comrades would only hear whispers concerning Sewsunker Sewgolum, the man who unwittingly became the symbol of the anti-apartheid sports movement.

BOYCOTT

More pressure was brought to bear on the SA authorities when in January 1965, Mr Hayden Banda, the Zambian Minister in an interview stated: 'This territory is to cut all sporting ties with South Africa. We will have no dealings with them as far as sport is concerned. South African teams cannot play here nor will Zambian teams be allowed to compete there.'

After being denied a place in the 1964 Olympics, SA was booted out of the Olympic Committee, with India being the prime advocate for their expulsion. In 1965, the Springboks faced stern criticism for their refusal, as on all previous tours of New Zealand, to play against a Maori representative team, and doubts were raised about the English cricket tour scheduled for the end of the decade.

However, Papwa's next big achievement happened in 1965 as he was set to rock the world once again.

BEATING THE WORLD CHAMPION

At the start of January 1965 (*statistics record this as 1964) Papwa lost the Natal Non-European Open which he dominated for the last eight years to 22-year-old, former caddie, Raydmuth Rajdaw (whose brother was the equally well known 'Anooplal').

The news of Papwa's defeat poured from the sports pages to the front pages of the Indian newspapers saying that he lacked the fighting qualities needed for competing on a professional level and called for opportunities for other black golfers to play overseas such as Rajdaw and Hlapo. But other newspapers saw it differently: 'His defeat will make him shake off his complacency. Up till now, he has been having it, more or less, his own way.'

Some critics were inclined to suggets that the champion was on his way out. That of course, was ridiculous. But it did show that Papwa was human, and his defeat was a tonic to his brother professionals, who had become supreme pessimists when there was talk of beating Papwa. Now they said, 'If Rajdaw can do it, so can I.'

Papwa was in a slump, and his defeat had also smashed the myth of his invincibility, and there was now a growing contingent of black golfers eager to beat the master at his game. Chowglay was widely believed to be equal to or better than Papwa. Vincent Tshabalala, a 23-year old furniture-store delivery driver for Dlamini, was another, and during the January SA Non-European Open, all three came together on the East London Golf course in a thrilling battle for ascendancy.

The temporary setback made Papwa all the more determined that he would preserve his near-unbeaten stroke play record on the SA fairways.

While waiting for his train from Bloemfontein as he travelled to East London, Vincent placed his suitcase down next to another, near a bench. When the train came in, nobody claimed the other suitcase, so Vincent told a railway policeman about it. The cop immediately took him, and the case to the station charge office.

'That's what scared me,' said Vincent. 'I remember the Johannesburg station suitcase bomb incident, and I thought I was being arrested. I was so upset, I nearly caught a train home.' It was just as well that Vincent went to East London as he played sparkling golf.

Ramphal Tiney took the lead equalling the Alexander CC course record with a 69, followed by Percy Mazibuko on 70, Hlapo 71, Ranjith 72, Tshabalala and Lee 73, with Papwa languishing behind with 77.

After Round Two, it was Tiney 69 73 (142), Papwa was 77 74 (151) nine behind. By lunchtime on the last day, Papwa had a one-stroke lead over Vincent, with Chowglay and Tiney following close behind him. Vincent took the lead between the 10th and 15th hole; however, he 3-putted the 16th, and they were once again tied.

The mixed crowd of spectators cheered every stroke played by the leaders, and by now the hot money was on Vincent. But Papwa was playing brilliantly, as was Vincent. At the final hole, Vincent was on the green for three within a foot of the pin and then sunk his putt.

Now it was Papwa's turn, he was ten feet away, and the gallery was silent as he stalked the hole, and settled himself knowing full well that the shot would determine the tournament. Nervelessly he potted it. They were tied, and players and spectators rushed over to congratulate both players. Papwa had done it again, with Chowglay, following a course record 69, one-shot behind, and Hlapo scoring a hole-in-one at the 14th.

As they had only been allotted a three-day permit for the event, there was no chance of a play-off, and the result was declared a draw.

Papwa received a total purse of R160 for coming second in the Natal and tied first in the SA Non-European Opens. But his application to play in the Natal Open was turned down.

Gary Player said he was disappointed with the ruling that Papwa could not play, declining to comment on the political aspect of Papwa's situation. However, the ruling was reversed, and one of the greatest duels in SA golf was allowed to commence.

Aged 29 in 1965, Gary Player became only the third golfer in history to win the Career Grand Slam. He accumulated nine major championships on the regular tour and nine Senior Tour major championship victories, and 165 tournaments on six continents over six decades.

The year 1965 was a big one for the king of SA golf, Gary Player, his 'golden year', when he was probably the 'Number One golfer in the world', and over this period together with Jack Nicklaus, Billy Casper, and Arnold Palmer, one of the top four golfers in the world. Together with Harold Henning, that year he won the Canada (later the 'World') Cup including the individual title beating the Americans for the first time, as well as the US Open to complete golf's Grand Slam of Majors. He took his third SA Open, his fourth Australian Open, and notched up wins in the World Series, World Matchplay (legendary comeback win over Tony Lema), and the NTL Challenge Cup.

Gary Player was at the peak of his career, he was 'walking on water', the National Party's white champion, and with a record that by then included three Major wins (including the 1959 Open Championship and 1962 Masters). Player was finally due to participate in the 1965 Natal Open alongside Papwa for the first time in SA, and despite his achievements, there was enormous speculation about how he would fare against Papwa.

Huge similarities. Both grew up poor boys, starting their passion for golf in their early years, with Papwa losing his father and Player his mother while both were very young.

As the world watched one of the most controversial fights in the sport's history, the re-match between the former underdog Muhammad Ali, the 'The Louisville Lip', and big bad Sonny Liston for boxing's World Heavyweight Championship. In SA, sports lovers waited for the duel which had all the ingredients of a heavyweight match for the four-round golfing champion of SA!

Muhammad Ali

Thursday, 14 April 1993: Ali lay down on the bed in a cramped cell in which Nelson Mandela lived for most of his 19 years he was incarcerated on Robben Island: 'I would have gone crazy in there', said Ali. 'But for a cause like he had, I would do it. I can just imagine how lonely he was in there.'

To win you need four commandments: consolidate, dominate, subjugate, and annihilate.
Danie Craven

In the white corner, the champion, standing 1,7m tall, weighing in at 69kg, age 29; the white 'Black Knight', a heavyweight giant of the fairways with three Majors, three SA Opens, and four Australian Opens, having once again been victorious in the SA Open, and a previous winner of four Natal Opens.

In the black corner, playing out of Durban, the Indian contender, standing 1,7m tall, weighing in at 65kg, aged 37, classified non-white, the only person of colour in the white field, the heavyweight of non-European golf with nine Natal 'Non-European' Open titles, six SA Non-European Opens, three Dutch Opens, and the Natal Open. This shack-dwelling, illiterate, former caddy, who was not allowed to play pre-tournament practice rounds, had won at home and abroad despite the seemingly insurmountable obstacles, with the 'Papwa Army' of Indian fans following his every move.

The hot money was on the white guy. But who would win and be the champion golfer?

This was 'war', a chance for blacks to prove that the black sportsmen were the equal of white sportsmen, and break down the government's perception of invincibility. Prime Minister Hendrik Verwoerd was confident that finally Papwa would be put in his place. Papwa's supporters told him that he could win despite not being able to practice on the course prior to the tournament. Speculation abounded, and the fans held their bated breath.

Papwa, unlike Player, did not like the rigors of practising and hitting hundreds of golf balls as he did not have to concentrate in the absence of competition, causing mutterings that he was lazy. So with Player pounding away on the practice range, he went fishing to relax and prepare himself.

Once again he would have to change and eat in his car and use the caddy facilities for his other needs. The stakes got even higher when Papwa returned to his vehicle in the car park before the tournament and found a dead Indian myna bird placed under one of the windscreen wipers.

The common 'myna' bird, derived from the Hindi language mainā, is a bird of the Starling family native to India, although several species had been introduced to SA. The plumage is dark, brown, with yellow head ornaments. Clearly this was both an ominous warning to Papwa were he to try and beat Player, and cause emotional distress to him before teeing off. Deeply disturbed, Papwa tried to wipe out the memory as he focused on what he had to do.

The Durban Country Club, established in 1922, overlooking the Blue Lagoon estuary and the Indian Ocean, saw an astounding feat that week. For three days, Gary Player, Harold Henning, and Papwa Sewgolum went head-to-head as their supporter bases swelled and became increasingly vocal and animated.

The first five holes were considered among the games most taxing starts. The appealing ripples found down the first fairway already lined with spectators, a 351 par-4, had the hole swinging left around the dunes with a hint of the glories that were to come. The approach shot to the green sat atop a dune with a swale in the front of the green, while behind the green the views highlighted how close the course was to the Indian Ocean.

Denis 'Hutch' Hutchinson took the round one lead shooting a 70, followed by a group of players on 71 including Player. Papwa also on 71, was still a distinct threat and like Bobby Jones, he preferred someone else to set the pace in the opening rounds. He played against the course, never against the field.

During round two, a stiff southerly wind sprang up late

in the morning, and the late starters faced difficult conditions. Papwa again wasn't putting well and holed nothing of significance. However, he 3-putted only once – at the 7th.

He dropped shots at the 1st hole, and another at the 7th, but picked up one at the 10th, 13th, and the 14th, but lost shots at the 12th, 15th and 17th for a 73, and now trailed Player by one shot.

His impassive face showed nothing of the turmoil inside him, knowing that a mishit shot might mean the loss of hundreds of rands. After he had finished the second round, he was more content because he felt that he now had the measure of the course and himself.

By the third and final day, as the sun came out, Papwa's game, too, came out of the shadows. With every stroke he played he seemed more certain as his golf became a thing of graceful, effortless beauty. All the old confidence was back, and there was an uncanny air of finality in the way he paced himself.

Sensing a battle between the white's favourite sporting son and their hometown hero, Durban's Indians flocked to the white-only course in droves.

Papwa's army of Indian supporters among the gallery consisted of black, coloured, Indian, and white, was growing into thousands, swarming across the fairways, most having never been onto a golf course, let alone knowing the rules of golf. They were unruly, kicking balls around and making a lot of noise, even while the players were playing their shots despite the marshals' attempts to control them, and as soon as Papwa had played, they were off not waiting for Player to finish putting.

Papwa had edged up the board to be one of the tournament leaders, as he burned the course from tee down the fairway and scorched even the greens. He and Player were paired together for the last two rounds, with Papwa one-shot behind. It was more like match-play between Papwa and Player.

As spectators jostled for a better view, tempers flared and muttered curses of 'coolies' were heard betraying the titanic battle they were watching, a match between races and cultures – between the darling of the white suprema-cists and the living hope of the oppressed.

Off the course, Papwa, like many of his supporters was severely disadvantaged. The golf course was the one place that allowed him a chance at equality, and he was deter-mined not to let his 'army' down.

The only shot that matters is the next shot. Focus 100 per cent on the shot in hand. What's happened is history. You don't want to get too excited or start thinking ahead. Stay in the present. One shot at a time!

A titanic battle was developing as Henning blitzed the field with a brilliant 69, pulling level with Player and Pap-wa shooting 72 and 71 respectively. All three in the running going into the final round, and the knowlegable money re-mained on Player.

The fourth round, Player immediately picked up an-other shot after a magnificent drive saw him birdie the first, Papwa was now two shots behind the leader Gary Player and equal second with Harold Henning after they both dropped shots at the first.

Player immediately picked up another shot – now three behind – clearly the occasion was too big for Papwa as the white members of the crowd cheered loudly while the Indian army was quiet.

The seething gallery knew that he was closer to defeat

than he had ever been in his short playing career. He was not only playing against the skill of his opponents, but against years of experience, but never for a moment did Papwa change his tactics.

These enthusiastic and partisan supporters contrasted with Player's reserved white gallery. Well-dressed whites many wearing their short khaki pants with long socks, and the colourful flowing saris of the Indian women as they followed their maestros, streaming down the fairway after their 'man'.

Player and his caddy walked ahead of Papwa, there was no talking, as they focused on what lay ahead. The second was halved in par-4s as tension gnawed away with both spectators and players. They understood what was at stake.

There was something inhuman about his play that afternoon. He churned out a stream of perfect strokes from the production belt that was his swing. He was hitting his drives further than he had been doing for some time, but the foundation of his score was the straightness of his second to the flag and his short game.

Then trouble found Player on the par 5 third hole, a possible 'eagle' hole, when he cut his ball landing in a small stand of bush and thick tropical trees as the suns rays streamed through the undergrowth, and small black faced silvery-grey vervet monkeys chattered in the treetops above. An Indian man picked up a ball and took it to Player: 'Is this your ball?' Player rounded on the man for picking up the ball, and there were mutterings among the Indian crowd, but it was not his ball.

After the five-minute allotted time, the ball was declared lost. Even if found it would have been unplayable, nevertheless he was a little upset when it was reported that an Indian spectator had pocketed the ball, and so Player returned to the tee with a two-shot penalty, clearly rattled, such that he signed for an eight to Papwa's par-5. A turning point of the tournament. A huge swing – now they were even as they matched each other stroke for stroke.

By the 14th they were both two shots behind Henning, then the pressure began. After Player had shot three birdies in a row to draw level, word filtered back that Henning now had the lead and they only had five holes to play. This was where champions kick in. Papwa seemed to be playing as if in a trance.

Inspired, Papwa, mopped his brow and replied with an eagle 3. His supporters who had swelled to a few thousand erupted, running over the green before Player had completed the hole. Player countered with a birdie then commented: 'If this goes on I just cannot play in these tournaments any more,' Clearly the pressure was on.

Mutterings from Player's supporters included that Papwa had taken too long to play his third shot, but it was that eagle at the 14th in the afternoon round that finally clinched the title for Papwa, the second turning point, and Papwa must have thought that this par 5,442m – 14th, was his Eldorado.

In the morning round, he gained a hard-earned par-5 when everything pointed to him dropping at least two shots. He had driven into the rough, saw his iron to the green kick left and back into the rough, played a weak third, and then chipped his fourth over the back of the green. But to everyone's surprise, he calmly chipped the ball into the hole as if he was doing it every day.

The afternoon effort was even more amazing. A good drive was followed by a magnificent three-wood to the back of the green, and then he sank the 15-footer for his two-under par eagle 3. They matched each other with pars over the next two holes - pressure and Papwa missed a 7-foot (2m) putt on the 17th and audible groans and worried looks. Player missed – the atmosphere was electric.

Papwa was being followed by hordes of enthusiastic

fans, noisily rooting for their hero. 'Come on Papwa,' yelled a young fan as the marshals' tried to take control as they moved to the 18th tee – the same hole where Papwa nearly lost the 1963 Natal Open.

Crowd control was not of the best and Player was somewhat unnerved by Papwa's jostling fans, as he began complaining about being 'put-off' by the talking jostling Papwa Army when he was lining up vital putts, but none of this detracts from Papwa's achievement.

Admonished by Player, they informed him that they were there to watch their hero, Papwa, not Player, while Player's supporters were willing him to pull a rabbit out of the hat and win again. Was it too late to save the game? And the government took notice.

So, by the 18th, Papwa held a one-shot lead over Player who was level with Henning. By then, spectators ran across fairways and encroached onto the green, refusing to heed the marshall's warnings when confronted to get a better spectating position. Seven thousand were lining both sides of the fairway.

His body felt tight but strong, pumped up, heart pounding, grimly focused, Papwa had the honour, launched his drive, came up on it rather quickly, the ball faded – far right, gathering momentum as it rolled down a slope, well below the green.

Papwa had an awkard up-hill pitch to play and instead of being in a position to win outright, now he was battling for a tie. His wedge pitch shot flew into a greenside bunker to the right of the green.

Ignoring the muttering from the crowd, as in anticipation they held their breath, he calmly exploded from the sand, and the ball sailed up over the lip of the bunker, landing with a thud, released, and rolled a few feet from the pin. It would require another superb putt for him to avoid a tie as Player had driven the green and was lying handy to repeat his eagle of the first round.

In silence as he walked up and down the line of that vital putt. A cine camera whirred. Papwa motioned to the offender and there was complete quiet. Again he surveyed the line. There was a nasty drop from the top of the hole. It was so easy to be short, yet too much strength and the downhill slope would carry the ball off line. The ball as guided by a magnet never left the line of the hole. Papwa dropped the putt for his par-4.

In the enormous cheer echoing over the course, Player heard the death toll of defeat. Player was faced with a three-metre putt to force the play-off. He clipped the putt in total silence as everyone held their collective breath. It rolled gathering pace straight for the cup, then slackened loosing momentum, taking the slope and at the last moment veering left, and lipped the cup.

Papwa, despite all the indignities and challenges, had stared down the champion and become the finest golfer in all of SA (for that day, at least) as with scores of 71 73 71 70 (285) he defeated the great Gary Player 71 72 72 71 (286) head-to-head and Harold Henning 73 73 69 71 (286) by one-shot to take his second Natal Open in three years.

For the first time in those grim holes, Papwa allowed his face to ease into a happy boyish grin of delight.

Once again the SABC refused to broadcast 'mixed sports' news of Papwa's win, despite 'David's' victory over 'Goliath', although it filtered back onto the Riverside streets, so that they were ready to cheer him on his way home, as friends and neighbours started to throng outside his home in a mood of defiant revelry.

Gary Player was in scintillating form making Papwa's feat all the more remarkable. This time it was not raining, only drizzling, and a red carpet was laid out on the 18th green where all the players received their prizes.

Afterwards, Gary Player sportingly commented that he

had no excuse and that Papwa: 'On today's showing Papwa deserved his victory, he chipped like a genius. Every time I thought he was in trouble, back he came to pull one out of the bag.'

Subsequently discussing this with Rajen Sewgolum, Papwa's son: 'It was a big thing your father beating me then because I was the champion. He beat me when I was playing very very well. His mind was outstanding, and he was one of the greatest gentlemen.'

Despite not winning, Player was happy for him as they stood to receive their prizes with Papwa's Army of 1,200 supporters looking on, as it meant Papwa could now go and play in Australia.

The word was out among the Indian community when it dawned on them that Papwa was going to beat Player and others. It showed that if a man of colour was given a chance, he could beat the whites, and even if he could not articulate their desires, they had their man who could embarrass the government, and delirious, they mobbed Papwa.

'You're a symbol. And when you beat Gary Player, beat the best golfer in the world, you sent out a message, the message that maybe whites aren't automatically better than you and I,' said Louis Nelson. 'They can't stomach it. Gary is their blue-eyed boy. Now they will see you as a troublemaker. They just don't understand. How can it be, a nobody from Riverside can beat their man.'

When interviewed after the victory as to how he found playing with Player: 'I have found Gary to be very friendly although one might think he is not so while he is busy concentrating on the greens, particularly. He was always quick to compliment me when I had a good shot.'

Papwa added that the gallery – all of them, white or non-white – were real sportsmen. They never failed to show their appreciation. When questioned further about the crowd, he said, 'it is always difficult to control a crowd like that, but I did not find any real problems with them. On the whole, I think they were good.'

The white press reported 'Papwa deserved to win despite the disgraceful behaviour of the gallery', but then went on to add that clearly Player was out of form (despite shooting 286).

Papwa's victory was earned the hard way playing with Player over the last 36-holes, and he never allowed himself to get flustered. In fact, he showed absolute determination throughout, never permitting his opponent to unsettle him. When Player turned on the pressure with three birdies in four holes, Papwa replied with an eagle. It was Player who became unsettled by Papwa's army of supporters.

Herbert Warren Wind wrote: 'I have an idea that it will be only a matter of time now before a major title falls to the world's greatest cross-handed golfer – Sewsunker Sewgolum.'

Papwa won because he was the best golfer in the field, and the best tactician. He knew that accuracy was needed above all else and, except for the second round, his play was straight and true from tee to green.

This victory should not to be taken lightly, as Player would go on to win the US Open later that year and complete the Grand Slam.

There were no celebratory drinks at the club – it would jeopardise the club's liquor licence, so Papwa went home to enjoy a sumptuous meal, with the trophy on the table, and a bottle of Cain-spirit to fill the glasses. He retold his victory hole by hole to the children late into the night – he had achieved the impossible!

Slazenger, the sponsor of his clubs, sent R60, and Dunlop provided an additional 150 free golf balls for the year and money for expenses. The Castle Wine and Brandy Co. (Pty) Ltd sponsored him to the tune of R150, the Indian Community of Greytown presented him with a radiogram, while Coca-Cola sponsored him with R200 for the following three years.

This happened at a time when there was deep depression amongst blacks, as the Indian Congress had been banned, and all the black leadership jailed, with Robert Sobukwe, Nelson Mandela, and Oliver Tambo shipped off to Robben Island. This was the vacuum into which Papwa stepped unintentionally. Now they had their champion who was going to embarrass the national government which maintained blacks were inferior to whites.

This was just too much for the apartheid government; the bubble of invincibility of their white sportsmen compared to black sporting heroes had burst. His victory was seen as a symbolically threatening event by the apartheid leaders. Papwa was regarded as a man looking for trouble instead of an athlete passionate about his game. An illiterate man was beating a white icon to boot.

Within two weeks the government clamped down on mixed audiences. Papwa's supporters had distressed many white spectators, and the government was concerned about the ramification of Papwa's progress.

Although Player retracted and denied some of his beliefs later on in his life, at the peak of his career, he was an apartheid-sympathiser and identified with the regime. Despite this, Papwa considered Player a friend and they both shared a common interest in their country.

'My father was never bitter despite all the things that happened to him. He was very humble on and off the course, and he always controlled his temper. He was a good man.' said Rajen Sewgolum.

'Papwa's win may have widespread implications. There is a danger that any ban may result in the world blackballing SA sportsmen,' stated the Cape Times.

Days after this magnificent feat, the National government saw it necessary to further restrict 'non-white' audiences from attending certain sporting events decreeing that mixed sport would not be permitted, and in so doing, effectively blocking Papwa's army of supporters from attending the SA PGA Championships. Prime Minister, Hendrik Verwoerd then took matters further by warning New Zealand that they would not be allowed to tour SA with mixed-race Maoris in their squad. The world took notice, and a number of new boycotts were implemented.

This prompted an international outcry causing a re-action from those blindly following apartheid who were determined not to make any 'concessions' and explicitly thwarted Papwa's chance of representing his own country in golf.

Papwa still had permission to play in some tourna-ments, and after opening with a 71 in the fourth position, he finished twelfth behind Player in the SA Open at Royal Cape GC and third in the SA Masters at Royal Durban GC. He was fifth in the PGA Tournament at Houghton, fifteenth in the Liquidair '5000' at Kensington GC, and fifth in the 1965 Flame Lily tournament in Bulawayo.

Clearly, Papwa's performances placed a severe and very public dent in the government's fantasies of white suprema-cy. Papwa's success embarrassed them, and his play became a matter of national security. Permission to play in a string of events were denied, and all appeals failed

He continued winning the non-European tournaments by large margins, but this earned him a pittance. His aver-age monthly income was around R35 in 1965.

At the end of all this period, and despite not playing in the Transvaal and Western Province Opens, Papwa never-theless finished third on the South African Order of Merit for the 64/65 season.

Gary Player	12 rounds	70, 25	R 1 750
Harold Henning	28 rounds	71, 03	R 2 940
Papwa Sewgolum	20 rounds	71, 90	R 1 448

This result should have been sufficient for Papwa to be selected to represent South Africa and partner Gary Player in the Canada (World) Cup, but instead Harold Henning partner Player to a sensational eight stroke victory over the Spanish team of Angel Miguel and Roman Sota, followed by Jack Nicklaus and Arnold Palmer to win the Canada Cup, with Player winning the individual low player of the tournament two shots ahead of Nicklaus.

1965 RESULT COMPARISON: 'PAPWA'

'PAPWA' SEWGOLUM		GARY PLAYER	
S.A Non-European Open	1st	US Open	1st
Transvaal Non-European Open	1st	SA Open	1st
Natal Non-European Open	1st	Australian Open	1st
Natal Thunderbird Classic	1st	NTL Challenge Cup (Canada)	1st
Griqualand West N-E Open	1st	Piccadilly World Match Play	1st
Natal Open	1st	World Cup & Individual Trophy	1st
SA Masters	3rd	World Series of Golf	1st
SA Open	12th	The Masters	2nd
SA PGA Championship	5th	Natal Open	2nd
Flame Lily (Rhodesia)	5th		
Carling World Golf Championship	8th		
1964/65 Order of Merit	3rd *	1964/65 Order of Merit	1st

despite being denied permission to play in the Western Province & Transvaal Opens

HOW TO WIN A MAJOR

Gary Player's letter dated 4 September 1965 to a friend shows what it took to win the 1965 US Open, and what would be required if Papwa was to push on and become a superstar.

Akron Ohio, USA
4ᵗʰ September 65

Hello There,

Bravery your intelligence. I will follow up my last letter written to you out of the blue, and the North Pole, with others from different parts of the world.

Just think of it – when the blue print for the design of the human being were laid down, he was geared to travel at 5 miles per hour, and here we are tearing around often at speed everything at 600 miles per hour! To my mind, therefore, the ability to adapt myself to an efficient, but this undoubtedly helped me to win the US Open this year! In golf rhythm is important, correct pacing is vital for proper match approach and physical coordination. The composed golfer who arrives early on the tee is better equipped to play than the one who scrambles on the golf course after a 40 mile p h dash in a motor car. How I pace myself in my travels also is illustrated on the JHB. NY. JHB run which I do attend 6 times a year. I take the fastest flight from JHB to NY with a stopover of a couple of hours in Frankfort. Take a little exercise even if it is walking or deep breathing, and sometimes I stimulate circulation. I round this off with a massage which the Lufthansa officials kindly help me to organise , as indeed they do any other requirement that I or my family may have in Frankfort from time to time.

The ... is so invigorating that I thoroughly enjoy the flight across the Atlantic and feel that I have a restful sleep each time. To describe my feelings on being welcomed back to South Africa after the US Open is difficult. They were not the feelings of triumph at all really, but of tremendous pride in the people and the country to which I belong with the inevitable pressure of event following my US Open win.

*I am now trying to slow my entire metabolism down to a nor-
mal pace and to apply my own maxim – "When pressure and
tension become too much don't brace yourself pace yourself!"
Well having written a little more than intended, I must now
RUSH – SLOWLY – to the practice tee!?!?!?!?*

TOTSIENS,

Gary Player

In January 1966, now aged 37, Papwa resigned from his
factory job to dedicate himself entirely to golf, practising
every day on different golf courses as well as doing stren-
uous exercises and regular 6km runs to keep his weight in
check at 65kg.

As the lone 'darkie' on the white professional circuit,
Papwa could enter their tournaments, but not the clubhouse. He gambled everything by giving up his job and
going into strict training for full-time golf. On the black
circuit, if he won everything – the South African, Natal,
Transvaal, Western Province, Kimberley, and Port Elizabeth Opens, he could earn possibly R500.

With no wealthy sponsor such as many white professionals had and no private club to pay him, he could barely
support himself and his family on this, let alone fund the
cash to play on the big circuit overseas.

He hoped this year would be his big year, after all, he
had beaten Gary Player. He entered a string of white tournaments where winnings added up to as much as R20,000 and
aimed to make enough to invade the US the following year.

But the sports authorities of the apartheid era had other ideas, and again set their sights on him when as the defending champion, he applied for a permit to play in the
Natal Open in 1966 and initially they refused him permission to participate.

Papwa now had a new manager (since 1964) in the modest loyal Fred Paul (or FM as he liked to be called) with his trademark moustache, a successful insurance salesman (Louis Nelson was now also the President of the Durban Golf Club having jumped ship opting for a higher leadership role in the labour movement) and they were escorted to the Security Branch offices for a 'chat'. They wanted answers as to why they were continually applying for permits for Papwa to enter tournaments, suggesting that they were troublemakers. After hours of answering the same questions, they were released.

His rejection letter stated that the permit allowing 'Mr Sewgolum (Indian) to occupy the Royal Durban Golf Club is refused'. No reason was given.

There was much consternation that this might lead to SA golfers being blackballed worldwide, and a special plea was made to the Minister of Planning to reverse the decision.

A few days later this decision was reversed, with permit permission for Indian and coloured spectators approved, but not Africans. The problem was how to keep the indian and white spectators apart.

Again permission to play arriving so late, created mental strain, brought about by the uncertainty, as he desperately needed to play to qualify for the Carling World Championship.

And so he was subsequently allowed to defend his Natal Open title at Royal Durban GC, finishing strongly on scores of 75 73 73 71 (292), for fourth place, losing to Gary Player's score of 286 followed by Cobie le Grange and Tommy Horton in second and third. Behind him were Tony Jacklin (future multiple Major winner), Ryder cup George Wills, Lionel Platts, and Bobby Cole.

It was not a particularly good tournament for Papwa who, despite his lack of practice improved each round, but he was not at his best and weak on his chipping that was usually very accurate, and perhaps the strongest phase of his game.

To complicate matters, given that Papwa was playing under the threat of banning, official efforts at separating the races soon collapsed and possibly with them, any hope of Papwa getting government approval for the next tournament.

The decision by the government was that Papwa could only play in events in which he had previously played up to the end of the previous year, and then still only subject to the issue of the necessary permit.

The professional circuit in Rhodesia (that is the former Southern Rhodesia following the break-up of the Federation and the declaration of Unilateral Declaration of Independence (UDI) by Ian Smith) in 1966 and subsequent years consisted of three events, the Dunlop Tournament, the Bata Bush Babes Tournament and the Haig Flame Lily Tournament.

These were all open non-racial events, and Papwa Sewgolum took the opportunity to play in all three, but he was the only black golfer to do so, as Rhodesian black golfers were not allowed to participate.

There was a strong representation of South Africa's best professionals, and Papwa was able to compete with the best. In the Dunlop he finished fifth (71 75 71 71 (288)) five shots behind winner Allan Henning, he won the Bush Babes (71 73 72 69 (285)) by three shots from Trevor Wilkes, and he finished eighth in the Flame Lily (72 69 75 72 (288)).

This relatively busy, and one must add, lucrative schedule clashed with the SA Non-European Championship. Accordingly, he did not play in the 1966 Non-European Open held in Bloemfontein which was won by David 'Bobby Locke' Motati.

While playing in the PGA at Germiston, he was informed that he was banned from the following WP Open, and he appealed. More bannings were to follow to prevent him from qualifying for the lucrative $200,000 Carling World Championships in Canada in September, as selections were based on the important SA tournaments, in case he succeeded on the world stage and drew attention.

Worse was to follow. Upon his return home, Papwa was informed that Riversdale, where he lived, had now been declared a 'white area' under the Group Areas Act, and he had to relocate to Mobeni Heights. This was an area set aside for Indians in Chatsworth consisting of 11 neighbourhoods and a total of 20,000 sub-economic and low-cost houses reserved exclusively for Indian occupation; a buffer area between white and the black Umlazi township.

It was evident that any efforts to compete in predominantly white tournaments was an exercise in futility. To add insult to injury, Papwa now discovered that the Security Branch, which had monitored his movements for some time, had a thick file on him, and this knowledge must have placed considerable pressure on him. Intelligence agents started moving into their area and began looking for any sinister things trying to dig up 'dirt' on Papwa, for instance, that he was an insurgent carrying mail to different underground 'terrorists'.

Still awaiting a response to his appeal, and while preparing in the hope of competing in the WP Open in Cape Town burly security police burst through the door in District Six, hauling him out of bed in the dead of night while staying at the home of prominent activist Sissy Gool. They demanded to know what Papwa was doing in Cape Town, and warned him that he had become an embarrassment to the SA government, threatening to do something about it if he continued to compete in white tournaments.

Papwa responded that he had come to play as the minister had yet to make his pronouncement concerning his appeal. 'You banned, boy. You not allowed to play! Didn't you know that? Have you seen all the trouble you make?

We know what to do with troublemakers, Robben Island is just out there. Continue and we going to get you!'

Shortly afterwards, still shaken, Papwa and Fred Paul drove to Port Elizabeth for the General Motors Open. The organisers had had arranged a caravan for the two on the course as well as two 'white' security guards whose presence suggested they were more likely to be security police, supposedly to keep them safe from agitators and fans.

When darkness set in, the clouds rolled in and blotted out the moonlight, Papwa suggested Fred take the guards some hot tea, but when Fred peered out of the caravan, the guards were nowhere to be seen. They felt alone and in the eery pitch-black night, Fred's gut was sending him a message as during the day they had also noticed some men with closely-cropped hair watching their movements and the caravan.

Still disturbed by their Cape Town experience and the chilling message from the security police, Fred suggested that they quietly depart the caravan, especially given the isolation of the club. They checked into a non-white hotel in the city.

The next crisp breezy morning, as the sun was rising, they returned showered and refreshed, feeling a little foolish and teased each other about their stupidity and fears. The security guards were back outside the caravan, and for just a second, Papwa thought he saw a puzzled look on their faces as they caught sight of them.

Chatting, Fred suddenly stopped as he opened the caravan door, and a strong wave of gas hit them. The caravan was reeking of gas. But neither of them had touched the stove, and surprised, they backed away rapidly waiting for an explosion.

They walked over to the clubhouse and sought out the manager. Together, with the maintenance manager, and on further inspection, they discovered that the gas pipe leading to the stove had been tampered with and cut during the night. Gas is a silent killer. The assassination had failed!'

CHAPTER SEVEN

Reaction

BANNED

Because of his success, and as part of an increasing clamp down on all forms of interracial sport, he found it tougher, despite the newfound respect among his peers, to raise money to play overseas. Playing abroad was no longer as successful, and the 'Papwa Trust Fund' was drying up.

Meanwhile, companies used his fame, getting him to promote their products, but in return, instead of cash payments, one prominent liquor company simply offered him a case of 'Cain spirits' every month as payment. No corporate sponsored a player of colour, no matter how famous.

Cracks slowly, sometimes agonisingly slowly, appeared in the SA sports wall that kept black sportsmen out of the establishment. Pressure was brought to bear, both externally and internally when in 1966 Senator Robert Kennedy (President John F Kennedy's brother, and the previous USA attorney-general prior to his bid for the USA Democratic nomination and his subsequent assassination) addressed UCT. His inspirational Day of Affirmation speech at the University of Cape Town is widely considered one of the greatest American civil rights speeches, where he spoke out about his belief that all people have a basic human right to participate in the political decisions that affect their lives.

Now changes for which Papwa had been one of the catalysts, but were too slow to benefit him, opened the way for younger sportsmen to inch their way into open participation.

And then it happened, the severest of all blows. The ban which golfers of all races from all over the country feared came at the end of the 1966 season – irony: the year of Verwoerd's assassination. The government declared Papwa, now 38 and still in his prime, ineligible to play in white tournaments. This continued until the 1971/2 season. Papwa was effectively banned, and when asked for his comments, Gary Player said, 'I do not meddle in politics.' Later he did speak out in support of Papwa saying he should be allowed to play in SA golf tournaments.

As Drum magazine headline put it: 'Is Sewgolum Sunk?', and 'Papwa – Ghost of Golf?'

A golfing ghost, a dark shadow drifting about white golf courses, among the white professionals, but not one of them. They, the best of them, led exotic lives, pursuing golf balls halfway across the world. He, who ranked with the best of them, rented two rooms in a Durban shack for himself, his wife and four young children, and scraped around to find extra cash to support his blind mother.

Once he had a shack of his own, but that was swept away with the building of the new Northern Freeway. He holds unquestionably one record: the world's poorest professional golfer who has won three National Opens.

The outlawing of Papwa clearly affected the standing of SA's best ambassador-of-goodwill, Gary Player. Player was a hero in America and treated with respect, yet the last thing he wanted was to have his name connected with a 'racial' incident. But this is what happened. Player's remarks that in SA, sport and politics were one and the same game simply meant that black, anti-South African groups now targeted him.

There were just a few tournaments for blacks, and although he was good wherever he played, how could he be expected to be competition sharp? With his soul amputated, Papwa became very ill, depressed, and worried as to how he would make ends meet and support his family, he began declining.

The politics of sport entered the SA sporting arena

more forcibly and on a much larger scale than ever before: multiracial versus multinational.

Papwa had become a severe embarrassment for the National Party government, which faced growing international scrutiny, particularly in the wake of the 1960 Sharpeville massacre. However, instead of easing its race laws, it was determined not to give in to the growing pressure

The government, which had decreed that mixed sport would not be permitted, lashed out at the global community, but the country was now almost certainly wholly isolated during the 1970s and 1980s.

When Papwa was barred from competing in the Transvaal Open, it effectively prevented him from qualifying and competing at the lucrative championships overseas. He took his plea to Vorster but never received a response.

> This humble letter is designed to bring to your notice the many difficulties I am faced with in order to play in the South African Golf Circuit... I am proud to be South African and I shall always remain loyal to my country. This banning order preventing me from playing golf for a living will indeed cripple me financially and as a result my family will be destitute. In this dark hour of crisis, I can only appeal to you to consider my plight and the plight of my family. I close this letter with the fervent prayer that my pleading will not go in vain.
>
> *Papwa Sewgolum*, South African golfer and Dutch Open Champion, in a letter to Prime Minister John Vorster in December 1966, requesting that the ban on his participation as an Indian in golf tournaments reserved for whites-only should be lifted. He was ignored

Player was approached for comment in the heart of the Transvaal tournament by a writer friend, John Hildyard of the Johannesburg Star.

'I don't know, John, what should I say?' Player asked. Hildyard suggested he just say that golf was his game and not politics.

'That should not offend anybody,' said Hildyard.

But the reply did offend or at least got caught in the crusader's craw of an opposition newspaper's woman columnist, Molly Reinhardt, the crusader of SA. Molly seized the opportunity to tee off on Player for not standing up for Papwa.

'I have the greatest admiration for Papwa's impeccable behaviour throughout his golfing career. No golfer in the world has suffered the insults that have been handed out to this first-class sportsman.' Player tried painfully hard to make plain his belief that the Verwoerd government was doing the best it could in a difficult situation

He called Molly Reinhardt a 'sweet old lady'. Molly pounced on that one, too. She now had the most popular SA name in the world on the tip of her épée, and her readership soared. She said she did not mind being called old, or a lady, but sweet she never was. Letters to the editor, pro and con Player, glutted the mails and were run every Sunday under a streamer 'MOLLY-GARY LETTERS'.

'Not good enough', according to some newspapers who thought that Player should have taken a stronger stand and in some way he condoned the treatment that was being handed out to Papwa.

On 6 September 1966, SA was rocked to its core with the assassination of the so-called architect of apartheid, Prime Minister Hendrick Verwoerd in the House of Assembly, who was stabbed to death by a court messenger Dimitri Tsafendas.

Verwoerd was replaced by Balthazar Johannes Vorster, who oversaw the abolishment of the coloured's voters' role and escalation of SA's border wars, and further alienation of Sewgolum and other sports people of colour.

BACK TO THE SOUTH AFRICAN NON-EUROPEAN OPENS

Through the summer of 1966/67, Papwa had continuing success on the non-white circuit in SA. The SA non-white golfers played for their richest prize in the 1967 SA Non-European Championship hosted at the King David Country Club. Cigarette manufacturers, Cavalla Ltd, presented a purse of R1,000 for this SA Open Championship meeting and provided extra funds to help with the organisation of the tournament.

The tournament was met with success, and the club willingly offered its course, and to provide all the accommodation possible for the comfort of the black officials and competitors, and attracted a vast gallery. At this time, Ismail Chowglay was still regarded as the best non-white golfer in the Western Province.

Golfers travelled great distances to attend and took part in the tournament even though there were few if any sponsors, consequently the entry fee was allocated to make up the purse: 'It is these people we can really class as sportsmen', stated Louis Nelson.

The King David CC closed the clubhouse for the duration of the tournament, and no European members or spectators were allowed on the course, much as they might have wished to see the play. This tournament was won by Papwa with scores of 70 69 72 71 (282) from Chowglay 74 74 70 72 (289), Mogoerane, and Hlapo.

Fred Paul continued writing applications for permits, and the press kept reporting that they had been turned down, embarrassing the government such that they were now deemed a threat to national security and possible treason. Security police knew he was not a troublemaker and that he just wanted to play golf, but it was his followers who brought politics into the sport with their uncivilised behaviour, which made the country look bad.

Papwa then received a special invitation to participate in the Carling World of Golf Championships in Canada, which was played at Royal Birkdale in 1966, on the basis that he had been denied the opportunity in SA to accumulate sufficient points to qualify.

The Carling World Golf Championship aimed to stage a true world championship for golf and make another contribution: 'to international understanding by bringing together golfers of all races, creeds and colours in friendly competition.'

In 1966 the brewery tournament board had expanded the qualifying field to include the champions from eight zones. Zone 1 USA, Zone 2 Canada, Zone 3 Mexico, Central America, South America, and the Caribbean, Zone 4 Great Britain and Northern Ireland, Zone 5 Europe, North Africa, The Middle East, Zone 6 Africa, Zone 7 Asia, and Zone 8 Australasia.

Six other South Africans, Harold Henning, Cobie le Grange, Barry Franklin, Trevor Wilkes, Bobby Verwey, and Denis Hutchinson also qualified. Papwa finished sixth against the world's best on 293 - the winner was Bruce Devlin on 286 - and by so doing, qualified for the event again the following year, returning to SA some R2,500 richer.

Sir Seretse Khama

It's a good thing to be able to laugh at yourself now and again. Well, the Prime Minister of Botswana, **Sir Seretse Khama**, managed to do this when he opened the new Gaborone Golf Clubhouse. He told the dismal story of his attempt to play golf. He was only 18-years-old at the time and confessed to weighing 89kg.

With his weight and size he thought he could do better than the others of a slight build. But when he took a swipe at his ball ... he fell flat on his face.

He had no intention of 'repeating the dose' he told the audience. So instead of taking a full-blooded swing at the ball, he was quite satisfied with a gentle swish that landed about 30 yards towards the fairway.

Club secretary, S.A. McCalgon, presented Sir Seretse with a book, 'How to Play Golf and Stay Happy', so that one fine day a crowd of interested golfers might observe the Prime Minister of the Republic, Mr John Vorster, and Sir Seretse at daggers – sorry, should have said drivers – drawn on a golf course doing friendly battle.

— S.A. Golf July 1967

After receiving medical treatment, he returned to the
UK in July for the 1967 Open Championship. The venue
was Royal Liverpool (Hoylake), and he got through the
qualifying stages quite comfortably on a score of 143, but
failed to make any headway in the championship proper
and came fifty-seventh, with Roberto de Vicenzo winning
on 278.

On the Rhodesian pro circuit, Papwa made a strong
showing in the second event, as the defending champion,
the Bata Bush Babes (R2,000) Tournament, finishing in
a tie for fourth place on 286. This was won by Graham
Henning on 282. In the third and final event, the Dunlop
Tournament, Papwa again finished in a tie for fourth (72
72 71 72 (285)) but a long way behind back-to-back winner
Graham Henning on 276.

THE ROYAL CALCUTTA GOLF CLUB

Papwa accepted an invitation to compete at a tournament
in Calcutta, where he was widely popular as a hero and
feted wherever he appeared. He had become a household
name in India where there were few or no international
sporting heroes, and there was a great deal of interest in
the treatment he had endured as an Indian in a country
with a 'white' government.

Fred Paul and Papwa were garlanded at the hotel in
accordance with the custom. The Indian people were anxious to meet a son of their soil who had shown the rest of
the world that golf was not beyond them. No expense was
spared in ensuring that Papwa was looked after.

Contrast his coming from a shack with holes in the roof
and newspaper stuffed into the windows, with an unbear-
ably hot corrugated iron roof in summer. Now they were
provided with an air-conditioned bungalow and a servant.

The saga of Papwa's poor treatment in SA at the hands

of the golfing authorities and government had received great prominence in the Indian press over the years, and the Indian people took Papwa to be a national icon, such that his company was highly prized. Mobbed by fans and reporters, he could not even buy the simplest item without causing crowds of people to gather.

Organisers at the Royal Calcutta Golf Club were perplexed, given the treatment Papwa had endured, when he patriotically insisted that the SA flag be flown alongside the Indian and flags of the other competing nations. This flag had been deliberately removed as the Indian government had forbidden the presence of the SA flag as there was no diplomatic recognition. Ordinary Indians could not understand his loyalty given all the injustices perpetrated against him and other social minorities in the country.

Several big names were in the field – Peter Thompson from Australia (five time British Open champion), Guy Wolstenholme and Malcolm Gregson from England, however, it was a little known Japanese player, Kenji Hosoishi who took the title beating Gregson in a play-off.

The press commented on his skill around the greens, and large crowds of spectators followed him around enraptured by his reverse grip, and marvelling at his game, especially the proficiency of his chipping.

But, in the strange conditions, he struggled with the fierce, unrelenting heat and exhaustion, and only managed a sixth place in this top-field tournament, not such a bad result in these conditions.

Banned from playing in SA tournaments, and with only small purses available in Rhodesia and on the non-white tour, he had no alternative but to look further afield to try and support his family. There were a few more forays overseas. He first went to Toronto in Canada to compete in the Carling event, but with a score of 152 for the first two rounds, he failed to make the cut.

Then it was on to his long-awaited debut at the US tour in 1967, and he signed up to compete in tournaments in Dallas, Houston, New Orleans, Oklahoma City, Dublin, and Toronto.

Among his spectators at the Huston event during the opening round was the previous year's US tour money leader, Billy Casper (ranked seventh all-time US Tour with 51 victories and winner of three Majors, runner-up in three), who wanted to see for himself the upside-down grip that he'd heard about.

'It was amazing,' Casper told the press that day.

His performances had disappointed. By then he was homesick, so when he came down with food poisoning during the Huston Open, Papwa threw in the towel, cut short the trip and returned to SA for medical treatment.

'He was always homesick,' recalls Verwey. 'He was just never very happy whenever he was away from Durban.'

To succeed in golf, you have to be a good traveller and have a management team around you. Papwa had always been a somewhat reluctant traveller, often feeling homesick and struggling to find his preferred vegetarian meals. The continuing refusal to acknowledge his achievements and allow him to play against the best of his own countrymen, however, wore him down and profoundly demoralised him.

Meanwhile, Graham Wulff was invited to spend two days as a guest of the Indian Government in acknowledgement of the help he had given his former employee, Papwa.

Unexpectedly, The Royal Calcutta Golf Club offered him the position of club professional with a monthly salary of 250 pounds plus a house, the first Indian offered this position since the club was founded in 1829. Much more than he could earn in SA. He was now 38, with probably only another five to eight years of competing at the top level ahead of him.

The Royal Calcutta Golf Club situated at Tollygunge is affectionately known as the 'Royal' and is synonymous with the game of golf in India. Founded in 1829, the Royal is the oldest golf club outside the British Isles. The oldest is the Royal & Ancient, St. Andrews in Scotland, the home of golf. The golfing heritage and history of the Royal have created a truly hallowed place for the game of golf.

Ladies were very reluctantly admitted to the club meant exclusively for the use of gentlemen in 1886 when the committee voted 43 against 13 on the condition that female members are allowed to use the course only in the mornings.

Being the first golf club in India and where the game of golf was introduced and started in the country, it had a policy of encouraging the local lads working as caddies to become some of the best professionals in the country.

The area over which The Royal Calcutta course is laid was originally paddy fields, and the course is consequently very undulating. Successive committees built mounds and planted thousands of trees and shrubs to enhance the beauty of the property. However, The Royal's conspicuous features are its strategically located water tanks and natural water hazards. Greens at The Royal are quite large by modern standards, and their undulations make them tricky. The par 4s are long and challenging to score on where approach shots require long and medium irons to be hit which test the skills of all the golfers.

Membership of the Club stood at over 2,500. A milestone in the Club's history was the election of the first Indian Captain Kamal Kumar Mitra Esq in 1963.

Over the years, The Royal had become a very popular venue for many prestigious amateur and professional events including the Indian Open. Later many renowned International golfers would walk these fairways – the most significant ones being – major winners Walter Hagen, Peter Thompson, Bobby Locke, Payne Stewart, Charles

Schwartzel, Louis Oosthuizen among others. Indian greats – I.S. Malik, H.S. Malik, Billoo Sethi, Ashok Malik, 'Bunny' Lakshman Singh, Jeev Milkha Singh, Arjun Atwal, Jyoti Randhawa, S.S.P. Chawrasia, and Anirban Lahiri, have all been a part of the Royal golfing heritage and history!

The question was whether he should leave SA, as not being able to play regularly in tournaments, he gave himself no chance by staying in the country where he was limited to non-European matches. He just was not able to compete enough.

'In this game, you have to play a lot of tournaments,' stated Dale Hayes.

However, Papwa was not allowed to play many contests. His career was such that when he got to the first tee, he still would not know if he would be allowed to tee it up.

At this time in his life, Papwa Sewgolum had reached a crossroad. Should he stay in Durban and his familiar surroundings, family, and adulation from especially the local Indian population, but where the government had banned him from playing in white tournaments, even merely becoming a member of or just playing on a white-golf course; where he was treated as a second-class citizen with no rights, and where the policy of apartheid was rife with security police following and frightening him and his family?

Or accept the offer of becoming the first Indian club golf professional at the famous 'Royal' Calcutta Golf course, following the election of the first Indian club captain in 1963, the oldest club in the world outside the UK? Here he would be paid a respectable regular salary, receive a comfortable home, mix with the cream of Indian society, be respected and admired for what he had achieved, and given time off to play in certain events. A place where he would prosper, with no apartheid (although the caste system existed) and where he could provide his growing children with all the advantages life could offer.

The decision seemed obvious, yet like those Jews who remained in Germany when the Nazis came to power, so Papwa believed the nationalist government would relent and allow him to once again play in the white SA tournaments. He did not want to leave his friends and family. His destiny was decided as he declined the offer!

He always felt his illiteracy as an embarrassing burden and to some extent, he was an outsider. Although this decision may have turned out to be a devastatingly poor decision for the Sewgolum family, in hindsight, it was a wonderful decision for black-SA, as Papwa's trials and tribulations continued to dominate in the spotlight of world opinion as the chisel continued to break another brick in the apartheid wall.

Equally, this was a pivotal moment for the nationalist government. Papwa, through his exploits, exposed SA's golf and golf courses to potentially thousands of tourist golfers every time he played abroad proudly flying the SA flag. Do they engage with him by reaching out and using this non-political hero to help break down world opinion, and as a buffer between the races for dialogue and harmonious interaction? The moment was lost. They decided to turn the screw further!

He then returned overseas and played in a number of other events in the UK and on the Continent, including the July 1967 Dutch Open at the Hague where he opened with rounds of 72, 69 to be trailing Guy Wolstenholme by one-shot together with Peter Townsend and Barry Coxon.

Eventually he lost the Dutch Open at the Haagsche by a single shot, shooting 72 69 73 69 (283) to Peter Townsend's 72 69 69 72 (282), with Graham Henning third (284), and in the French Open he came fifth on a score of 281, finally returning home with a windfall of 1,500 pounds.

| 1967 | Peter Townsend | | England | Haagsche | 282 | 1 stroke | | Sewsunker Sewgolum |

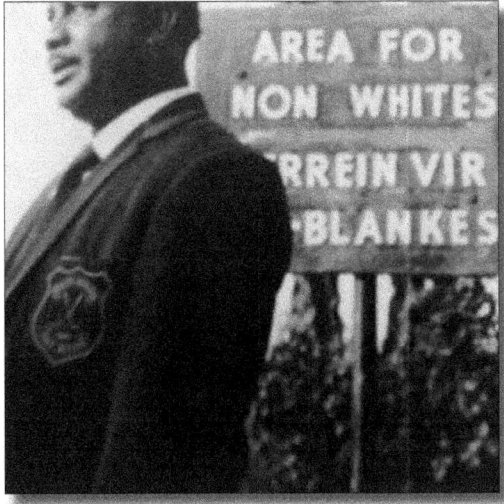

In the background in 1967 was South African-born 'coloured' cricketer Basil D'Oliveira from Cape Town who was as talented at cricket as Papwa was at golf, and who had left to play professionally in England. When he was selected for England to play in SA, the Vorster government stopped the tour. The resultant worldwide outcry, with slogans such as 'No normal sport in an abnormal society!' pushed a reluctant cricket establishment to find a way to include playing opportunities for local players of colour.

There was an outcry in the British House of Commons when Pretoria ruled that 'teams comprising whites and non-whites' could not be allowed to compete in SA. The tour was called off, and SA cricket which was enjoying a golden era at that time found itself isolated.

Two years later, Dawie de Villiers led his Springbok rugby team to the UK, where they faced the full wrath of the anti-apartheid movement.

Attempts by the authorities to soften race laws for soccer had mixed results, and later in 1974 tensions peaked during the final of the 'mixed-race' Chevrolet Cup between

Kaizer Chiefs and Hellenic when a riot broke out leading to a pitch invasion. Two years later, Soweto erupted in flames, and the revolution began in earnest.

By clamping down on all interracial sports in 1967, the government made it impossible for Papwa to play in any 'white' tournament golf in SA ever again, nor was he allowed to enter any golf course, not even as a spectator.

Meanwhile, Papwa's erstwhile manager, Louis Nelson's ambition knew no bounds as not content with his positions as Chairman of the Durban Golf Club, and President of the Natal (N-E)GU, he ascended to the presidency of the SA(N-E)GA.

Restricted to playing in non-white tournaments in SA and neighbouring countries, Papwa turned his attention to the 1968 SA Non-European Championship at the Circle Country Club with R1,000 prize money sponsored by Grosvenor Motors BP on offer. By now he was going on 40 and had already peaked as a golfer. The standard of his game slowly ebbed over the years and was now on the decline.

Nor were the apartheid laws of the land confined to matters of black and white. They embraced all races. Thus it was that the Circle CC being in Natal and situated in nominally a 'black' area, a permit was needed, and obtained from the Department of Planning, *'to allow Coloured, Chinese and Indians to take part in and to watch the event'*. At the same time, non-whites were not allowed to use the clubhouse or any other facilities that were reserved for whites only.

A surprise entry for this 1968 SA Non-European Open championship at the Circle Golf Club, was 'Eddia' Johnson-Sedibe, winner of the title in 1951 and 1952, now living in Germany where he was resident professional at the Verband Golf Club.

By now, since going to compete in the 1959 British Open, Eddia had become the most popular teaching professional in Germany, regularly competing in Europe and finishing within the top 30.

In 1969 there were also reports in the black press of his having built his own golf course and driving range at gut Waldhof near Hamburg, but this was a gross exaggeration as he had merely conceived the idea after his car stopped on the cobblestones of gut Waldhof and told the owner Bernhard Kroger that he wanted to build a golf course there, and that he had already planned the course in his head. Kroger then engaged him to consult insofar as the construction thereof.

However, by the mid-1970s he had reached a stage where he also wanted to participate in the 'struggle', the reason he had left SA, such that he returned to SA, and was subsequently killed in Angola. (His nephew is Lieutenant-General Aubrey Sedibe, SA's Surgeon General. A medical doctor who served in Umkhonto weSizwe (MK), the military wing of the ANC during the liberation struggle, and transferred to the SA Defence Force when MK was incorporated into it in 1994)

Unfortunately, he did not witness liberation from the apartheid regime. Today he is still a role model for many young black golf enthusiasts.

This time Papwa won with scores of 70 70 71 74 (285) from Tshabalala (293) and Hlapo, and followed that with a win in the Spa Open in Swaziland where he set a new course record with a 69. In Rhodesia, he finished ninth in the Dunlop shooting 74 72 75 73 (294), followed by a tie for third place with 281 in the Flame Lily. He then won a sponsored tournament in Mbabane, Swaziland, carding a winning 218 against Cox Hlapo's 223

What did it matter that he continued to dominate in the black tournaments? A golfer is only as good as his opponents. And while there were a few outstanding black players, they too were curtailed in that they were forced to compete against the same pool of players over and over.

There was undoubtedly an awareness that something needed to be done about black golf and in December 1968 Gary Player played a large part in organising a R1,200 Gary Player Invitational golf event, the most lavish ever held in SA for black golfers. Papwa was an easy winner with Tshabalala second (293). His first prize was R500.

Papwa also won the R.L. Bambata Boodhan trophy over 36 holes at the Springfield course, named after the grand-daddy of non-white golf run by Durban Golf Club in his honour since 1948. Back home, Papwa had become a popular speaker at school prize-givings and other community functions inspiring them to rise above their station and dream.

The black golfers had a small circuit from the end of December 1968, all played on European courses. First, there was the Natal Non-European Championship at Kloof CC, December 25–26. Next, the South Western District Non-European Championship at Oudtshoorn on December 28–29, and then the SA Non-European Championship January 1-2.

1969, and once again Papwa was the winner of the SA Non-European Championship, this time at the only black 18-hole club in the country, the new Athlone Golf Club in Cape Town open to all races with scores of 71 76 73 75 (295) from A. Hartzenburg (298). Clearly, the fairways were still rough and ready, the greens challenging, and the south-easter was blowing.

'Papwa' Sewgolum finished yet another year playing for small change. Banned from playing on the rich all-White circuit in SA, and being too poor to travel overseas, Papwa faced a bleak future.

His total earnings for 1969 was a meagre R840. At least 20 per cent had to be deducted for travelling costs, caddie fees and other expenses. That left him with just R672, making his monthly income R56. The three tournaments staged by the Natal(N-E)GU carried a total cash prize of R1,700.

Papwa won all three tournaments. His purses were R100, R100, and R140. Unmistakably, Papwa got a raw deal in 'non-white' tournaments. But he had no choice. By then, he was also coaching as the professional attached to the Durban Indian Golf Club.

His manager, Fred Paul, made attempts to get him a job but had little success. The highest paid job Papwa could get was for R40 per month, with no time off for golf. This meant that Papwa was better off playing golf. The extra R16 kept Papwa in golf – the sport in which white South African, Gary Player, was making a million.

Papwa now criticised the standard of the organisation of the non-white tournaments and the small purses in the press.

When articles appeared criticising the association, including Papwa's own comments concerning the poor first prize purse disbursement, Louis Nelson, now president of the SA(N-E)GU went on the attack:

> *Papwa is not the only non-white golfer struggling in South Africa and should stop relying on public sympathy to raise money. Wealthy Indians have dug deeply in their pockets on three occasions to send Papwa overseas and have not got a thing back for it. It is about time he stopped complaining and did a day's work himself. The media should stop paying all this attention to one player - you – when there are other younger players emerging.*

Papwa could hardly credit that the friendship with his former manager was over, and Nelson had wanted the limelight all along. The rift between Papwa and his former manager Louis Nelson was growing.

As Chairman of the Durban Golf Club, the club sent Papwa a letter criticising him for not carrying out his coaching duties, alleging that he was not interested in coaching beginners. The 'club' was not satisfied with his response, reviewed his position as club professional and terminated his position.

Soon afterwards, the UN General Assembly called on all its member states to suspend sporting ties with SA. In the UK, the Halt All Racist Tours (HART), which was headed by SA-born activist Peter Hain, began baring its teeth and, in 1969, severely disrupted a rugby tour of the UK by an all-white SA team.

After the 1967 All Black tour to SA was withdrawn by the New Zealand government because of the apartheid regime's refusal to grant visas to Maori players. The 1970 tour went ahead with four Maori players included.

The propaganda was unsuccessful. SA having been excluded from the Tokyo Olympics in 1964, was formally expelled from the International Olympic Committee in 1970. There would be many more sporting boycotts to come. According to the famous dictum of the anti-apartheid SA Council on Sport, there could be 'no normal sport in an abnormal society'.

The 1970 SA Non-European Championship was held at Benoni and the Ohenimuri Country Clubs where the winner, Papwa, won R250 for his efforts with scores of 77 67 69 74 (287) – the 67 equalling the course record – from Tshabalala 75 70 74 76 (295) and Mogoerane (302).

Meanwhile, there was a problem insofar as the obscure distinction among blacks between amateurs and professionals. Relatively little control was exercised to separate the two codes and a major problem was that, unlike their white equivalents, the blacks did not have separate bodies for the paid and amateur ranks.

GOVERNMENT RESPONDS

With the ban on black golfers continuing, the SA Non-European GA, under the presidency of Louis Nelson, sent six black golfers to compete in the 1970 British and Continental circuits and included Vincent Tshabalala, Ismail Chowglay, Martin du Preez (manager), and Richard Mogoerane. The intention was to make the presence of black golfers recognised in international golf. 'We want to ensure a continuity of participation of non-white golfers in international golf following the breakthrough made by Papwa Sewgolum.'

Chowglay, now 37, shooting 71 74 72 77 (294) came a credible sixth, winning R250 in the German Open at Krefelder GC won by France's Jean Garaialde on 276 from Valentine Barrious and Ettore Torre, impressive especially when considering that golf courses are actually designed for golfers playing right-handed. He missed the cut at the French Open by one shot shooting 72 71 (143).

The night before The Open qualifying tournament each player sat working out his round for the next day. Unfortunately, it did not proceed as planned, as the morning dawned cold, windy, and drizzling. Chowglay opened with a 74, Tshabalala a 75, but Martin du Preez and Richard Mogoerane were well off the pace. They all missed the cut.

Once again it demonstrated that had Chowglay been given the opportunity in his prime locally and been able to travel overseas, who knows what he may have accomplished. He certainly could win. Meanwhile, reporters and others were keen to interview them concerning political issues but were given short shrift.

'What goes around, comes around'. And so it was in July, that Chairman Louis Nelson was suspended by his own Durban Golf Club for his refusal to comply with the requirement of the committee in connection with a number of matters concerning the running of the club and the unacceptable manner in which the records were kept, unsatisfactory condition of books of finance, and the general reports of the club.

The club had convened a general meeting for March, but Nelson obtained a Court Order at the last moment that prevented the meeting from being held; he claimed it was to protect his rights as a member and chairman of the club.

Up until 1964, Nelson ran the golf club with a group of officials who supported him in all his actions. But from 1965 after a complete overhaul of officials except for him, marked a change and the beginning of friction between the chairman and new officials and members of the committee.

In 1969 a sub-committee was appointed to make a full inquiry into the whole matter and regularise the club's record. But the majority of the past officials refused to provide any assistance, including the chairman Nelson himself, leading to his suspension until he complied.

Nelson reacted by taking the golf club to court after making it a personal issue between himself and the members of the committee and demanded they be held personally liable for all legal costs. He then settled this matter on the Supreme Court doorsteps, and the committee was not found liable for any losses in their personal capacity. He had involved the club in legal costs in the amount of R2,000, and certain members then generously paid these expenses on behalf of the club.

The general feeling among the 162 registered members of the club was that Nelson had involved the club in unnecessary litigation and legal costs and that the committee had the competency and right to suspend him.

In July 1970, the general membership of the Durban Golf Club decided to elect new officials at the annual general meeting. Fred Paul, Papwa's manager, was elected as secretary, with Ken Singh as the new chairman.

Louis Nelson, after ten years at the helm, was bundled

out of office together with all his supporters. The meeting was the first of its kind in the history of black sport in SA, following his contemptuous disregard for the club's constitution and failure to produce the information required in connection with the records of the club, and the scant respect in his treatment of the committee.

Nevertheless, Louis Nelson was still the President of the SA(N-E)GA where earlier in the year he had attacked Papwa for trying to raise funds for a trip abroad. By now the golf guru, such that when he passed away in 1973 the tournaments started to disintegrate.

Paul meanwhile retained his faith in the golfer and continued in his efforts to raise funds through begging, borrowing, scrimping, scrounging, and saving, and eventually, his labours were rewarded.

Following his annual trip up north to compete on the three-tournament 1970 Rhodesian circuit, Papwa was back in the UK for his last Open Championship played at St. Andrews. There were several SA black players in the field including Durban caddy Lawrence Buthelezi and the long-hitting Vincent Tshabalala. Papwa shot a record-breaking 64 in the qualifying tournament. However, he shot 72 and 78 in The Open proper to miss the cut by one shot. On the cut-line, one-shot ahead was Player who was playing day-in-day-out, while Papwa had little tournament and competition play worth the name, going from 'bush' golf to the atmosphere of St. Andrews; validation that Papwa was still a golfer of international standards and could not be written off as some people had written about Papwa as a 'has-been'.

At the same time, Buthelezi made history in that he was the first Zulu to play at St Andrews, and the first Zulu to play in the Open Championship.

Papwa was also invited to play in the John Player Classic, worth R130,000. Later in the year Papwa played for the Rest of the World against Britain, losing his match to

Brian Barnes by one hole. Clearly he was still good enough to represent the 'Rest of the World' but not SA.

But for Papwa, there was no one speaking out for him, no protests, no boycotts when he was explicitly banned from playing in the Natal Open. Out of sheer malice the apartheid government 'revoked his passport', trying to limit the amount of exposure he could receive overseas and the resulting reflection on their policies, thus closing off any possibility of competing internationally, meaning that he could not make a living playing golf in the international arena either. Checkmate!

In the ensuing years, denied the right to play the game he loved, Papwa was said to be a broken man, who struggled to survive and stared forlornly at his golf trophies.

Earlier that year, there had been a number of professionals from Britain and Ireland on the SA circuit, and most of these golfers had decided to skip the Rhodesian tournaments in favour of the more lucrative Zambian circuit. Seven of them were promptly thrown in jail when they arrived in Lusaka because they had been to SA. This was in the years of sanctions and boycotts, and sporting contact with SA was verboten. The matter was eventually cleared up, but the seven had to spend a night in jail.

Two other players were based in Zambia and one of them, Simon Hobday, was served with deportation orders because he had taken part in tournaments south of the Zambezi.

BREAKTHROUGH

South Africa was struggling to build a professional circuit of international repute and in recent years had put up prize money significant by all standards outside of the US. However, in its efforts to consolidate and project the country as an established stopping-off point on the world circuit, at least in the minds of some of the best players, there was still a long way to go.

So, in 1971, the government, evidently smarting from the hostile reaction from governments and organisations around the world concerning its race policies, and in the face of mounting pressure to allow non-racial golf, introduced the concept of 'Open International Tournaments'. These competitions allowed top black golfers to play in a few leading tournaments including the SA Open, provided always that they were players of adequate standard, which led in August 1971 to the formation of the Non-White Professional Golfers' Association.

There were three Open International Tournaments, the PGA Championship, the SA Open, and the General Motors Classic.

In this context, the season beginning with the PGA championship at Huddle Park on November 24, provided 'another crack in the wall' and made history in the professional game. Among the black qualifiers who played all four rounds were Solly Sepeng, L. Letsoala, Daddy Naidoo, Richard Mogoerane, and with the best score, Ismail Chowglay.

As was reported in the press: 'For the first time in a tournament field there will be players of mixed race - several non-white players from SA, including Indians and Africans; an American Negro, Lee Elder and a Chinaman from Formosa, Lu Liang Huan' ('Mr Lu').

For four days, blacks and whites mingled on a 'Whites Only' golf course as though it were the established South African way of life. For four days, they sat together in the stands; for four days, they played together on the course; for four days, they ate and drank together in the clubhouse – although they still had to use separate toilets – and for four days, nobody gave it a second thought.

Sadly, Papwa, the shuttlecock of sports apartheid for so many years and the man who had done all the front-running for mixed golf, was now too old to savour the honours out there on the fairway.

Interviewed in the comfort of the clubhouse lounge: 'Look at all the golfers, Black and White, mixing freely. It's marvellous to be treated as a golfer for a change and not some sort of freak. I'm very happy for the young non-Whites who have their golf careers ahead of them. But it's come too late for me. I'm now 43. There's nowhere for me to go but down in this tough game of nerves. I'm just about all washed up.'

A large group of his own people told him that he must not play in multinational tournaments, but golf was his only livelihood. Then there were some who said he should play because as long as you play, you embarrass them. As long as you humiliate them, it will tell the world that this multinational thing doesn't work. But neither of the two forces would meet.

Four black players qualified for the GM Classic, Vincent Tshabalala, Ismail Chowglay, Ronald Anooplal, and Richard Mogoerane, while Vincent Tshabalala played all four rounds in the SA Open which was played at Royal Johannesburg. He finished in twenty-sixth place with a score of 288.

The 71/72 season had not been particularly good for Papwa, and he lost the SA Non-European title at Benoni Country Club to Vincent Tshabalala. Papwa Sewgolum's long reign as the SA Non-White golf champion ended on the 72nd green at the Benoni Country Club.

Papwa had been held to a tie by Vincent Tshabalala in 1965, and finally, it was to this same golfer, that he eventually relinquished his stranglehold on the SA Non-European Championship when Tshabalala came through to beat him by a single shot.

Vincent Tshabalala is the new champion heralded the news report. He beat Papwa by one shot - yet he came so close to losing the title. Tshabalala had a four-shot lead on Papwa going into the third round after a par-71, but Papwa whittled down the lead to a nail-biting finish.

Both had good drives at the last hole. Tshabalala had a tough third onto the green while Papwa was on the edge of the green for his second, and was left with a reasonable putt for a four. He missed, and Tshabalala holed to win by one shot.

Final scores: Vincent Tshabalala 292; Sewsunker Sewgolum 293; Daddy Naidoo 294; Ronald Anooplal 296; Johnson Chetty 302; D. Mukwevu 303.

His best showing was at Mbabane in the Swaziland Holiday Inns tournament, March 1971, where after a final round 67 he finished third behind Denis Hutchinson and Cobie le Grange. Precluded by the laws of the land from competing in the 'white' circuit in the Republic he, as Hutch put it at the prize-giving, 'came in well from the cold.'

After 63 holes it was clear that the top spots would go to Hutch and le Grange, so the fight was on for the third position. At least five players were in real contention, but in the end, it was Papwa who stood up best under strain. His final round of 67 not only secured third place for him but was the best return for the entire day.

A decision was taken that Papwa would not return to the UK and Europe in 1971 but that the possibility of his playing in New Zealand and Australia was being considered. This did happen towards the end of the year, in fact, he travelled with Gary Player, who discretely sponsored him and helped fund that trip.

On 17 November 1971, he entered the Christchurch Garden Classic in New Zealand where he displayed a grand performance as an 'Indian First' in golf. Player also arranged a number of invites to tournaments in the US, but unfortunately, Papwa once again became homesick and returned home after only competing once. He simply did not have a proper manager and support team.

CRACKS IN THE WALL

Suddenly Papwa was not the only sporting hero increasing pressure on the apartheid government – 'a country at war with itself'.

RUGBY: THE ALL BLACKS

In 1960, nearly 160,000 people signed a petition opposing that year's tour by an 'all white All Blacks' team. Groups like the Citizens' All Black Tour Association campaigned with the slogan, 'No Maoris – No Tour'. Others argued that politics had no place in the sport. In the end, Wilson Whineray's team left as planned, their aircraft narrowly missing demonstrators who were sprinting across the runway at Whenuapai airport. Despite protests, the controversial rugby tour went ahead. The issue of sporting ties with SA would eventually split the country in 1981.

For the 1970 tour of SA, a solution in the form of a compromise was devised for Māori (and Pacific Island) players. They would be considered 'honorary whites'. It was a term applied by South Africans to certain ethnicities, giving them most of the rights of white citizens. However, while this placated some, many were angered. Protest organisation HART was formed in 1969 with significant Māori input. The tour went ahead with Sid Going (who was Māori) and Bryan Williams (Samoan) participating as honorary whites. While the New Zealand Māori Council saw this compromise as acceptable, the Māori Women's Welfare League opposed the tour.

In 1973, the government under Prime Minister Norman Kirk effectively forestalled planned protest actions when it intervened to cancel a planned Springbok tour of New Zealand, as the team was to be selected on the grounds of race rather than merit.

In 1976, the All Blacks toured SA, with the blessing

of the then-newly elected New Zealand Prime Minister, Robert 'Piggy' Muldoon (who subsequently acted as the narrator in the Rocky Horror Show after his term as Prime Minister ended).

Twenty-five African nations protested against this by boycotting the 1976 Summer Olympics in Montreal. In their view the All Black tour tacitly supported the apartheid regime in SA. The five Maori players on the tour, Billy Bush, Sid Going, Kent Lambert, Bill Osborne and Tane Norton, as well as ethnic-Samoan Bryan Williams, were granted honorary white status in SA.

It was a goodbye to innocence in terms of separating rugby and politics for New Zealand rugby players because there is no glory in playing rugby against a country that treats more than half of his population as substandard humans. This tour was an eye-opener for the New Zealand rugby people (players and administrators). As the teams prepared for the first test, in Durban, it was announced that Egypt had become the twenty-ninth country to boycott the Olympic Games in Montreal – a direct protest against the All Black tour.

A month earlier, the Soweto Township erupted in violent protests against Afrikaans being used as a medium of instruction resulting in the shooting of hundreds of schoolchildren as police panicked while dealing with the protestors, and 176, mostly schoolchildren, died as a result of police gunfire in Soweto. By the end of the tour, some 3,000 black and coloured people had been killed or injured in the escalating violence.

In 1981, a Springbok team was permitted to tour New Zealand, and protests against the tour reached a level unparalleled in New Zealand history. This reflected the fact that both the Māori protest movement and anti-apartheid movement HART had developed significantly. Many protestors were arrested and charged as demonstrations became increasingly militant.

The tour was a cross-over for many New Zealanders. It was a goodbye to the idea that sporting relations can be maintained on the basis that sport and politics should be kept apart. Families split apart, as older rugby-loving parents supported the tour, while younger non-rugby players fought bitterly at home about the rights of people of colour.

The government decided not to interfere due to their public position of 'no politics in sport'. Major protests ensued, aiming to make clear many New Zealanders' opposition to apartheid and, if possible, to stop the matches taking place. This was successful at two games, but also had the effect of creating a law and order issue: whether a group of protestors could be allowed to prevent an official match taking place.

The controversy also extended to the US, where the SA rugby team continued their tour after departing New Zealand. Apartheid had made SA an international pariah, and other countries were strongly discouraged from having sporting contacts with it.

The 1981 tour was the last time the All Blacks and SA rugby teams would play while the country remained under an apartheid system.

President Nelson Mandela remembered that when he was in his prison cell on Robben Island and heard about the cancellation of the Hamilton game in 1981 due to protests, it was as if 'the sun had come out'.

CRICKET: THE BASIL D'OLIVIERA AFFAIR

In 1968, Basil D'Oliveira, a mixed-race SA player who had represented England in Test cricket since 1966 was included by England in the proposed tour to SA. Having moved there six years earlier, D'Oliviera was considered part of the team, but for SA under apartheid, the potential

inclusion by England of a non-white South African in their tour party became a political issue.

John Vorster's government had different ideas about the 'coloured' cricketer - prompting a crisis that shook apartheid.

D'Oliveira left SA primarily because the era's apartheid legislation seriously restricted his career prospects on racial grounds and barred him from the all-white Test team. Manoeuvring by cricketing and political figures in both countries did little to bring the matter to a head. The Marylebone Cricket Club's (MCC) priority was to maintain traditional links with SA and have the series go ahead without incident. South Africa's Prime Minister B. J. Vorster sought to appease international opinion by publicly indicating that D'Oliveira's inclusion would be acceptable, but secretly did all he could to prevent it.

D'Oliveira was then omitted from the England team to tour SA; they insisted that this was based entirely on cricketing merit, but many in Britain voiced apprehension and there was a public outcry. After Tom Cartwright's withdrawal because of injury on 16 September, the MCC chose D'Oliveira as a replacement, prompting accusations from Vorster and other SA politicians that the selection was politically motivated. Attempts to find a compromise followed, but these led nowhere.

Sporting boycotts of SA were already underway by 1968, but the D'Oliveira controversy was the first to have a severe effect on SA cricket. The SA Cricket Board of Control announced its intention to remove racial barriers in SA cricket in 1969 and formally integrated the sport in 1976. Meanwhile, the boycott movement escalated sharply, leading to SA's near-complete isolation from international cricket from 1971.

Dr Ali Bacher, the former head of SA cricket, told the BBC. 'He showed conclusively that black people in SA, given the same opportunity as whites, had that ability, talent, and potential to become international stars.'

Negotiations broke down, and the MCC announced the tour's cancellation on 24 September. The D'Oliveira affair had exposed SA to the world as a racist state. More than two decades of sporting isolation would follow coming to an end only in 1991 after the release of Nelson Mandela.

Gerald Majola, the chief executive of Cricket SA, said: 'The circumstances surrounding his being prevented from touring the country of his birth with England in 1968 led directly to the intensification of opposition to apartheid around the world and contributed materially to the sports boycott that turned out to be an Achilles heel of the apartheid government.'

The significance of the Vorster's decision was that D'Oliviera, irrespective of the fact that he was now holding a British passport, was born in Cape Town of mixed race, and, therefore, unacceptable lest other black South Africans living abroad think they too could compete against white SA.

Vorster approved the inclusion of Maori players in the New Zealand All Blacks as they had been included the previous year. Further, the difference was that Vorster made a distinction between those born in SA and those born abroad – satisfying his own views of foreign and domestic players.

Just as Papwa had put a human face to the realities of petty apartheid when he was forced to accept his prize in the rain, the D'Oliviera affair exposed the lengths to which the SA government would go to achieve the acceptance of apartheid to watch their nations favourite sport, and by extension their nation's approval, thereby perpetuating the system that now so many South Africans took for granted.

OPEN INTERNATIONAL TOURNAMENTS

Following a few dismal years, re-energised by his 1970 European tour and his sixth placing in the German Open, Ismail Chowglay was once again the SA Non-European Open champion at Kroonstadt where he shot 74 74 75 74 (297) winning from Tshabalala 79 73 74 72 (298) and Mogoerane (298) who tied for second.

Overall control of golf in SA at this time was in the hands of an organisation called the SA Golf Council. Its intention was presumably to establish some sort of working relationship between black and white golfers and to coordinate the activities of the various controlling bodies. Amateur golf was under the control of the SAGU (white) and the SA(N-E)GA (black), while professional tournament golf was under the control of the SA Professional Golf Association (white) and the SA Professional Players Association (black). Another body called the SA Bantu Golf Union was considered not to represent Bantu interests throughout the whole country and was denied membership of the SA Golf Council.

It has been made evident that the two professional bodies did not always see eye to eye, each one jealously guarded its own domain and demanded absolute loyalty from its members. Notwithstanding these differences, it is of interest that it appears that Papwa was able to play in events under the control of both of these professional bodies and also those under the control of both of the amateur bodies. The Vavasseur Natal Open was under the SAPGA, the Masonite Tournament was under the SAPPA, the SA Open was under the SAGU and the SA (N-E) Open was under the SA(N-E)GA.

Meanwhile, Papwa who was unhappy with the direction in which the organisation of black golf was heading, boycotted the Oris Stroke-Play Championship at Houghton. 'I refuse to be a political football,' said Papwa. 'I'm getting tired of non-white golf officials who put themselves above the game.'

In Natal, Daddy Naidoo and 16 other golfers refused to take part in an event carrying a R300 first prize.

What was this all about?

The reason was that Louis Nelson as chairman of the SA(N-E)GA had now become instrumental in the formation of the Non-White South African Professional Players' Association that insisted that all black golfers should be members of that Association or barred from tournaments under its control.

Papwa and the others refused to join an organisation whose officials were making personality issues of in golf, and not affiliated to the white PGA. Participation under these conditions might get them barred from the multiracial tournaments.

The SA Professional Players Association fought back suspending eight professional golfers for two years for taking part in multinational events, and Papwa was fined R50.

Papwa was still a force on the non-European circuit winning the Transvaal Non-European Open, and the Luyt Lager Open in 1972, who were the sponsors of this tournament for blacks to the tune of R1,000 played at the Ohenimuri Country Club. This 72-hole event was won by Cox Hlapo (now 48) in a sudden-death playoff from Papwa. Hlapo ended the tournament with a tremendous 25m putt for a birdie on the first extra hole.

The leading scores were:

290	— S Hlapo	S Sewgolum
293	— I Chowglay	
294	— R Mogoerane	
295	— R Letsoalo	
296	— V Tshabalala	

The government announced that five events in the 1973/74 season would be designated as 'open internationals' and the top four black golfers on the Order of Merit would not be required to qualify for multinational tournaments on the SAPGA circuit.

These open international events attracted the usual entry from the leading black players.

In the PGA championship, Papwa and Chowglay were the best, tied on 299 but a long way back. The SA Open was played at the Durban CC won by Bob Charles on 282 from Bobby Cole, Vinny Baker, and Graham Marsh, with Papwa finishing eleventh, and those making the cut in the General Motors Classic at Wedgwood CC were Richard Mogoerane, Ismail Chowglay, Solly Sepeng, and Z Manunda.

October 1973 the Masonite Africa Ltd with R1,500 prize money was won by Papwa after a tense fight back by Theo Manyama. Plans were afoot that this would be one of ten tournaments for black golfers in the following season.

But Papwa was not yet finished, and in 1974, he once again showed his dominance and won the SA Non-European title played at Glendower Golf Club for a record tenth and final victory when he made up 10 shots on Tshabalala in the final round to win by 1-shot.

He also won the Tournament of Champions, Natal Non-European Open, R3000 LTA Masters, and Griqua Gold Cup, and came 13th in the Natal Open after shooting 292 (Chowglay shot 294 and Daddy Naidoo 295). Meanwhile, Gary Player was winning The Masters (USA) and The Open (UK).

Mr Sam Geelay presents the Masonite Cup to Papwa after his success in the Tournament of Champions in Durban.

Chowglay (now 41) was perhaps still the leading player after Papwa and was part of a group of professionals sponsored by Becks Lager touring the country giving golf lessons. A newspaper report states that he qualified for the 'White' PGA circuit and would be eligible to compete in eight tournaments.

During 1975, Papwa competed in as many of the former white-only tournaments as possible but though he often made the cut, he routinely finished outside of the top ten. He was losing weight, and did not play as much golf as before, preferring to spend the day fishing at the nearby Umlazi River, where he had good memories of fishing with his father as a young boy.

Still the Papwa era hadn't ended, not by a long chalk as the old maestro confirmed once again that he was still the best black golfer in the country when he took first prize of R300 in the R1,500 Natal N-E Open, nine shots ahead of his nearest rivals Ismail Chowglay and Ram Rajdaw on 303, followed by A Collins (306) and J. Ranjith (307).

Richard 'Boikie' Mogoerane, the winner of the SA Non-European Open in 1973, won again in 1976 played at Durban, while Papwa won the Western Province Non-European Open

With his killer instinct fading, and weight ballooning, Papwa became a shadow of his former self, but he took a central interest in the establishment of a strong association for black golfers, and the encouragement of young talent.

With his passport returned, he again travelled to the UK in 1976 and, among other events, appeared in the Kerrygold Tournament at Waterville in Ireland. This was the last trip he made overseas.

The 1977 SA Non-European Championships was won again by Vincent Tshabalala in Durban with scores of 73 75 73 70 (291) and for a fourth time in 1983 shooting 74 74 75 74 (297).

Papwa's final tournament was the 1977 Natal Open for 'non-whites'. He won it for at least the seventeenth time in a minimum of 21 starts.

By then, he was ready to concede that his career was effectively over. Interviewed with sportswriter Norman Canale in 1978, Sewgolum noted that while it was heartwarming that golfers of all races were beginning to mix freely, 'it's come too late for me.'

Canale observed: 'Sadly, Papwa, the shuttlecock of sports apartheid for so many years and the man who did all the front-running in the movement for mixed golf, was now too old to savour the honours out there on the fairway.'

That same year Gary Player won his ninth – and final – Major championship, the US Masters at Augusta. While it marked the end of an incredible chapter in Player's life, a new one was opening as he would win a further nine Majors – on the lucrative seniors' Championship Tour – ironically started by Brian Henning, who in 1976 as president of the SA PGA banned Vincent Tshabalala after he refused to partner Player in the World Cup following his victory in the French Open.

PAPWA'S DEATH

Whether it was the shame of the Natal Open saga, the discouragement he felt at not being able to compete, or years of prejudice held against him, Papwa's health and career were never quite the same. He faltered in the tournaments where he could compete and never properly recovered, both on and off the golf course.

On the 5th of July 1978, Papwa Sewgolum died. He was relatively young, only 49 years old, but he was not always in the best of health, and, perhaps most significant of all, he had had enough. 'The struggle for him had ended.'

He was a champion.

Our Champion!

'What counts in life is not the mere fact that we have lived, it is the difference we have made to the lives of others that will determine the significance of the life we lead'.
Nelson Mandela

The difference between Player and Sewgolum was that the doors that opened for Player to enter the golfing world and carve out his remarkable story were bolted shut for Papwa.

I lost my mother when I was eight, my father worked in the mines, and I had a three-hour round trip to school every day before coming back to make my own supper,'

Player said. 'But even though I went through all that, it was nothing compared with what Papwa had to endure.'

Papwa was, in the best sense of the word, a simple man who saw himself neither as a symbol nor as a political flag-waver. He asked only for the chance to express his talents

As the first black man to play in a white tournament he competed at the 1961 SA Open at East London trailing not clouds of glory, but red tape in the form of a group areas permit which excluded practice time, drinks at the bar, and the opportunity to change his shoes in the locker room. Such was Papwa's introduction to first-class tournament golf, and it says much for his character that he rose above these indignities and got on with the job of earning a living in the only way he knew.

He was a golfer who spent too long on the sidelines to achieve his full potential, and his early death emphasises this sad fact. He has, however, a place in the game's history not only for what he did, but how he did it, and colleagues will doff their caps in memory of a gentle, unassuming man - who achieved far more than ever he realised.

On his untimely death, the National Party Minister of Sport, Dr Piet Koornhof in an ironic twist sent a telegram to his family paying tribute to this 'grand master of golf' in these words 'I am very sorry to hear of your great irreparable loss. He was a fine golfer, a great man and will be sorely missed.'

'South Africa has produced many Champion Golfers but few the equal of Papwa. A genius around the greens. It was a privilege to know Papwa as a Champion and as a Gentleman.' Dale Hayes, Golf World Cup gold medallist and winner of four national Opens on the European Tour

'From a hundred yards in, Papwa was dynamite. His short game was undoubtedly his greatest strength. The fact that he is relatively unknown to South African golfers today is a great shame.' Gary Player.

'I always had the impression that he could have gone down as one of the best golfers in the world had he been blessed with the right opportunities from a much younger age.' Bobby Verwey.

It's one of golf's great traits that, irrespective of class, colour or upbringing, the only conflict is between a man and the ball. Sure, there are challenges, like the weather, and opponents, and internal fears, but they have only as much influence as you allow them to. When you stand over a stroke, it is just you and the ball. When he played a shot he switched off, there was nobody around him, nobody in front of him. He had a very relaxed way of playing and accepted the bad times.

Player and Papwa might have shared a course on only a few occasions, but their shared adversity meant they had more in common than most, even as they were reminded of their differences all too often. It was an ironic role-reversal, in that Player's trouble started when he left SA, and Papwa's occurred whenever he came back.

That's the beauty of sport. Even after the greats pass on, their legend grows with time and their legacy is there for all to see, forever.

This unassuming son of a farm labourer dared to dream and succeed in the face of overwhelming adversity, which included a racist golfing establishment and - in a classic irony of apartheid logic – a government which actively undermined his accomplishments and outrageously humiliated and scorned him.

Beating Player in the Natal Open and matching the golfing cream in the SA Open attested to the quality of Papwa's ability. Who knows what heights he would have reached as a golfer were it not for apartheid? Yet, because of apartheid, the lives of Player and Papwa panned out so differently.

While Player went on to become one of the greatest players the game has known and a multi-millionaire, Papwa died in 1978, penniless, a pauper, and broken man because he was denied the opportunity to do what he loved most in life – play golf at the highest levels.

'And he was very, very talented. He was relatively short

off the tee but had a very good short game, and was, in my opinion one of the best and most accurate players I have ever seen within 40 yards (36m) of the green, and he had a very good temperament. He's been an extremely controversial subject in South Africa. It was tough for him. He came along at the wrong time, unfortunately. But in the meantime, he's given a lot of people, particularly young Indian golfers, a lot of encouragement. Any young Indian golfer coming along can have Papwa as a hero.'

'And he faced enormous restrictions to his freedom throughout a short career that was sabotaged by the racist regime. How do you ever say what a man's future would have been?" asks Player, finally. But then he proceeds to do just that: 'If you want to make a comparison, he was just under a Harold Henning. Harold Henning was just a little better than him. He would have had a very nice future.'

Unfortunately, we will never know just how far Papwa could have gone had he been given more opportunities. In his prime during the 1960s, he lost that period from 1966– 1972 when he was banned. While his victory over Player in the 1965 Natal Open could have been a stepping stone to greater things had he lived in any other time or circumstance, it was seen as a symbolically threatening event by the apartheid leaders of the time.

Discussing his father, Rajen Sewgolum notes that Papwa 'thrust South Africa into the glare if the international spotlight and marked a significant turning point in South Africa's relationship with the civilised world when he won the 1963 Natal Open'.

Papwa was regarded as a man looking for trouble instead of an athlete passionate about his game. An illiterate Indian man beating a white man at an elitist sport was merely unacceptable – what if this defeat eradicated the misguided notion of white supremacy? In the government's eyes, Papwa had to be stopped.

To complicate matters, although non-political, Papwa suddenly found himself thrust into the political limelight as the 'symbol of the anti-apartheid sport movement'. The sport's boycott that followed led the fight to end apartheid and helped bring about the day when Nelson Mandela would honour Papwa Sewsunker. 'Papwa' Sewgolum still remains one of the greatest golfers to come out of SA.

In 2004, the changing tides of democracy ensured Papwa was honoured for his excellent achievements in the field of golf and his perseverance and courage in the face of debilitating apartheid laws. He was awarded the 'Order of Ikhamanga in Silver' from President Thabo Mbeki, South Africa's highest honour for achievement in the performing arts and sport.

In 2005, Judge Christopher Nicholson's biography of Papwa Sewgolum: From Pariah to Legend was published, followed by Maxine Case's book 'Papwa Golf's lost Legend', while a documentary film about his life, 'Papwa: The Lost Dream of a South African Golfing Legend', had its premiere in August 2005, a life that was lived 'in triumph and in loss', Craig Urquhart also dedicated one chapter to Papwa as one of the ten best South African golfers in his book 'The Kings of Swing'.

South Africans will be able to reflect the ignominy, hurt and shame that the crippling racial laws inflicted on the emotions of the majority of South Africans restricted from participating in the broadest possible opportunities – such as to play the golf they wanted to, loved and played well.

In 2009, Sewsunker 'Papwa' Sewgolum was inducted into the Southern Africa Golf Hall of Fame, ironically alongside Gary Player and Bobby Locke, Nick Price, Sally Little, Ernie Els, and Retief Goosen, all multiple major winners, and in 2010, the Durban Golf Club was renamed the 'Papwa Sewgolum Municipal Golf Course', one of the few municipally-owned tracks in SA.

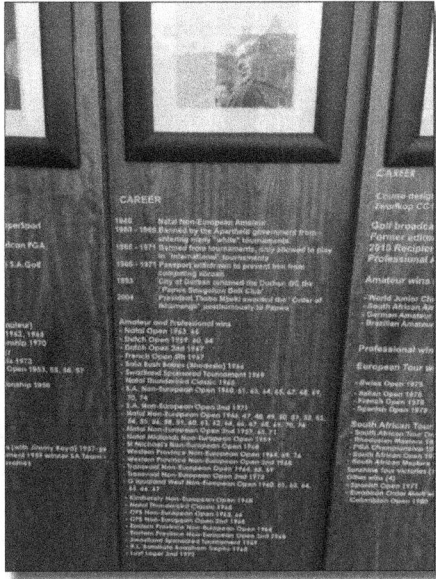

Sewsunker 'Papwa' Sewgolum citation and record displayed in the Southern Africa Golf Hall of Fame.

Durban Country Club, where the infamous prize-giving ceremony took place, unveiled a memorial plaque in 2005 on the outside wall of the clubhouse, facing the 18th green, honouring Papwa.

In Honour: Sewsunker "Papwa" Sewgolum

This plaque was commissioned by the members of the Durban Country Club to commemorate local golfer Sewsunker 'Papwa' Sewgolum's historic victories in the 1963 and 1965 Natal Open Championships, making him the first person of colour to win a professional golf tournament in South Africa. We salute the talent of this self-taught legend of the game.
The plaque concludes:

"The club apologises for what had happened four decades earlier".

Durban Country Club chairman Ray Lalouette described the 1965 Natal Open awards ceremony as 'an ignominious debacle that must have been the source of much embarrassment and humiliation for a fellow human being at a time when he should have been experiencing joy and jubilation'.

'No matter what the background, or the rules of the land, it must have been an experience that caused hurt and shame for him and his family'.

'It is therefore fitting and appropriate that I, as the current chairman, take this opportunity on behalf of the members of the Durban Country Club, to apologise to Mrs Suminthra Sewgolum and to Mr Sewgolum's son, Rajen, and his family for the suffering you have endured as a result of that most unfortunate incident'.

'We have commissioned this plaque to serve as a permanent reminder to all those (and especially golfers) who walk this way, that 'Papwa' Sewgolum was a remarkable man.'

However, the plaque does not take into account all Papwa's victories on the supposed parallel non-European tour as 'professional tournaments in South Africa', nor does the Durban Country Club 'where people matter and values count', make any mention on its website of its most famous former employee, home-grown champion and local hero.

As Craig Urquhart, in his book 'The Kings of Swing' comments, 'A good man, a great golfer and a beacon for all of South Africa, Papwa Sewgolum may not have won a Major, but the role he played in levelling the courses in this deeply fractured land can never be underestimated'.

Whatever the truth of the conflicting details of the prize-giving, the incident was just one of countless apartheid assaults that Papwa endured. But as a potent symbol of exclusion, it turned into a firestorm, starting with press commentary at home and abroad.

In 1966 Gary Player went on to pen his infamous lines: 'I am a man of Verwoerd and apartheid' in his book, Grand

Slam Golf. Player – the 'white champion' – although he changed his public position as circumstances changed in SA, he was at that time deeply involved in the apartheid-support system established by the state, and as such, at that time never challenged the fact that one of the few golfers in the world capable of beating him was banned by racism from even making a living out of golf, while Player went on to become a multi-millionaire.

Papwa — the 'black champion' — on the other hand, even embarrassed his hosts in India by insisting when he played there that the SA flag is flown alongside those that represented the countries of the other players in the tournament.

However, the memory of Papwa remains strong and continues to inspire a new generation of golfers. He was a symbol of the sports-boycott movement. But thanks to this country's laws at the time, which were subsequently declared a crime against humanity by the UN, his achievements were limited.

'I have always admired people who achieved in spite of adversity. He did a lot in spite of what he had, and had to deal with.' Sally Little, twice LPGA major champion.

The prohibition that black sportsmen faced continued until the abolishment of apartheid in the 1990s, when the sporting walls that Papwa had first, and most spectacularly pounded on, would, at last, be reduced to the rubble of history.

In the years since liberation, the golf establishment and government have worked to bring golf to black youngsters. Academies and bursaries have been set up and talent identified and given opportunities. The majority of black golfers, however, still face the obstacles of poverty, a lack of facilities and limited opportunity. It is a measure both of how far the sport needs to move forward, and of the stature of Papwa's achievements that no other SA golfer of colour, other than Vincent Tshabalala has so far won a major national open tournament either in SA or overseas.

He was a champion!

SEWSUNKER 'PAPWA' SEWGOLUM
(12/1928 – 07/1978)

1. Mother was blind. Lived in a shack — didn't go to school — could not read or write
2. Went to work at 11 following the death of his father
3. Taught himself to play golf with a wooden stick
4. Played with the 'wrong' reverse grip
5. At 16 won the Natal Non-European Amateur Open
6. Later shot 59 in a caddy competition at Beachwood – only the 2nd sub-60 in SA
7. First black golfer to win a European National championship tournament - the Dutch Open
8. Won the Dutch Open (3) runner-up (1) - first player to win it three times (in 4 attempts)
9. Won the Natal Open (2) – beating Bobby Verwey and Denis Hutchinson in 1963; Gary Player and Harold Henning in 1965

Citations

- 1960 Member British PGA
- 1970 Rest of the World vs. Britain
- All Tournaments won – 77 (at least)
- Open tournament wins – 10 (excludes non-European titles)
- Lesser SA Tournaments (18)
- SA Non-European Open (10) 2nd (1) - Provincial titles (38) 2nd (9)
- SA Non-European Sportsman of the Year 1959, '63
- SA Order of Merit 1964/65 3rd – despite being prevented from playing in two events
- 2004 awarded the Order of Ikhamanga in Silver

- 2009 Inducted into the Southern Africa Golf Hall of Fame
- 2010 Papwa Sewgolum Municipal Golf Course named after him.

Disadvantaged by apartheid — prevented from playing the SAPGA 'white' tour – LATER BANNED/PASSPORT CANCELLED.

Record

Amateur

- Natal Indian Amateur Open 1946

Professional – Open tournaments

- Dutch Open 1959, 1960, 1964, 1966 4th, 1967 2nd, 1970 6th
- The Open 1963 13th, 67 57th
- SA Open 1963 2nd, 64 3rd, 65 12th, 70 11th
- Natal Open 1963, 1965
- Grand Prix Series First Leg 1963
- Grand Prix Series Second Leg 1963 2nd
- Kensington Open 5000 1964 8th
- Cock 'o North (Zambia) 1964
- SA Dunlop Masters 1965 3rd, 66 11th
- LiquidAir 5000 1965 15th
- SA PGA 1965 5th, 66 11th
- Natal Thunderbird Classic 1965
- Flame Lily (Rhodesia) 1965 5th, 66 8th
- Carling World Golf Championship 1966 6th
- Bata Bush Babes (Rhodesia) 1966
- Rhodesian Dunlop Open 1966 5th
- French Open 1967 5th
- India Open 1967 6th
- Swaziland Spa Open 1968
- Mbabane Holiday Inn 1971 3rd

Professional – Non-European TPA tour

- SA Non-European Open 1960, 61, 63, 64, 65, 67, 68,69, 70, 74
- SA Non-European Open 1971 2nd
- Natal Non-European Open 1954, 55, 57, 58, 59, 60, 61, 62, 63, 65, 66, 67, 68, 69, 70, 74, 75, 77
- Natal Non-European Open 2nd 1956, 64, 71, 76
- Griqualand West Non-European Open 1960, 61, 63, 64, 65, 67, 69
- Western Province Non-European Open 1960, 64, 69, 76
- Western Province Non-European Open 1968 2nd
- Transvaal Non-European Open 1964, 65, 66, 67, 69, 70
- Transvaal Non-European Open 1972 2nd
- Eastern Province Non-European Open 1964
- Eastern Province Non-European Open 2nd 1963, 68
- OFS Non-European Open 1966, 69
- OFS Non-European Open 1968 2nd
- Natal Midlands Non-European Open 1959, 60
- R200 Sponsored Invitation 1964
- R.L. Bambata Boodhan Trophy 1965, 2nd 66
- Thunderbird R500 Classic 1965
- Transvaal Invitational 1966
- Gary Player Trophy 1967
- Gary Player Invitational 1968, 69, 70
- Kimberley Non-European Open 1968, 69
- St Michael's Non-European Open 1968, 71
- Luyt Lager 1972 2nd
- Tournament of Champions 197?
- Coca-Cola Open 1974 2nd
- LTA Masters 1974, 2nd 75
- Griqua Gold Cup 1974

*Records incomplete

CHAPTER EIGHT

Repercussions

ANTI-APARTHEID DEMONSTRATIONS AND OPEN TOURNAMENTS

Meanwhile, Gary Player was the all-too-visible target of anti-apartheid demonstrators. Wherever he played, he was regarded as a spokesman for apartheid – or at least the one tangible target its opponents could easily attack.

Did he have death threats? 'Every week,' he says. 'Every week!' And once more, now with resignation: 'Every week. In America, Australia, Europe, for about two years. It was not easy. At the PGA Championship in 1969, in Dayton, Ohio, they threw ice in my eyes. They threw telephone books at my back. They charged me on the green. They threw balls between my legs as I was about to putt. You know, it's hard to comprehend. And I lost the PGA by one shot. This was my best tournament I ever played (he told the author). And I had it everywhere I went. Everywhere.'

Player talks of the injustice of it, and of the black players he supported and sponsored during the 1970s, including Papwa and Vincent Tshabalala, another talented golfer whose opportunities were curtailed by apartheid

Player also mentions his iconic one-white-leg/one-black-leg pants that he wore at the 1960 Open at St. Andrews. They were, he says, 'a quiet protest, of bringing white and black together.'

'We were brainwashed,' concedes Player.

1960 The Open: Youthful Gary Player's black and white pants

In 1970 Player went to the US to play a series of exhibition matches with Black players to benefit the United Negro College Fund.

Meanwhile, the Black Panther movement denied it had made threats on Player's life, and Arthur Ashe, barred by the apartheid government from playing in the SA Tennis championship, added fuel to the fire saying that he feared for Player's safety.

In 1971, entries of SA Golfers were turned down. Sally Little was persuaded not to enter the British Amateur championship because the organisers feared demonstrations.

At the same time, a professional golfer for the first time was refused permission to play in a tournament because he was a South African as Bobby Cole's entry in the Volvo tournament in Sweden was turned down. The Tournament Director, Mr Tom Liden, informed George Blumberg, who was acting on behalf of Cole, of the news in a cable which read: 'Since Cole is from South Africa we are unable to have him enter our tournament. Sorry.'

'I'm still often asked why I stopped playing tournament

golf at such a young age. It was politics. Hugh Baiocchi and I arrived in Athens to represent South Africa in the World Cup of Golf, played a practice round and took part in the pro-am before being told that we would not be allowed to tee up in the tournament. In fact, we were given 48 hours to leave Greece – I got fed up with the uncertainty of playing under such conditions.' stated Dale Hayes.

Although no golfers were affected as severely by the politics of SA as Papwa Sewgolum, Vincent Tshabalala, Richard Mogoerane, Ismail Chowglay, Edward Johnson-Sidebi, and Simon Hlapo, there were others that were also affected, albeit in a smaller way.

Gary Player missed out on huge money by not being allowed to play in Jordan.

In the late 1970s Sweden stopped South Africans from competing, and when they arrived at the borders of France, Spain and the Netherlands, they were never sure if they would be allowed in.

1976 The British PGA tried to withhold payment of prize money to Simon Hobday because of his Rhodesian/SA connections.

GARY PLAYER'S INVOLVEMENT

Verwoerd's replacement was John Vorster, a keen golfer and enthusiastic supporter of the Nazis during World War II. Player was a regular golfing companion – something else that attracted a great deal of criticism.

John Vorster served as the Prime Minister of South Africa from 1966 to 1978. He was known for his staunch adherence to apartheid, overseeing (as Minister of Justice) the Rivonia Trial in which Nelson Mandela was sentenced to life imprisonment for sabotage, and as Prime Minister, the Terrorism Act, the complete abolition of non-white political representation, the Soweto Riots, and the Steve Biko crisis.

He conducted a more pragmatic foreign policy than his predecessors in an effort to improve relations between the white minority government and South Africa's neighbours, particularly after the break-up of the Portuguese colonial empire. Shortly after the internal settlement in Rhodesia, in which he was instrumental, he was implicated in the Muldergate Scandal and resigned the premiership.

—Accessed online Wikipedia

One day Player went into Vorster's office. 'And I said to him, please, I'd like to break down the apartheid barrier in sport,' Player recalled. 'You know, to go to a man like that was tough. And I said I'd like to invite Lee Elder, the black American golfer, to South Africa. I thought he was going to tell me to get out. Instead, with those thick bushy eyebrows and head still bowed, he said, go ahead. And that was a start. I'm very pleased I did play golf with Vorster, because had I not, I could not have gone into his office and achieved that. I was able to contribute a very significant thing to our country.'

'I had set a trend, but once we could get an international player of colour here, there is no doubt that was the start of breaking down apartheid for all sports.'

It was 1971 and Elder said he would play in SA, but only under certain conditions: Other black professionals must be allowed to compete, in front of mixed crowds, and have full access to all the amenities, such as the clubhouse. Player – and Vorster – agreed.

In other quarters, the National Party government branded Player a traitor for inviting African-American tennis star, Arthur Ashe and his compatriot, golfer Lee Elder, to SA.

Three tournaments that year would be classified as 'international' events that were open to golfers of colour, with more to follow in subsequent years. Similar initiatives took place in other sports. Selected hotels and restaurants were also accorded 'international' status. Papwa played in these golf events, but his best years were gone.

There were still restrictions, however. Dale Hayes recalls that black players weren't allowed to use the same toilets as whites. And for many, this kind of 'reform' was nothing but tokenism: government propaganda intended to counter the rising international outcry against apartheid.

'Those tournaments were really just a window dressing on the situation in South Africa,' says Dennis Bruyns, ex-

ecutive director of the SA tour from 1981–1991. 'The black players in South Africa couldn't go to any of our main venues for 51 weeks of the year, but in the fifty-second week, when the tournament was on, then they could go and play and have a drink in the bar. Basically, the Group Areas Act didn't apply for that one week. It was all part of a grand plan at the time. There was a huge effort to try to sell this to the world.'

Bruyns, a former tour professional, choose his words carefully concerning Player's role in creating the 'international' events: 'I think to an extent he was used,' he says. 'He was doing it from his heart. They were more political than he was. They saw an opportunity.'

Gary Player, the super-fit, small, neat man dressed in dark outfits (he liked westerns and wanted to dress like his cowboy hero) was known as the Black Knight. His working rules were strict and uncompromising — health, diet, practice, and physical strength, something he advocated long before it became popular.

He was denied a place in the Commonwealth Ryder Cup team because he would have represented a pariah state, and he did much to narrow the race gap as the true reality of apartheid struck home

Player found himself embroiled in the race issue. In his 1966 book 'Grand Slam Golf', he had written: 'I must say now, and clearly, that I am of the South Africa of Verwoerd and apartheid ... a nation which ... is the product of its instinct and ability to maintain civilised values and standards among the alien barbarians ... The African may well believe in witchcraft and primitive magic, practise ritual murder and polygamy; his wealth is in cattle.'

These words, phrases, and inferences were deemed patronising at best, racist at worst, and his image suffered in some quarters, possibly unfairly as it was fashioned by the time and place in which he lived, and not contrived by the author, but by his ghost-writer. Player claimed he simply did not read the proofs before they went to press.

Judge Christopher Nicholson is less charitable. In his book 'Pariah to Legend', he says the events were 'a charade. This kind of thing was nothing but an attempt to put a positive face on apartheid. Gary Player was part of that.'

Nicholson also criticises Player's role in the '70s in the so-called 'Committee for Fairness in Sport', and the conservative newspaper, The Citizen, both of which, he says, were government-funded operations.

At that stage, according to SA writer Christopher Merrett: 'It is a matter of undisputed historical fact that Player was a notorious apologist and propagandist for apartheid', as seen in his book in 1966, the year after he was beaten in the Natal Open by Papwa, although there is no mention of Sewgolum.

Player goes onto say he won an amazing comeback victory against Tony Lema in the Piccadilly match-play tournament in 1965 because he got to thinking about his country, 'maligned, misunderstood, pilloried by people who can tell us how to order our affairs from a range of 6,000 miles without ever coming down to South Africa and seeing for themselves and trying to understand.'

Certainly, his political colours were still firmly nailed to the National Party flagpole more than a decade later when it emerged Player had been a member of the secret clique assembled by Eschel Rhoodie and his 'Infogate' pals to back the launching of the English Nationalist voice piece, The Citizen, during the BJ Vorster regime.

However, Player subsequently felt he played a large part in lifting the lid off the whole business because when rumours first circulated about various payments being made, everybody denied it; but when the television people asked him if he had been paid he straight away admitted it. It was one of the first pieces of hard evidence.

Nicholson continues, insofar as golf slacks featuring one black leg, one white leg Player wore during the Centenary Open of the British Open in 1960. The caption, referring to this: 'Seems to me the one black leg, one white leg rather was an endorsement of the separateness apartheid espoused.'

Both Player and Sewgolum professed only to be golfers, uninterested in politics, but as Nicholson shows, Player – the 'white champion' – although he changed his public position as circumstances changed in SA, and as more pressure was brought to bear when abroad, was deeply involved in the apartheid-support system established by the state.

However, in hindsight, one needs to reflect upon the 'white society' South Africans were brought up in AT THAT TIME. A white person growing up in SA, separated from Africans due to apartheid policies, unless they were interacting on a personal level, were brainwashed through the apartheid controlled media, and for Player, who was never exposed to university politics, to be asked to play golf with the Prime Minister was viewed as an honour.

Liberal universities in and around the early 1970s saw UCT student Geoff Budlender, the SRC President, reject Vorster's insinuations 'with the contempt it deserved', as for the first time police beat up white students demonstrating for free black education at St. Georges Cathedral, and then violently carried protesting students off UCT's Jameson stairs. Neville Curtis, NUSAS President, having been tipped off, escaped through the mountains to New Zealand via Lesotho, while Steve Biko at Fort Hare was telling touring UCT law students that they wanted a clear polarisation between blacks and whites, and white liberals merely muddied the water. Meanwhile, the law student moot room was a breeding ground for Anton Lubowski and others. Outside of the university no one was the wiser except for some newspaper headlines.

Growing up with a father working on the mines, and no mother, Gary Player was not part of this world.

In Player's case, it should also be remembered that from 1961, Helen Suzman was the sole voice of South Africa's oppressed until 1974, when six colleagues joined Helen in Parliament. Suzman became known for her strong public criticism of the governing National Party's policies of apartheid at a time when this was unusual among white people. She found herself even more of an outsider, as she was an English-speaking Jewish woman in a parliament dominated by male Afrikaners.

At that time, the Progressive Party was the lone voice speaking out in parliament against apartheid, with the 'white party' only supported, in the main, by affluent liberal English-speaking whites, especially the Jewish community, and for the rest, the vast majority supported the apartheid policy.

It is likely that Player had a double purpose for initiating the invitation for Lee Elder to play in SA, both in an attempt to deflect political contempt aimed at him while playing in international events abroad, as well as to help create the impression of trying to break down barriers within SA by enabling leading black golfers to participate in white-only tournaments. Similarly, in the 1970s, he started to assist Sewgolum and especially Tshabalala financially, and through tournament invitations, to break into the international arena (he had already started assisting white golfer Cedric Amm in 1964 by sending him to play in Europe and the USA).

In 1974 he appeared to modify his political views in his

autobiography 'Gary Player World of Golf', where he goes on to say: 'As in every country, there are things that are obviously wrong, and a great many of us are working hard to rectify them. I must say, however, that in all my travels across the world I've never seen a country where white and black get along as well together as in my country.'

The question, however, must be asked why is it that only Player is targeted for not assisting black golfers, especially Papwa Sewgolum? Other great SA golfers were playing competitively such as world champions like Bobby Locke (four-time major champion – top 20 all-time list of golfers) and Harold Henning (over 50 worldwide victories).

Player was also asked by government officials to entertain a few very important overseas businessmen by playing golf with them when they came to SA. He says it seemed harmless enough and nothing more than a good public relations exercise. At first, he declined as he had an arrangement to appear in Australia for a sizeable fee, but then they also offered albeit a lesser fee, so being a patriot, he agreed. He goes on to say that if they had told him it was to advance the cause of apartheid he would not have done it.

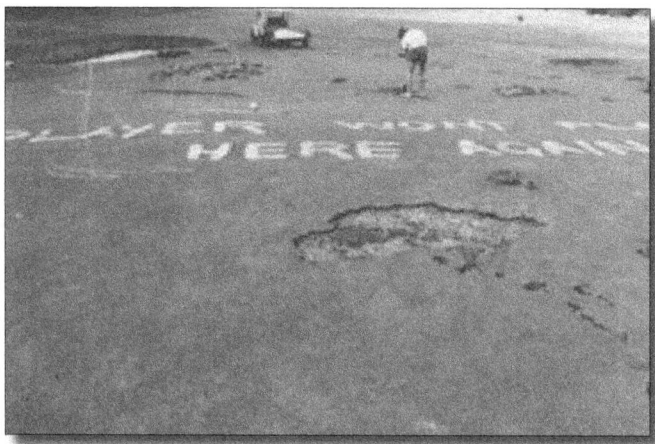

1974 Australian Open Royal Melbourne GC

Later in the 1980s as the reality of apartheid was appreciated by Player, it dawned on him that as a sportsman of his eminence in SA, that it was not possible to separate politics from sport. There is no doubt that he both changed his views, and subsequently spoke out forcefully against apartheid and inequality, while at the same time raising millions of dollars for the disadvantaged as well as funding his own school for disadvantaged children: 'then suddenly I realized that it wasn't equal, apartheid was a dreadful policy.' But this was too late for Sewgolum and Chowglay.

In 1987, in an interview with the LA Times, Player disavowed the system of apartheid, stating 'We have a terrible system in apartheid...it's almost a cancerous disease. I'm happy to say it's being eliminated...we've got to get rid of this apartheid,' and 'the wind of change has at last reached South Africa, and our country will be the better for it.'

While in an interview with Graham Bensinger, Player discussed his early support for apartheid stating that the SA government had 'pulled the wool over our eyes' and that the people were 'brainwashed' into supporting these policies.

Reflecting, and in Player's defence against accusations levelled, one must take into account that Player nevertheless did make significant attempts to assist black golf:

- 1968 Player played a large part in organising a R1,200 Gary Player Invitational golf event, the larg est purse ever offered for black golfers.
- 1971 Player took Sewgolum to Australia and the USA where he got him invitations to play in tourna ments
- 1974 Player assist the Athlone Golf Club with the fi nancing of their new clubhouse by playing an exhibi tion match where Player/Chowglay beat Sewgolum/ Tshabalala 4/2

- 1974 Player sponsored and took Vincent Tshabalala to Australia and the USA to play in a number of tour naments
- 1976 Player financed Tshabalala's trip to Europe and arranged for tournament participation invitations
- 1980 The brainchild of Gary Player, then the SAPGA President, was a mini-circuit for black players spon sored to the tune of R24,000
- He launched a competition in South Africa for black caddies with the winner accompanying him to Eu rope each year to work with him
- 1986 saw the inaugural TPA Tournament, another of Gary Player's initiatives and carrying sponsorship of R100,000, which he donated, restricted to black golfers only, and as such drew a lot of criticism as 'apartheid in reverse'. This led to Player resigning as President of SAPGA in protest after a clash with other SAPGA officials.

'Without Gary, I would not have started in golf. Gary is the only one who has helped me a great deal. He taught me the basics, how to think right, how to save strokes around the greens and how to keep fit.'
Vincent Tshabalala.

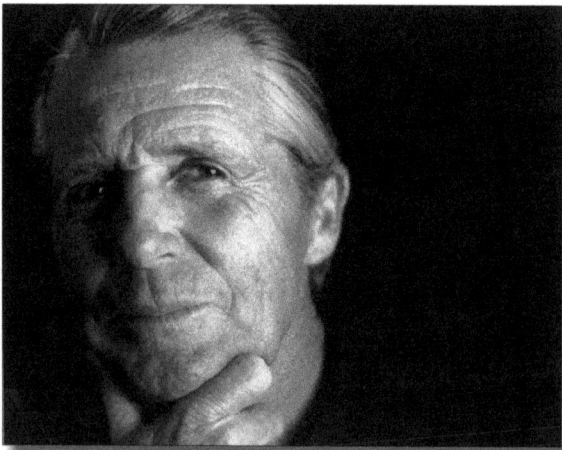

However, Player's more recent recollections are interesting: 'Protestors of South Africa's apartheid policy gave me grief for a couple of years. I didn't believe in apartheid, and I surely wasn't responsible for it, but I was a ripe target. They burned awful statements into the greens where we were playing. I got death threats at my hotel every day. At the 1969 PGA Championship, a guy screamed just as I stroked a 10-inch putt, and I missed and lost by one. At Merion, during the 1971 US Open, we kept guns in the house where I was staying. I struggled through it, and you know something? It's easier to fight than to run away. It was a tough two years. But Nelson Mandela, who spent over 20 years in prison, had it a whole lot worse.'

Player was awarded the 'Order of Ikhamanga in Gold' for exceptional achievement in 2003 by President Mbeki for excellence in golf and contribution to non-racial sport in SA.

Possibly he could have done more to assist Sewgolum (who was seven years his senior), but in later years, he certainly played a significant role in breaking down apartheid as his understanding and appreciation of the ills of apartheid changed.

Lee Elder recalls that distant summer of 1971. 'Gary asked me to come,' he says gently. 'We were good friends, and we still are today. I wanted to try to help in any way I could.' Elder, a year older than Player, is something of a pioneer. At a club with a complex history in matters relating to skin colour, in 1975 he became the first black person to enter the grounds at the Masters as a competitor, opposed to a caddy or waiter.

Elder decided to take in some other countries during the African expedition. 'I had a US State Department advisor, Fletcher Martin,' says Elder. 'He told me that a lot of people wouldn't think highly of me flying directly into South Africa from America.' So Elder was made a 'goodwill ambassador', and, over a period of two months and travelling with an entourage of a dozen people, he played in Liberia, Ghana, Nigeria (where he won the Nigerian Open), and Uganda.

In SA, he played in tournaments and exhibition matches with Player, including one in Durban where the proceeds went to a school for black girls.

Elder's lasting memory of the trip is a big dinner one evening at the famous Wanderers Club in Johannesburg.

Vorster was part of the receiving line, shaking hands with all the guests as they arrived. Right before it was Elder's turn to meet the prime minister, Vorster abruptly left the receiving line, walked over to the main table, and sat down.

'It was in the newspapers there the next day – Vorster snubs American golfer,' says Elder. 'The reason he gave was that the proceedings were taking too long, and he wanted the festivities to start on time.' Elder shakes his head.

'The thing about Gary. He was always proud to be South African. He's a good friend. He didn't deserve to be targeted. These things are a lot different now.'

Is there still racism in golf, in America? 'Oh, yeah,' replied Elder to the rhetorical question. 'You have a generation that's been taught a certain way by their parents. A lot of improvements, but it's going to take time, generations until we get to the day when we don't see the colour, we see the person.'

Outside of SA, Player made substantial goodwill gestures such as handing over his entire prize money for winning the 1965 US Open, a major portion to cancer research (his mother died from cancer).

'You know what,' says Johan Immelman, former commissioner of the Sunshine Tour, 'We sit here in Cape Town today, and I'm thinking, did that really happen? How did they get away with it?'

'Mandela taught us to look forward,' said Player. 'He said you cannot live in the past. You cannot have bitterness in your heart. It's like when you play golf -- if you make a bogey, you better forget it and get a birdie on the next hole. There's a great spirit in South Africa. We've made bogeys. We're making birdies now.'

ISMAIL 'BOY' CHOWGLAY

With the assistance of Cape champion golfers Phil van Dieman and Polly November who first recognised and furthered Ismail's talent, Chowglay was widely believed by 1962 to be the equal or better than 'Papwa' Sewgolum after annexing the 1962 SA Non-European Open. However, it was only in 1972 that Ismail, the 6' 2" reigning Western Province champion, regained the SA Non-European Open, beating Tshabalala and Mogoerane into second place.

Four years apart, what a journey Papwa and Ismail had travelled! Rivals, both of Indian descent, both playing with the back-to-front grip, both denied the ability to compete on the white SA tour until they were in their 30s, and both near the end of their careers.

Still there was a little fire left, with Ismail winning at least one further WP Non-European title in 1973, beating

Papwa in their final battle into second place for the 1976 Natal Non-European title, and in 1983 at the senior age of 51 amazingly winning (oldest player to win on the TPA Tour, but alas no senior tour available to him), for probably the last time a provincial title when he won the Transvaal Non-European title (fifteen years after his previous triumph). In all, he won 14 provincial titles (despite holding down a full-time job), which was only bettered (substantially) by Papwa.

Ismail, wearing his pointed straw hat (which made him look even taller), hit his 3-wood 240m and never bothered with a driver. He also preferred not using a tee, and would merely push up some turf or make a tee from sand. His short game was legendary, even though his bag never contained the full set of 14 clubs. His back-to-front grip enabled him to steer the ball low to the flag, or high when he wished, and he was exceptional straight off the tee landing on the fairway time-after-time.

At that time, the caddies at Clovelly played with rolled up bent wire, and used the pods growing on the branches of the katoki tree in which they placed stones to increase the weight, and which made a 'whirring sound', said Abe van Rooyen (1970 WP Non-European Open winner). He then stated that Ismail was possibly the best left-handed golfer in the world at that time (with the exception of Bob Charles).

Known for his flashing smile (in which sat a gold tooth), Ismail was a real ladies man. Wherever he played, the caddies would follow, and Ismail smiled and joked his way through the game, always helping others. He had a special friendly charm and especially took time to assist junior white school children by playing golf with them.

Ismail died, like Papwa, poverty-stricken in 1992 at the still youthful age of 59, possibly South Africa's best left-handed golfer.

ISMAIL 'BOY' CHOWGLAY
(1933 -1992)

Citation

1. Caddy Royal Cape GC before 1963
2. Caddymaster Clovelly CC 1963–1979
3. Coached Clovelly Juniors 1965–1970
4. SA Non-European Open (2) 2nd (5) - Provincial titles (14) 2nd (7)
5. Only allowed to play in his first SA 'white' tournament 1964 aged 31, and then sporadically

Disadvantaged by apartheid – prevented from playing the SAPGA 'white' tour.

Record

- German Open: 1970 6th
- The Open: 1970 56th
- Natal Open: 1974 15th

Non-European TPA

- SA Non-European Open: 1962, 72 (*62 - Oppenheimer Cup best qualifier)
- SA Non-European Open: 2nd 1956, 63, 67, 73, 79; 3rd 1961, 65; 4th 1964
- SA Non-European Open Foursomes: 1962 (with P. van Dieman)
- WP Non-European Open: 1956, 63, 65, 66, 67, 68, 71, 73
- WP Non-European Open: 2nd 1961, 64, 4th 1955
- Eastern Province Non-European Open: 1963, 68; 2nd 1964
- Griqualand Non-European Open: 2nd 1963, 64
- OFS Non-European Open: 1964
- Transvaal Non-European Open: 1968, 83; 2nd 1969
- Natal Non-European Open: 1976; 2nd 1975
- Kroonstadt Non-European Open: 1964 3rd
- OFS Special Strokeplay 1964 3rd
- Luyt Lager: 1972 3rd

> - Marley Classic 197?
> - LTA Masters 1975 2nd
> *Records incomplete*

How could it be that Papwa Sewgolum and Ismail Chowglay, who regularly had pages and pages of copy written about them locally in primarily the Indian, Coloured, and Black-read newspapers and magazines in both SA and India, heroes and icons to millions of blacks, coloureds, and Indians, would be abandoned by both black and white, as well as the golf bodies, and be allowed to pass away in abject poverty due primarily to apartheid?

LIGHT PEEPING THROUGH

Discussions between the two amateur bodies, the SAGU and the SA(N-E)GA led to the first 'Open International' SA Amateur Championship

The first 'open international' SA Amateur Championship was the 1972 event held in East London. In the Stroke-Play those that made the cut were Reggie Mamashela, Ronald Ngquka and Shan Dorasamy, while Ngquka got through to the match play stages and made history when he beat Springbok Johann Murray 5/3. He lost to Kevin Suddards in the second round, but his performance was an indication of things to come.

Later in the year, it was announced that, with respect to the 1972/73 season, the SA Amateur would again be designated as 'Open International', as would the SA Open, the SA PGA, and the SA Classic. There was still a majority of professional tournaments that were denied to black golfers, as also the various provincial amateur championships. Nor had there been any relaxation of the complex Government regulations and permit requirements in and around multiracial sport.

Lee Elder had played in the 1972 PGA Championship

and accepted an invitation to play again in 1973. As part of his tour, the plan was that he and Gary Player would play an exhibition match in Cape Town.

It appeared that the challenge match could only be held with the approval of the Minister of Sport and the conundrum was that, if such approval were to be given, it would entail a major amendment to the 'open international' concessions granted over the previous two years. These concessions granted permission for non-whites to compete only in full-scale tournaments classed as 'international'. This match would be between two people. There was, however, a precedent. The year before Yvonne Goolagong played what was classed as a challenge match against Margaret Court on the Rondebosch tennis courts. In the end, the Player/Elder match never took place. No suitable date could be found that did not clash with an SA PGA tournament and the matter of the permit fell away.

In 1974 to assist the Athlone Golf Club, Cape Town, with the financing of their new clubhouse, Gary Player played an exhibition match featuring Sewgolum, Tshabalala and Chowglay. As the Cape Times put it: 'Athlone will be one of Player's sternest tests in his golfing career'.

Prior to the challenge match, Player held a golf clinic for the spectators who had come to watch this epic encounter.

By then, Papwa (with A. Hartzenburg, runner-up in the 1969 SA Non-European Open on his bag) had a thickset build, compared to the lithe, slim 'boyish' ladies man Chowglay (with Abe van Rooyen, 1970 WP champion carrying his bag). Long-hitting left-handed Chowglay scuffing up the turf instead of a tee, using only a 3-wood, outhit Papwa who was a little shorter than Player. But that did not matter, and despite the sandy lies off the fairway and poorly conditioned fairways, once Papwa got near the green, he put on a short-game display.

The challenge caught the public's imagination, and was watch by a mixed-race gallery of more than 2,000, and together, Tshabalala, Chowglay, and Sewgolum more than held their own against Player, with Player going round in approximately 67, Papwa was also round in 3-under par-69, Chowglay 71, and Tshabalala 72, with Player/Chowglay beating Sewgolum/Tshabalala 4/2.

All three, Sewsunker Sewgolum, Ismail Chowglay, and Vincent Tshabalala were later to be inducted into the Southern Africa Golf Hall of Fame.

Sadly, by 1978, the Bob Grimsdell designed Athlone Golf Club was not able to maintain its course, and it was apparent that the course would have to be closed down. There was opposition to the idea of commercial development on the property, but there seemed to be no alternative. The belief that the course was more suited to recreational usage and housing was proven correct. The sadness was that the course did not survive.

The anti-lobbyist Fitz Sonnenberg on the City Council way back in 1962 was proved right. The course was a white elephant. Golf is an expensive sport that the rank and file of the coloured community – and most whites – could not afford to play. Money was thrown away and the valuable land would be better suited for building. It did indeed cost more than the members could afford to keep it in order and, unless maintained as a public facility by the municipality as suggested by Ken Elkin, it had to close down. At this time there were eight coloured golf courses in the Peninsula, albeit established in the bush.

The Athlone Golf Club continued as a member club, and when they finally lost their course, the Jewish King David CC stepped in to help. King David CC was one of the few clubs in the country that had been granted international status and to accommodate the golfers from Athlone was, therefore, no problem. This is the first mention of a club given this status.

Within the concept of open international events and the fact of black golfers being restricted to these, it was for the most part business as usual for the next few seasons.

The names of the leading black golfers competing in the designated tournaments tended to repeat from year to year, tournament to tournament – Chowglay, Tshabalala, Mogoerane, Naidoo, Manyama, Sepeng, Motati, Mamashela, Mavundla, Chetty, Molefe and, Papwa Sewgolum. Chowglay was perhaps the leading player.

1975 Vavasseur Natal Open in January was one of the open international events. Papwa finished on 77 73 70 72 (292) for a share of thirteenth place. Also doing well was Chowglay (294). A major breakthrough came in September 1975 when the Minister of Sport Piet Koornhof announced that all racial barriers on the professional golf tour were to be lifted. This was the first proper multiracial golf tournament in SA.

By this stage, Sewgolum was already 46 and Chowglay 42 with their best years behind them. As Sewgolum stated: 'It has come too late for me'. Interestingly, Papwa was invited to play in neither of these tournaments. Outside of such events the usual personal, legal and sporting limits, oppression and segregation continued.

It was now time for Vincent Tshabalala to take up Papwa Sewgolum's mantle...

CHAPTER NINE

'Vive la France'

*The profile of a champion is rather like a complex jigsaw puzzle. There
are many pieces, and without all of them he is incomplete. Sound
technique is only one of the pieces. Another is fitness.
There has to be peace of mind, proper diet, patience,
courage, an ability to enjoy the adversity of pressure,
intelligent playing strategy ... Perhaps most important of all,
there must be this commitment to excellence.*

Gary Player

VINCENT TSHABALALA

Another golfer showing his potential and making his
mark was Vincent Tshabalala. Born in 1942, six
foot one, Vincent started working out as a caddie
after school at Rietvlei Golf Club, including caddying for
Gary Player, who also spent time coaching him, and saved
up for golf clubs to pursue his passion for golf, a sport that
was historically a white sport. Later he got work as a very
gifted mechanic before he devoted his life to his greatest
passion. When he turned professional it was with a mixed
set of clubs bought 1 by 1.

During the 1960s on the non-European Tour, he had
six wins, four second-place and one-third place finish. He
was however barred from the Southern African Tour in his
prime during the 1960/70s as a result of apartheid.

Like 'Papwa' and Chowglay, Tshabalala used a
cross-handed grip to good effect with his long irons and
was ranked the number one long-iron player on the 1976
Sunshine Tour. He also had a magical short game.

He tied the SA Non-European Open with Sewgolum in
1965 and won the title in '71, '77, and again in '83.

The problem remained that black golfers including

Vincent had great difficulty in raising the finances for competition. Many of them worked outside the game during the off-season to raise cash to fund their competitive play. Vincent worked as a mechanic when not on tour.

Then in 1974 Gary Player sponsored this young black African and took him overseas to Australia where Player won his seventh Australian Open in spite of enduring anti-apartheid demonstrations who ventured on to one of the putting greens in the middle of the night and wrote 'Go Home, You Racist Pig' in white lime powder. It was the beginning of further troubled times for SA golfers abroad where they faced a hostile reception when interviewed and on the golf course, with some of the greens vandalised by demonstrators prior to playing.

'After all, I was there', said Vincent. 'And I was also targeted by Australian racists, who referred to me as 'smoke'.

'I remember standing on the tee at a par-3 – 160 metres from the pin – and they were saying things like, 'The smoke won't get it over the water.' I stepped back to recollect myself, and then I hit a 5-iron at the flag, two feet from the hole. Vincent never lost for words, 'I turned around and said, this smoke can play!'

It was the beginning of more troubled times for SA golfers abroad. Later they went to America, and Player arranged for Vincent to play two PGA Tour events – the Kemper Open and the IVB-Philadelphia Golf Classic. In those two tournaments, Tshabalala only broke 80 once.

Tshabalala then competed in the US Open – the first SA black golfer to do so. No mean achievement!

Tshabalala had learnt the game not on the emerald, tree-lined courses that proliferated throughout 'white' SA, but on a scrubby, eight-hole course laid out on waste ground. The greens were not green but dusty brown, and the concept of a hazard was unknown because the whole course was a hazard.

He did well in the 1976 Dunlop Masters at Kensington, finishing fifth on a score of 273 (Papwa finished on 289) and also in the Rhodesian Dunlop Masters on 285 for a share of eighth place.

Vincent was unable to play in the majority of tournaments on the Southern African Tour in his prime, but once again with the assistance of Gary Player, who financed his trip, he gained entry to tournaments on the European Tour in 1976.

And so it was that he made his European Tour debut at the Madrid Open at Puerto de Hierro finishing tied for the forty-fifth place. Then onto The Open, won by Johnny Miller, where Vincent came fifty-sixth.

This coming week, on an extremely tight budget, not having money for a caddy, Tshabalala would have to pull his own golf cart and judge his own distances. Touring professionals during practice rounds would attach a wheel to their cart with an odometer measuring distances as they made their way around the course, judging these and writing them down in a little notebook for reference during the tournament.

As a former caddy, he never needed to consult with a caddy for the line as he had developed a flair for 'reading' the green. So Vincent set out for France, and the famous Le Touquet Golf Club.

Set within superb natural surroundings – between the forest and the sand dunes – Le Touquet Golf Club is one of the most beautiful of European courses, surrounded by a vast forest and an opaline sea, and only two hours from Paris. The 18-hole La Mer Course, a typical British links course, was built in 1931 by the renowned architect Harry Colt together with Charles Alison, and ranked in 1976 as one of the top 20 courses in Europe.

Measuring 5,648m (now 6,343m), this par-72 golf course started in the flat land soon threading its way into the ever larger dunes as the round progressed, undulating fairways, prolific pot bunkers, not to mention the awaiting gorse and heather rough, which demanded concentration and precision. All this and the blustery wind that funnelled down the Channel whipping across the exposed links, seldom benign and could seriously damage any score card, and with wonderful sea views of the Channel from elevated tees.

Opening with a 434m par-5, followed by a long 187m par-3, then a short 324m par-4, and a short 410m par-5, allowed the golfer to get away with a fast start and then claw back the round with par-5s at the 15th and 17th holes.

04 May 1976, at the French Open, Vincent knew he was in 'the zone', the clubhead moved all the way back to the top of his swing as he rhythmically swung the club back, he felt every little motion, and then the momentary pause. It felt like he had all the time in the world, amazingly smooth and mechanical, as he aimed for the top of the flag, trying to drop the ball from the fairway directly into the hole as the clubhead made solid contact with the ball spraying up the turf. And his confidence grew as his short-game, his real strength came to life.

He opened with a solid 70 despite pulling his own golf cart, leaving him two shots behind the leader, Salvador Balbuena (winner of the Portuguese Open three weeks earlier), and in a group of players in fifth position with Neil

Coles, Sam Torrence, and Simon Hobday. It was still all smiles after the second round with another comfortable 70, which kept him in the hunt although Balbuena had pulled clear, now with a 6-shot lead over Vincent, but only three ahead of Hobday.

The third round was played on a crisp morning, which equalled Vincent's golf as he shot a brilliant 66 to move solidly into contention now only three shots back of the leader, tied with Simon Hobday who shot a 69. Roaring back through the field after a poor second round was Sam Torrence with a course record 63, now a shot back of Vincent and Hobday, together with English Ryder Cup star Neil Coles.

Thus Vincent started out three behind Balbuena, and after ten holes was 5-strokes adrift. But the Spaniard lost a ball for a six at the 11th, a turning point, and then ran up a three-over par-8 on the 14th after three times hooking into the rough, and like an Americas Cup yacht sweeping past all opposition, Vincent took the lead.

Balbuena and the gallery could feel Vincent advancing ahead of them tearing up the course, passing the leader in the fourth and final round as Balbuena playing conservative golf shot 72 to Vincent's scintillating magical 67 giving him 16 below par 272, and two ahead of Balbuena.

To put this into perspective previous winners of the French Open have included Jose María Olazabal, Colin Montgomerie, Retief Goosen, Sam Torrance, Robert Allenby, Nick Faldo, Seve Ballesteros, Bernhard Langer, Sandy Lyle, Greg Norman, Dale Hayes, Brian Barnes, Peter Oosterhuis, David Graham, Roberto de Vicenzo, and in 1951 Hassan Hassanien (Egypt's greatest golfer).

And so it was that, Vincent Tshabalala, a 35-year old black South African who had been working as a motor mechanic two years previously, while pulling his own golf cart, snatched a shock victory by winning the French Open, on

May 09, 1976, just two months before the Soweto uprising, with scores of 69 70 66 67 (272) (-16), beating a top
international field. He finished two strokes ahead of Salvador Balbuena, with Simon Hobday, Neil Coles, and Sam
Torrance sharing third place, and Seve Ballesteros 6 shots
adrift, winning E4,907 (Severiano Ballesteros won it the
following year, and Dale Hayes in 1974).

French Open 1976 winner Vincent Tshabalala

- TSHABALALA Vincent SA 69 70
  66 67 = 272 (-16) € 4,907
- BALBUENA Salvador SPN 67 66
  69 72 = 274 (-14) € 2,944
- COLES Neil ENG 69 69 68 70 =
  276 (-12)
- HOBDAY Simon RSA 69 67 69 71
  = 276 (-12)
- TORRANCE Sam SCO 69 74 63
  70 = 276 (-12)

A protégé of Gary Player, he said: 'Funny thing I have
achieved. I owe everything to Gary Player, who helped me
with my game and programme of physical training, and
helped my family. He will be over the moon about my win,
which means I will not have to pre-qualify for the British
Open. I played that in 1970 but I didn't make the last two
rounds.'

One of his training methods he said, was to follow the
precept of 'keeping dry'. He said that meant playing 18
holes and avoiding the 19th hole.

In 2010 Vincent was delighted to meet Sally Little for
the first time at his induction into the Southern Africa Golf
Hall of Fame at Oubaai, and he took her aside, drawing out a
torn well-worn old article from his wallet. 'I always wanted to

VINCENT Tshabalala, the powerful Soweto professional kisses the French Open Trophy he won at Le Touquet when he pipped Spaniard Salvador Balbuena winner of the Portuguese Open a couple of weeks before.

tell you that when I won the French Open, I drew inspiration from this newspaper clipping I carried in my pocket throughout the tournament. It told the story of Sally Little who earlier that month had become the first South African female to win a Major in the United States when you triumphed at the Women's International in South Carolina.'

The following months their careers were to be overshadowed by the tragic Soweto uprising.

Returning home to Soweto in July, and despite the 'necklacing', a common horrifying death for black collaborators (burning tyre containing petrol placed over the head), and with the '(Winnie) Mandela football club' in their yellow tracksuits terrorising the residents with kidnapping, torture and murder, Tshabalala was immediately selected by the SAPGA, headed by Brian 'Bruno' Henning (later one of the founders of the US Champion Tour), to partner Gary Player in the World Cup — the FIRST BLACK SPORTSMAN to be selected to REPRESENT AND PLAY FOR SOUTH AFRICA — which invitation he immediately turned down!

This was despite Gary Player being his friend and mentor, and irrespective of the money and status he would earn, he declined for good reason as Soweto went up in flames during the 1976 July student riots following an attempt to enforce Afrikaans language requirements on black African students, and the mood of the black population was sullen and threatening. Vincent lived in Soweto, the centre of the unrest, and an acceptance of an invitation to represent 'white' South Africa abroad was potentially dangerous to himself and his family. At the same time, he felt he was being used by the Apartheid government as he was only ranked fourteenth on the SA Order of Merit, that he did not deserve his place, and as such that his selection was merely for political expediency.

Furthermore, the invitation was to represent the PGA in this world event, even though they would not let him be a member, nor did he have the same rights as the other 'white' professionals to vote.

This was simply glossed over as it did not occur to them — they had allowed him to play under the new dispensation, and surely this was enough?

1976 Soweto Uprising

The upshot was trouble with the SAPGA, and its president Brian Henning. They had obviously wanted to put on a 'black' face in the world arena to deflect the criticism and banning now levelled at those white golfers playing internationally, and especially Gary Player. Furious, for no valid

reason, the winner of the French Open, Vincent Tshabalala's entry for the SA Open was turned down.

Further, he was suspended not only by SAPGA but now
by the black controlling TPA body for having taken part in
a 'white' tournament

In order to enable him to play in multiracial tournaments, and thus get around this ban by both the SAPGA
and the Black TPA Tour, he formed the 'South African Bantu Golf Union' on the advice of Minister Piet Koornhof.

But it seems he was soon forgiven as that season he
played nine events and would finish joint seventh in the
Sumrie-Bournemouth Better-Ball (with John O'Leary),
seventeenth at the Italian Open, and joint twenty-first in
the Piccadilly Medal.

In January 1977, Vincent won the SA Non-European
Open in Durban with scores of 73 75 73 70 (291) albeit an
event run by the amateur body, the SA(N-E)GA. However,
he was then banned from playing in the Zambian Open because he was South African.

In January 1981, George Blumberg quit organising
Black Professional Tournaments following Tshabalala's
controversial statements in the press that he was being discriminated against insofar as 'white' professional tournaments. That year he was also banned from playing in Kenya
Open because he was a South African.

In 1982 Tshabalala became a member of the PGA, and
later as President of the PGA in 1990, he played an integral
part in uniting the Professional Golfers Association (PGA)
and the Tournament Players Association (TPA).

Soon after, during the 1980s, his career was curtailed
by an injury. However, there was a reprieve of sorts. Despite a series of injuries, he made a comeback to the game
as a senior in the over-50s ranks, where he played on the
European Seniors Tour from its formation in 1992. He was
twice runner-up; behind John Fourie in the 1992 Belfast

Telegraph Irish Senior Masters, and behind Maurice Bembridge in the 1996 Hippo Jersey Seniors.

He was fortunate to have had this second crack as he finished in the top 20 on the European Senior Tour Order of Merit four times in the 1990s despite not winning any tournaments. In all, he finished in the top-10 ten times and in the top-15 sixteen times, counting both regular and senior events.

He also played on the Southern Africa Tour after racial restrictions were abolished in the early 1990s, but by then he was almost 50, and he didn't win any official money events, although he came second in the Kenya Open in 1997 aged 55.

However, in his 60s, he won the Nelson Mandela Invitational in both 2004 playing with Ernie Els, and in 2005 playing with Tim Clark, and then in 2009 aged 67, the Gary Player Invitational 4ball Alliance together with Thomas Aitken.

2004 Nelson Mandela Invitational. Ernie Els helping to chair Vincent Tshabalala (62) after their victory.

'As someone who was able to rise from my circumstances due to the kindness and support of Gary Player, I am delighted to come back and support the great legend. It is such an honour to be invited to support the Nelson Mandela Invitational. It gives me the chance to contribute to helping children have a better life meaningfully .'

In 1999 Vincent Tshabalala, now 57, accused the SAP-GA of 'anti-black sentiment' after they suspended John Mashego and Solly Sepeng for six months following a personal dispute brought on by the PGA's decision to reduce the number of black exemptions onto the previous all-white tour from ten to five with an emphasis on favouring youth at the expense of those who suffered under apartheid.

He accused Mashego of being a token black used as a pawn by the tour, who have told him what is good for blacks. 'Age should not be a factor. Any player who can make the cut should be considered.'

In the latter years, Vincent received several awards including:

- Presidential Sports Award from Thabo Mbeki
- Certificate of recognition from the City of Johannesburg in 2003 for his dedication to overcome racial barriers in sport and golf
- Lifetime achievement award from the Union of Golf Societies in 2005
- Golf award from SABC Sports for his excellent contribution to the promotion and development of golf as the premier sport in South Africa
- Inducted into the Southern Africa Golf Hall of Fame in 2010 (ironically together with Brian Henning)

After his active career, he became a dedicated teacher of golf, more of interest to help and see people gain than to earn money. For four years he worked as a pro at Malarbadens Golf Club in Sweden during the summers.

This eloquent charming larger than life elder-golfing

statesman passed away in 2017 at the age of 75, still hitting balls on the practice range, and looking for that comeback.

2010 Vincent Tshabala's induction into the Southern Africa Golf Hall of Fame: Barry Cohen, Hugh Baiocchi, Vincent Tshabalala, Sally Little, Dale Hayes, Cobie le Grange, John Bland.

VINCENT VESELE TSHABALALA
(1942 – 2017)

Citation

1. Prevented from competing in South African tournaments during his prime because of Apartheid.
2. 1976 Selected to partner Gary Player in the Canada Cup (later World Cup). First black sportsman selected to represent SA. Refused for political reasons.
3. 1976 formed the Bantu Golf Union.
4. Fighter for the rights of black golfers.
5. 1982 became a member of the PGA.

6.   1990 Captain of the SAPGA - he played an integral part in uniting the Professional Golfers Association (PGA) and Tournament Players Association (TGA).

7.   2010 Inducted Southern Africa Golf Hall of Fame.

- Professional wins (10) – 2nd (8)
- S.A. Non-European Open (4) – 2nd (5)
- Provincial Tournaments (3) – 2nd (4)
- Other SA Tournaments (2)
- European Tour wins (1) – Senior 2nd (2)
- Southern Africa Senior wins (2)
- On the white tour when he was allowed to compete from the 1970s, he finished in the top-10 (10) and in the top-15 (16) counting both regular and senior events
- Injured from c.1978 – 1991

Disadvantaged Apartheid — prevented from playing the SAPGA 'white' tour

Record

- French Open 1976
- SA Masters 1976 5th
- Madrid Open 1976 45th
- Sumrie-Bournemouth Better-Ball (with John O'Leary) 1976 7th
- Italian Open 1976 17th
- Piccadilly Medal 1976 21st
- SA Dunlop Masters 1976 5th
- Rhodesian Dunlop Masters 1976 8th
- The Open 1977 56th
- J&B All African Classic 1994 3rd
- Kenya Open 1997 2nd

Non-European TPA

- S.A. Non-European Open 1965, 71, 77, 83
- S.A. Non-European Open 2nd 1966, 68, 70, 72, 74
- Western Province Non-European Open 1963, 2nd 1969
- Natal Non-European Open 1971, 72, 2nd 69, 3rd 67, 4th 68
- Transvaal Non-European Open 1972, 2nd 66, 70
- Transvaal Non-European Matchplay 1966
- Far North & North East N-E Open 1966 2nd
- Gary Player Non-European Invitational 1968, 2nd 69
- Special 72-hole Tournament 1968 4th
- Swaziland Spa Open 1970 2nd

Seniors

- Belfast Telegraph Irish Masters 1992 2nd
- Hippo Jersey Seniors 1996 2nd
- Nelson Mandela Invitational 2004 (with Ernie Els), 05 (with Tim Clark)
- Gary Player Invitational 4Ball Alliance 2009 (with Thomas Aitken)

Records incomplete

2010 John Bland, Vincent Tshabalala (donating his 3-wood to the S.A Golf Museum on being inducted into the Southern Africa Golf Hall of Fame), and Denis Hutchinson.

Vincent Tsha-
balala's 3-wood
proudly dis-
played in the S.A.
Golf Museum

TOUR RESULT COMPARISON: NATIONAL AND PROVINCIAL

'Papwa' Sewgolum – Ismail Chowglay – Vincent Tshabalala

When Tshabalala came onto the scene, he together with Papwa and Chowglay featured in numerous Non-European
tournaments. In many of them, either one or two of them
simply did not feature, but it is interesting to note their respective records when they, in fact, did play against each
other, although some of Sewgolum's victories were by the
proverbial mile.

**Tshabalala was 14 years younger than Sewgolum and 10 years
younger than Chowglay.*

SA NON-EUROPEAN OPEN

1956		I Chowglay
1957		
1958		
1959		
1960	S Sewgolum 80 80 74 74 (308)	
1961	S Sewgolum (297)	
1962	I Chowglay 72 74 74 77 (297)	
1963	S Sewgolum 75 77 75 74 (301)	I Chowglay 74 77 80 83 (314)
1964	S Sewgolum 71 72 70 75 (288)	
1965	S.Sewgolum/V Tshabalala 77 74 69 71 (291) 74 74 73 70 (291)	
1966		V Tshabalala
1967	S Sewgolum 70 69 72 71 (282)	I Chowglay (289)
1968	S Sewgolum 70 70 71 74 (285)	V Tshabalala (293)
1969	S Sewgolum 71 76 73 75 (295)	
1970	S Sewgolum 77 67 69 74 (287)	V Tshabalala (295)

1971	V Tshabalala (292)	S Sewgolum (293)
1972	I Chowglay 74 74 75 74 (297)	V Tshabalala
1973		I Chowglay
1974	S Sewgolum 77 69 75 70 (291)	V Tshabalala 70 70 72 80 (292)
1975		
1976		
1977	V Tshabalala 73 75 73 70 (291)	
1979		I Chowglay
1983	V Tshabalala	

TRANSVAAL NON-EUROPEAN OPEN

1964	S Sewgolum (284) *63 course record	
1965	S Sewgolum 70 70 71 71 (282)	
1966	S Sewgolum 69,70,70,73 (282)	
1967		S Sewgolum
1968	I Chowglay 73 69 73 73 (287)	
1969	S Sewgolum	I Chowglay
1970	S Sewgolum	V Tshabalala
1971		
1972	V Tshabalala (295)	S Sewgolum (297)
1973-82		
1983	I Chowglay	

O.F.S. NON-EUROPEAN OPEN

1964	I Chowglay	
1965		
1966	S Sewgolum 69 70 70 73 (282)	
1968		S Sewgolum (304)
1969	S Sewgolum	

NATAL NON-EUROPEAN OPEN

1954	S Sewgolum	
1955	S Sewgolum	
1956		S Sewgolum *lost playoff
1957	S Sewgolum	
1958	S Sewgolum	
1959	S Sewgolum	
1960	S Sewgolum 74 72 75 73 (294)	
1961	S Sewgolum 73 73 71 73 (290)	
1962	S Sewgolum	
1963	S Sewgolum	
1964		S Sewgolum (294)
1965	S Sewgolum 72 71 73 75 (291)	
1966	S Sewgolum 70 71 73 74 (288)	
1967	S Sewgolum	
1968	S Sewgolum (286) *63 3rd round	

1969	S Sewgolum *by 21 shots	
1970	S Sewgolum	
1971	V Tshabalala	S Sewgolum
1972	V Tshabalala 73 69 69 71 (282)	
1973		
1974	S Sewgolum	
1975	S Sewgolum 73 73 77 71 (294)	I Chowglay (303)
1976	I Chowglay *play-off	S Sewgolum
1977	S Sewgolum	

WESTERN PROVINCE NON-EUROPEAN OPEN

1956	I Chowglay	
1957		
1958		
1960	S Sewgolum	
1961		I Chowglay
1962		
1963	I Chowglay	
1964	S Sewgolum 68 65 72 70 (275)	I Chowglay (302)
1965	I Chowglay	
1966	I Chowglay	
1967	I Chowglay	
1968	I Chowglay (297)	S Sewgolum (305)
1969	S Sewgolum 74 74 76 72 (296)	V Tshabalala (298)
1970		

1971	I Chowglay 79 76 72 75 (302)	
1973	I Chowglay	
1974		
1975		
1976	S Sewgolum 78 70 76 77 (301)	

EASTERN PROVINCE NON-EUROPEAN OPEN

1963	I Chowglay (309)	S Sewgolum (310)
1964	S Sewgolum	I Chowglay
1965-67		
1968	I Chowglay	S Sewgolum

GRIQUALAND WEST NON-EUROPEAN OPEN

1960	S Sewgolum 69 72 72 72 (285)	
1961	S Sewgolum 75 68 69 73 (285) *68 course record	
1963	S Sewgolum (285)	I Chowglay (293)
1964	S Sewgolum 77 72 74 72 (295)	I Chowglay 75 75 73 78 (301)
1965	S Sewgolum 71 69 70 71 (281)	
1966		
1967	S Sewgolum (300)	
1969	S Sewgolum 78 78 75 69 (300)	

CHAPTER TEN

Breaking down apartheid barriers

PRESSURE

In 1975 there was a split among black professional golfers, and two rival controlling bodies were formed, the 'SA Golf Association' and the 'SA National Golf Union'.

The fact that the two professional bodies did not always see eye to eye has been made evident, each one jealously guarded its own domain and demanded absolute loyalty from its members.

In 1980 these two reached an agreement to disband and form a single controlling body, the Tournament Players Association (TPA). Simon Hlapo was elected chairman, Bernard Gase secretary and Vincent Tshabalala and Reggie Mamashela committee members. The formation of the new body was apparently Gary Player's idea.

Overall control of golf in South Africa was in the hands of the SA Golf Council.

Meanwhile, amateur golf was under the control of the SA Golf Union (white) and the SA(N-E)GA (black) while professional tournament golf was under the control of the SA Professional Golf Association (white) and the SA Professional Players Association (black).

In 1977, the Commonwealth Tournament involving teams from Canada, New Zealand, Britain and SA, but not Australia, was scheduled for Royal Durban. Late in November 1975 and as a precursor to the event, a multinational amateur tournament was planned for Mowbray GC involving the visiting teams and including seven South African black amateurs, Shan Dorasamy (Natal), leading amateur in the 1975 SA Non-European Open in Kimberley, John Thetele (Transvaal), runner-up in the Open, John Baxter

(WP and Athlone GC), third in the Open, John Davids (WP and Athlone), Martin du Preez (Transvaal), Wellington Songqwigi (EP) and Josef Mofokeng (Transvaal).

However, the 1977 Commonwealth Tournament being played at St. Andrews was called off for fear of anti-apartheid demonstrations.

That year, the SAGU announced that in future non-white golfers would be eligible to play in the South African amateur, all provincial open championships, the country districts and under-23 tournaments. Non-White clubs would also be able to arrange friendly matches with White clubs as well as entering leagues.

At a provincial level, the WPGU made application for the WP Amateur and Stroke Play Championships to have multinational status, as well as the various club open tournaments, and teams were to be selected strictly on a merit basis only. No doubt the other provincial unions around the country were making similar decisions.

As it happened, the WP Amateur was duly granted 'normal' status and in April 1977 became the first provincial championship open to all races. Again, history was made. The following year one of the surprises of the WP Championship was Michael Meyer (*playing with the author), an Athlone member, who reached the last four of the match play. Without financial support, Meyer returned to caddying for those whom he triumphed over.

Alfred Makanda, a 21-year-old caddy at the East London GC, became the first non-White golfer to win a provincial title, beating Springbok Buster Farrer 4 and 2 in the final of the 1977 Border Match Play Championship

Except for the all-important matter of membership of golf clubs, amateur golf was to all intents and purposes non-racial. The 'de jure' fact was that it was the provisions of the Group Areas' Act that prevented non-whites from joining white clubs.

'NO BLACKS, NO JEWS, NO DOGS'

The slogan 'no Blacks, no Jews, no dogs' was a common slogan heard at numerous golf courses in South Africa right into the 1980s. Set among the valley flanked by mountains, sand dunes, and a river, other clubs may have their histories, but that of Clovelly, like the club itself, is unique.

Following a devastating fire which burnt down this nine-hole golf course clubhouse in 1932, Gus Ackerman and Michael Pevsner purchased the property for the sum of 3,000 pounds and in 1932 formed the Clovelly Country Club.

They purchased the club with definite aims in view because as Jews, they had been denied membership in Cape Town to private clubs such as Kelvin Grove, and a number of golf clubs (something that continued into the 1980s), and they decided that they would then form their own golf club.

The stated purpose in the constitution was 'that the aforesaid land shall only be used for sporting and other activities of the Clovelly Country Club from the membership of which no person shall be debarred by reason of race, religious denomination or creed.'

Many members of the former club who did not want to mix with Jews departed and formed the new club of Westlake Golf Club; ironically the land was purchased from a coloured dairyman named Hendricks who owned a small farm on the other side of the mountain.

Michael Pevsner became the first President of the Club and remained so until his death in 1941. Gus Ackerman became the first Chairman, a position he only relinquished in 1953 when he was elected Life President until his death in 1966. His son Raymond succeeded him in the President's chair.

Probably the most famous game of golf played at Clovelly was in 1947 when Maurice Bodmer (club professional with an outstanding amateur record) partnered Bobby Locke against 'Slamming' Sam Snead and Norman von Nida in an exhibition match which was won 2/1 by Bodmer and Locke. Subsequently, for many years Bobby Locke continued to sojourn to Clovelly for the three month summer period, and Bodmer was with Locke when he had his accident at Lakeside railway crossing where he effectively lost the use of his eye.

Raymond Ackerman playing with his youthful friend Rita Leveten (2010 Southern Africa Golf Hall of Fame inductee) at Clovelly thought he was a hotshot golfer with a possible career, that was until he played Denis Hutchinson in the SA Amateur and lost 10/8, so instead he turned his attention to building his Pick 'n Pay empire.

And so it was in January 1978 that Raymond Ackerman approached Prime Minister B.J. Vorster and Minister Connie Mulder, and informed him that he was opening Clovelly to all races. Mulder's immediate reaction was 'over my dead body', but Vorster sent him packing, telling him to 'get out of the office'. He then confirmed that Ackerman could proceed if 87 per cent (an arbitrary figure which he plucked out of the air) of the members agreed. Most of the members agreed, and the club became the first golf club in apartheid SA to be opened to all races.

Another chink in the armour!

Three months later, the new Minister of Sport, F.W. de Klerk, (the future Prime Minister who would release Mandela) used this loophole to allow all sports clubs to choose their membership, thereby opening sports clubs to all races.

2015 Clovelly CC Raymond Ackerman, Pat van Heerden, President FW de Klerk, Barry Cohen celebrating Ackerman's role in opening sports clubs to all races

By 1979 all the leading players of colour in the Western Cape, such as Stan and Percy Lendis (1963 WP Non-European Coloured Open champion), Wally Johannsen, Andrew Hess, Fred Weaver, Moses Mooi, a young 'Slamming' Sammy Daniels, Carl Mentoor, and Abe van Rooyen (WP Non-European Open winner 1970, second '71), were all playing league for Clovelly. Moses Mooi became the first golfer of colour to be selected for a SA Provincial white team when he was selected to play for the WP 'B' team.

Subsequently, Ackerman donated this very valuable real estate to the members of Clovelly, and further, set up the 'Raymond Ackerman Golf Academy'. This enables disadvantaged children straight from impoverished communities, who have never played golf, assists them daily at the club with their school work and life skills, teaching them to play golf, and enables certain students to study further at university.

This endeavour went relatively unnoticed until the Southern Africa Golf Hall of Fame awarded Raymond Ackerman the 'Harry Brews award' in 2014 for his selfless contribution to the betterment of golf.

ISOLATION AND PROTESTS

Golf World reported that allowing black players to compete on the Sunshine Tour is nothing more than 'window dressing' according to Bill Reid.

The SAPGA hit back saying black golf has made great strides, but until the black golf bodies stopped squabbling for ethnic power and formed one body, the white-controlled PGA would not admit them. The SA PPGA and the SA Bantu Union, decided to amalgamate and form a single controlling body, the Tournament Players Association.

Globally the campaign to isolate SA from participating from international events was led by Sam Ramsamy and Peter Hain from the office of SANROC based in London.

'No normal sport in an abnormal society' was still a key adage of SACOS both locally and globally. Sport in apartheid SA was a powerful medium which was used to achieve the ultimate objective for a non-racial democracy in the politics of liberation.

At about the same period the SA regime had changed their stance and promoted the concept of 'Multi-Nationalism' because of international pressure and the eagerness of white sports persons to compete internationally.

On the 13 July 1980, a campaign to ban golfers from SA competing in the US was launched with the Eisenhower Tournament in October as the first target.

Acting Secretary General, Dr John Dommisse, quoted by the Washington Post, 'Golfers represent one of the most segregated sports in South Africa but have rarely been challenged in the USA in recent years. Gary Player will also be a future target, though he would not be singled out for special attack.'

In 1981 more than 160 black golfers walked out of the Grahamstown Non-European Open held at Grahamstown Golf Club in protest over a humiliating racial incident involving a 'white' caddy, Clive Marx who was caddying for Philip Meke.

After 18 holes, the club manager approached Marx and informed him, 'White people are not allowed on the course while blacks are playing.'

They had a long argument, then Marx sat down in a chair with a cool drink and a sandwich. Organising secretary of Northwood club, Madikane Msiza, said that Meke, with Marx caddying, had arrived back at the clubhouse after completing the first 18 holes of a 36-hole tournament.

Msiza said the club manager told Marx that he could not sit there and threatened to call the police. He said Marx must also move his car right off the golf course. Marx then went and sat in his car.

The vice-president of Northwood GC, Count Attwell called all his club players together, and they decided to walk out of the tournament 'in protest at the humiliation of a member of our club'. All the other players felt the same, and they walked out too.

Count Attwell was then called into the club manager's office and told that the incident would 'harm relations' and the players should continue as if nothing happened. Attwell told him that 'our members were not prepared to play on.'

SEX AND PUBLIC SCHOOLS See Page 3

DAILY EXPRESS

Thursday March 12 1981 • 12p • Weather: Showers

THE VOICE OF BRITAIN

Beaumont, Faldo may be barred over S. Africa links

BLACKED

British sport stars facing a ban

ALL the sports men and women pictured on this page are on a United Nations "apartheid" blacklist, it was revealed last night.

It is the latest move in a publicity war that hit England's cricket tour of the West Indies and could now wreck all sport world wide.

THE OFFENCE

Golfer Nick Faldo and England Rugby stars Bill Beaumont and John Carleton top the British section of [illegible].

Their offence: They have recently played or are planning to play in South Africa.

In all, the list prepared by a U.N. committee names 185 athletes in 15 sports from 21 countries, including [illegible] Americans, 33 French, and 15 West Germans—and some Africans.

Golfer Lee Trevino and tennis

By PHILIP FINN in New York and MICHAEL O'FLAHERTY in London

players Stan Smith, Bob Lutz, Dick Stockton, Cliff Richey, and Guillermo Vilas are in the American section.

So are two black boxing stars—former heavy-weight champion Floyd Patterson and the present holder Mike Weaver.

French names include the entire international Rugby team, captained by Jean-Pierre Rives.

Among Australians is tennis player Kim Warwick.

THE HEARINGS

The UN Committee Against Apartheid is holding three days of hearings in Conference Room 4 of the General Assembly building in New York. More names—perhaps including cricketers—are expected to be added to the list.

There will be another meeting in Paris in May which will probably produce a [illegible] resolution.

Committee chairman Mr [illegible] Clark, U.N. Ambassador for Nigeria, said: "I think we are making perfectly clear what we feel about countries who go along with apartheid."

THAT MATCH

At home, England captain Bill Beaumont said: "I'm not particularly surprised or bothered. At the time I led the Lions in South Africa I made my views known—I don't support apartheid but I think South Africa has made advancements towards multi-racial sport, especially in Rugby."

But Beaumont and John Carleton are due to play in a special match in South Africa next month. "I will have to reconsider that if it is going to jeopardise my career with England," said Beaumont.

John Carleton agreed: "I might have to reconsider."

Golf star Nick Faldo, recently

Page 3 Column 1

BUDGET: MAGGIE IN WAR WITH THE WETS—PAGE 2

WORLDWIDE CONDEMNATION

In 1979, Calvin Peete (USA) played in the Kronenbrau Tournament at Milnerton, Moses Mooi was selected for WP 'B' provincial side, and in 1980 Noel Maart was selected for the WP Inter-Provincial team.

Also, in 1980, an exciting development, and the brainchild of Gary Player, now SAPGA President, was a mini-circuit sponsored to the tune of R24,000 and scheduled for October 1980.

The continuing application by the government of its apartheid policies and its pursuance of segregation of the races was anathema to the world, and sport in SA, not least golf, became the target of the world's condemnation

The Gleneagles Agreement, the UN resolution condemning apartheid and the OAU took a heavy toll on white SA golfers. With a stroke of a pen, the country's leading golfers were barred from major international competition.

To breach this stranglehold, the 'Sun City Million Dollar Challenge' was launched by Sol Kerzner in 1981 with a field of five men. For the rest of the anti-apartheid world, this event was appalling, and Jack Nicklaus became the target of the anti-apartheid activists, including a request from Arthur Ashe, the Wimbledon tennis champion, not to participate. Subsequently, Lee Trevino also bowed to this pressure when his sponsors threatened to withdraw their support.

John Hopkins of the London Sunday Times wrote: 'It's an affront to the dignity of millions of black Africans.' Describing Bophuthatswana, the SA homeland created by the apartheid regime as a self-governing haven for black people and home of Sun City as bleak, arid, riddled with disease and malnutrition, and a GDP of R150 per person, when comparing it to Lesotho, one of the world's least developed countries, which had a GDP of R240 per person.

Meanwhile, in February 1982, a R10,000 tournament

was scheduled to be played at the Pimville CC in Soweto run by the Tournament Players Association.

In Zimbabwe, Lewis Muridzo (Lewis Chitengwa's father) and Aida Alhadeff won the first multiracial, mixed Mashonaland Foursomes at Ruwa.

It had become obvious to the PGA committee that this was nothing more than 'window dressing', as black players could play with limited privileges, but could not be a member, nor did they have the right to play in events, as the Group Areas and the Liquor Acts were still a force.

The PGA then decided to let nine black players become members of the Tournament Players Division of the SAPGA: Vincent Tshabalala, Joe Dlamini (who was now emerging as the next dominant golfer), Richard Mogoerane, Theo Manyama, Shadrack Molefe, Ismail Chowglay (now 49), Peter Mkata, Daddy Naidoo and John Mashego – all enjoying full privileges including full voting rights, although they were still ineligible to join white clubs and generally restricted from playing at these clubs.

But the PGA was patronising about it, as they never consulted with the TPA including the selection of the nine players. The PGA made a mistake, as although they gave these nine players full membership, all non-exempt tournament players still had to go to the Tour School to compete for the top 50 tour cards.

Black players were very upset because they had not been consulted and contacted Gary Player who was playing abroad, calling for an immediate meeting. At a meeting at the Wanderers chaired by Player, the PGA and the TPA with Bernard Gase as president, the TPA had a spokesman with a clear political agenda who had a go at Player stating that were it not for black players, Gary Player would never have got to where he was. Player was furious: 'I got to where I got was because I worked and practised hard – nobody helped me. I also grew up poor without shoes.'

The TPA then ejected their spokesman, and Bernard Gase took over. By 1985 there were at least 29 qualified black members of the PGA. Of course, there were always grumbles concerning exemptions given to some invited players outside the top 50.

With the exception of those mentioned above, amateur golf was to all intents and purposes non-racial. The excuse used, despite the dispensation given to Clovelly, was the de jure fact that it was the provisions of the Group Areas Act that prevented blacks from joining white clubs.

This pressure only increased when SA golfer Jeff Hawkes, while competing in the Scandinavian Open in 1982, reportedly said: 'Negroes are like children – you can't teach people to drive before they can ride a bicycle,' and then went on to say 'You in Sweden don't know anything about apartheid. It's a good law. I support my government 100 per cent,' it went down like a lead balloon. When challenged he echoed the sentiments of many of the golfers, namely, 'I don't have anything to do with politics. I'm a sports player trying to make a living.'

Shortly afterwards the Netherlands closed the door to SA golfers when they banned 15 golfers from competing in the Dutch Open. Sweden banned all SA golfers a year later in 1983, and by mid-1983 they were barred from three European Tour events.   Similarly, they were banned from the Tunisian Open leading to some golfers abandoning this tour and heading for the lucrative US tour.

Likewise, SA was banned from participating in the Eisenhower Trophy and World Cup of Golf. Even Gary Player started to get worried. Wherever he went, he was greeted by angry anti-apartheid demonstrations - Britain, Ireland, Australia, New Zealand and the US.

In contrast to his comment some years before when he said he 'didn't meddle in politics', in 1985, with the country in the grip of a state of emergency and his future career under threat, he launched a scathing attack on the government and its race laws. 'South Africans must not cry because they are being isolated. Apartheid should be abolished in its entirety. South Africa is doomed as long as apartheid exists. I feel the South African government should admit it erred by adopting these race laws. It should say sorry to the world and formulate a new policy for the future.' But not even Gary Player could force a change of thinking.

NO WORLD CUP FOR THE SPRINGBOKS

By ADRIAN FREDERICK

SOUTH AFRICA was forced to withdraw from this year's World Cup golf tournament after a lengthy wrangle with the International Golf Association.

Jimmy Hemphill, executive director of the SA Professional Golfers' Association, reluctantly had to inform the IGA that the South African team of John Bland and Mark McNulty would not be playing in the prequalifying tournament at the Lagunita Country Club, Caracas.

The decision brought to an end months of negotiation between Hemphill and new IGA executive director Burch Riber in which South Africa:
* was excluded from the original list of countries invited to play;
* was then invited and informed that there was "never any intention of the IGA to drop SA" and that SA "will continue to be invited in the future";
* was advised "in the best interest of the SA team" to decline a "sincere invitation" to participate this year;
* turned down the original IGA request to withdraw on the grounds that "we (the SAPGA)

BANNED
—AGAIN

4   South African Golf, September 1985

In the mid-80s, Bob Malt brought 40 overseas players to play in the Phalaborwa Classic, and in return, he and the players were given an exemption into the tournament. Black players were upset by these exemptions as this event was virtually in 'their homeland', and this led to a boycott the following week, with the threat of necklacing if any black golfer played in the event. Despite the substantial purse, a scared big Joe Dlamini immediately withdrew. Only John Mashego played, but he slept the whole week in the PGA offices.

By now it was clear that the 'tail was wagging the dog', as for so many years black golfers had been treated with contempt from the time black golf commenced, when black players were not allowed to play in 'white' tournaments, nor on golf courses built with government tax money but re-served for whites, or become members of golf clubs. Now due to internal and external pressures, black amateurs and professionals had to be accommodated and quickly, failing which overseas golfers would not be able to play in SA, and the country's golfers would be isolated from playing abroad.

Mention needs to be made of the inaugural TPA Tour-nament in 1986, another of Gary Player's initiatives and carrying sponsorship of a whopping R100,000. This event was restricted to black golfers only and as such drew a lot of criticism. 'Apartheid in reverse' was the accusation, com-ing in particular from the SAPGA. Player was unrelenting and defended his actions and that of the TPA. The winner's cheque was R10,000 and with it, and with second place, went air tickets to London and hotel vouchers to enable the winners to try for a European Tour card. Joe Dlamini was the comfortable winner with scores of 71 66 73 73 (283) fol-lowed by Solly Mogare (292) and Noel Maart (293)

This tournament saw a clash between the SAPGA and Gary Player over his funding of the R100,000 TPA Tourna-ment, on the basis that the SAPGA constitution stated that it is multiracial and cannot sanction an 'apartheid in re-verse' tournament exclusively for black golfers. Player who organised the competition because he wanted to help black golfers then resigned as President of the SAPGA.

In 1986 the TPA organised a boycott by all black com-petitors participating in the Sunshine Tour Germiston Cen-tenary Classic because of its association with a 'celebration of a 100 years of the black man's oppression'. Daddy Naidoo was then expelled from the TPA for ignoring this boycott.

CHAPTER ELEVEN

A Final Push

PUSHED IN THE RIGHT DIRECTION

In spite of, in fact probably because of, the isolation of South Africa's sportsmen from the rest of the world, golf on the home front continued on its own steady way. Events such as the 1 Million Dollar Golf Challenge were affected as the leading professionals refused to make the trip to SA.

For the first time a black golfer won a 72-hole provincial title, as Sammy Daniels playing wonderful golf went on to win the 1987 Boland Open Stroke Play Championship, certainly the first time a golfer of colour had won a 72-hole provincial title, and then in 1990, in partnership with Michael Michel, he won the inaugural Western Province Foursomes Championship.

Simmering discontent came to a head in 1988 when all but one black golfer boycotted the 1988 Lexington PGA Championship which was played at the Wanderers GC under the banner of the SAPGA. The black players claimed that there was still widespread racial discrimination in golf, including the fact of an excessive influx of overseas players being allowed to participate, not being allowed to play on white courses during the week, and few blacks were invited to play in the Pro-Ams before each tournament.

Of the black professional golfers, Joe Dlamini, in particular, was enjoying some success. He won the 1988 Marley Classic, an all-black event under the control of the Tournament Players Association and played over 54 holes.

Leading scores were:

J Dlamini	73 73 68 (214)
T Manyama	76 72 70 (218)
H Mashego	72 71 76 (219)
M Gallant	73 73 73 (219)

June 1989, Dlamini followed this up by winning the Mitshushiba Pro Shop Swazi Pro-Am title.

Sunday, 11 February 1990:
Nelson Mandela released

On this day, **Nelson Mandela** was released unconditionally from prison after 27 years. Accompanied by his then-wife Winnie, he left the Victor Verster prison on the outskirts of Paarl and was driven the 60km to Cape Town by African National Congress'(ANC) Rose Sonto along a route lined by thousands of supporters.

On the balcony of the City Hall, he spoke to a crowd of approximately 50,000 people, who had waited for hours to see him. He expressed his sincere and warmest gratitude to the 'millions of my compatriots and those in every corner of the globe who have campaigned tirelessly for my release'.

In the 1990 Natal Amateur Championship, Basil Naidoo was the leading qualifier, and golf was under the radar with the government and the NSC, and yes, some players could not or would not come out to SA.

Following Mandela's release, messages went out in October to all the sport bodies that they must join with their black sports body counterparts and form one body.

Golf consisted of amateur and professional bodies. There were two main bodies, the TPA and the PGA with both having around 150 members each. If they did not join, then the government would place a moratorium on overseas players coming to SA. This was already October with tournaments due to start the following month in November.

The meeting was chaired by Dan Meyer (who had previously been sent to Robben Island) of the NSC (later SASCOC) with Vincent Tshabalala, as a full member, and captain of the PGA, sitting on the PGA side. At that time there was a joint government and joint South African Presidents.

It was suggested that they form one body with joint members. The TPA said, 'This was the best offer they had received all week.' A week later the PGA SA was formed with six members from each committee consisting of the new committee. Bernard Gase from the TPA became the chairman, and they met to sort out the constitution and details.

Professional golf never had a one-day moratorium. No other sport had this goodwill in coming together in only two weeks. That's what made professional golf so different.

Then to cap it all, in 1991 Mokgeteng John Mashego became the first black player (following Papwa Sewgolum's two Natal Open victories) to win a tournament on the Sunshine Tour when he won the Bushveld Classic defeating Steve van Vuuren and Ian Palmer in a playoff.

UNIFICATION: THE FINAL CHAPTER

On the 9 August 1992, SAGU and the SAGA met at the Holiday Inn, Jan Smuts Airport, to consider a draft constitution for the new unified controlling body which was to replace the SAGU and the SAGA.

The name of the new controlling body was the South African Golf Federation (SAGF), and the members were to be the Provincial Unions, plus the 'new men on the block' to be called The Golf Association.

The office-bearers at the inauguration of the SAGF were:

President (Year 1):	GJ Shuttleworth
Deputy President (Year 1) and President (Year 2):	H Govender
Senior Vice-President (Years 1 and 2):	CG Wells
Second Vice-President (Year 1 only – deceased):	R Ntshingila
Second Vice-President (Year 2):	M Pinto

Martin Pinto, Cecil Wells, GJ Shuttleworth

It was agreed that Clause 10.1.4 of the new Constitution should read: 'Golf clubs affiliated to members of the Federation should provide for at least 5% of their membership to people of colour without going onto a waiting list providing they have been recommended by The Golf Association.'

Following the resolution passed at the SAGU AGM meeting held on 23 September, the SAGU was dissolved on 26 September 1992.

Finally, the 'long walk was over' with amateur unification as the SAGF was founded to replace the SA Golf Association and the SA Golf Union, and in 1997, the name was changed to the South African Golf Association.

The struggle was over...

"IT ALWAYS SEEMS IMPOSSIBLE UNTIL ITS DONE."
~NELSON MANDELA

APARTHEID: GOLF TIMELINE

1952: Non-European golfers not allowed to be on the golf course at the same time as whites, or use the same facilities – nor can they join the SA PGA

1952: Indians not allowed to overnight in the Orange Free State without a permit

1959: Sewgolum not allowed to travel overseas on SAA

1961: Sewgolum allowed to play in the SA Open, but no other golfers of colour allowed

1963: Sewgolum allowed to play in the Natal Open, despite restrictions, which he wins but receives his trophy outside in the rain – worldwide condemnation. He becomes the figurehead of the anti-apartheid sport movement

1963: Sewgolum allowed to play in the SA Open where he finishes second

1964: Chowglay, the 1962 SA Non-European Open champion prevented from playing in the WP Open at his Clovelly Country club where he was the caddy master

1964: SA banned from the Tokyo Olympics

1965: Sewgolum beats Player in the Natal Open

1960/70s: Gary Player's role in supporting apartheid

1967: All Blacks cancel their rugby tour to SA

1968: Basil D'Oliveira banned from playing for England in SA

1970: Honorary 'white status' was given to the international black sportsmen

1970: South Africa expelled from the International Olympic Committee

1971: Gary Player targeted by demonstrators in the USA

1971: Sally Little prevented from playing in the British Ladies Open, Bobby Cole banned from playing in the Volvo event

1974: Player and Tshabalala targeted by demonstrators in Australia – Hayes and Baiocchi prevented from playing in the World Cup

1976: British PGA tries to withhold Simon Hobday's purse winnings due to Rhodesia's UDI

1976: Tshabalala wins French Open then refuses to partner Player in the World Cup and is banned from playing in the SA Open

1976: Student riots in Soweto

1977: Tshabalala banned from playing in the Zambian Open because he is a South African

1977: Commonwealth Amateur tournament at St. Andrews cancelled due to South Africa's participation

1978: Clovelly Country Club opens to all races

1980s: Gary Player does an about turn and becomes a vocal opponent criticising apartheid

1981: Springbok 'rebel tour' to New Zealand splits New Zealand population apart

1981: Tshabalala banned from playing in the Kenya Open because he is a South African

1982: Blacks still restricted from playing at white golf clubs

1982: Jeff Hawkes speaks out in support of apartheid in Sweden

1983: Sweden, Tunisia, and the Netherlands ban South African Golfers

1983: Eisenhower Trophy bans SA participation

1985: State of Emergency declared in SA

1985: South Africa banned from playing in the World Cup

1985: Leading international professional golfers such as Jack Nicklaus refused to play in the Million Dollar Golf Challenge at Sun City due to political pressure – Lee Trevino's sponsor threatens to withdraw its sponsorship if he plays

1985: TPA boycotts Phalaborwa Classic due to playing exemptions given the overseas players

1986: TPA R100,000 tournament – apartheid in reverse – Player resigns as SAPGA President

1986: TPA boycotts Germiston Centenary Classic celebrating 100 years of black oppression

1990: Vincent Tshabalala captain of the SA PGA

1991: John Mashego becomes the first black winner (since Papwa Sewgolum) on the Sunshine Tour

1992: Unification under one golf body

CHAPTER TWELVE

Black Diamond

All fathers live their dreams through their kids

THE TEACHER: LEWIS MURIDZO

In 1988, Lewis Muridzo informed Nick Price: 'Watch out, Lewie's coming after you.'

Muridzo-Chitengwa has churned out at least 65 golfers who eventually received scholarships to the US, but he remains one of the most underrated coaches in the country. It is virtually impossible to talk about Zimbabwean golf without mentioning his name.

First black Zimbabwean member of a white golf club, first black Zimbabwean golf professional, and extraordinary golf coach over 57 years

His journey in golf is one that was full of trials, tribulations and a fair share of success.

'I started playing in Highfield on makeshift courses in 1958 where we would dig our own putting holes. A caddy master, Phillip, at Royal Salisbury Golf Club urged us to start caddying there when I was just 12, and by 1961, I was already teaching others,' he recalled.

Lewis was one of the people who started Gleneagles Golf Club in 1959, situated in the now high-density suburb of Budiriro 5, the first black golf course in Salisbury (Harare), although it also had some white members. This was where blacks got a chance to play the game, and where Lewis began coaching from 1961–1985 (for free).

Gleneagles, ironically named after the world-famous Scottish championship golf course, was the first golf club for non-whites, who were then not allowed to play the sport, or be affiliated to the Mashonaland Golf Union, hence it was populated by mostly blacks, Indians and coloureds, and eventually was first to be affiliated to the Mashonaland GU.

Meanwhile, David Phiri, having received his Oxford Blue for golf, was the first black player to play at Royal Salisbury GC in 1963, returning home from Oxford University on his way to Zambia, where he became the Governor of the Reserve Bank of Zambia.

Lewis paid his dues but never hit the big time himself. He started as a caddy and was the first black Rhodesian to play in the 1974 Rhodesian Open at Bulawayo. There he played with Fulton Allem, who broke his club in a fit of fury, and his poor caddy feared for his own life!

After winning the Castle and African Distillers Championship, coming second in the Mashonaland Amateur in 1976, and winning the Coca-Cola Trophy in 1978, he became Wingate's (Harare) first black manager and golf coach.

He was the first black person to join a 'white' golf club when he became a member of Salisbury South in 1977, winning the club championship in 1980.

In 1982 he won the first multiracial, mixed Mashonaland Foursomes playing together with Aida Alhadeff at Ruwa and was one of the few black golf professionals in Zimbabwe, the former British colony. He turned professional joining the Zimbabwe Professional Golf Association (ZPGA) in 1985 aged 39, having grown up in an environment where blacks were not allowed to play golf at white-golf courses, let alone turn professional.

In 1987, he unsuccessfully tried to qualify at North Berwick, Scotland for The Open where the wind was blowing half-a-gale on the second nine.

As a caddy he contributed to former World Number 1 Nick Price's game, and coached another major champion and World Number 1 from Fiji, Vijay Singh, as well as Zimbabwe Presidents Cup player Brendon de Jonge, his former student.

'I taught Nick Price when I was still a caddy. I got the

experience from caddying and would help a lot of golfers on tour when I became a professional,' he said before telling the story about how he helped Singh.

'I worked with Vijay Singh on his way to becoming the first non-white golfer to win the Nigeria Open. I met him in 1989 in Nigeria when he decided to come to Africa to improve his game on the then Safari Tour after failing to qualify at the European School. When we came to Lusaka, Zambia he told me that he needed to finish in the top 15 of the competition and needed help with his swing. So we went to the tee-box for an hour, and we worked on his swing the following day, and that same Sunday he shot a 71 and finished in the top ten.

He gave me his shirt in gratitude. The following year he came here at Wingate, and I helped him round the course where he shot 68. The following week we went to Royal Harare, checked his swing again, and I helped him win the 1989 Zimbabwe Open at Chapman. After that, he decided to go to the PGA Tour.'

Such is Lewis's reputation in golf as player and coach that he made friends with some of the world's best golfing personalities such as Gary Player and world-renowned Zimbabwean golf instructor, David Leadbetter, to mention but a few.

Being a professional enabled him to travel the world to places such as the Philippines, Hong Kong, Thailand, India, Singapore and Malaysia, among others on the Asian Tour.

The European Tour ensured that he graced golf courses in France, Scotland, England and Germany, while the Safari Tour opened up trips to Zambia, Ghana, Kenya, Nigeria and Ivory Coast.

While he taught golf to all kinds of people, being the only Zimbabwean teaching professional who had played golf for a living on the PGA in Europe, Asia, and Africa, Lewis Muridzo, tall, articulate and immaculately dressed, decided he was also going to teach his five children. Rhodah Muridzo became the Zimbabwe Ladies champion, but it was his son who excelled — and his son's name was Lewis Chitengwa.

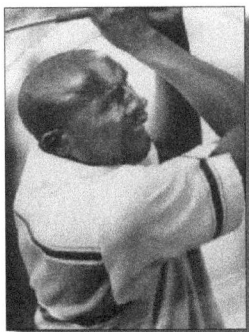

Alan Rae and Lewis Muridzo-Chitengwa

LEWIS CHITENGWA

Lewis had the unique combination of drive and compassion –
a fire in his belly and a softness in his head.
Nick Price

As Price, Johnstone, Watson, and McNulty began contemplating Champions Tour careers, Zimbabwe needed new talent to continue the country's golf legacy into the new millennium, and they found it in Lewis Chitengwa, who perfectly represented the country's demographics - a strong symbol of the changing face of Africa.

Chitengwa was born in Harare in 1975, and by the time he had reached his teens, it was clear the young golfer had the talent to follow in the spike-marks of fellow Zimbabwean golfing greats like Nick Price, Tony Johnstone, Teddy Webber, Denis Watson, and Mark McNulty.

Gifted in languages, he spoke fluent English, Shona and French and studied Japanese, Spanish, Italian and Swahili. After spending countless hours honing his son's golf skills at Wingate Golf Club, famed local golf coach, Lewis Muridzo-Chitengwa Snr was confident that he had uncovered a future Masters, US Open and British Open champion.

The only challenge left for a black golfer having overcome colonialism and apartheid, was to take on the world's best, Tiger Woods.

Lewie was already the Zimbabwean Amateur champion and had represented Zimbabwe at both the 1992 World Junior Golf Team Championship in Japan, and then the Eisenhower Cup in Vancouver, Canada (together with Terry Bowes, Nasho Kamungeremu, Sean Farrell, and Gary Thompson) – shooting 66, the lowest score for the championship.

'Nick Price asked me to host the Eisenhower Team that came to Vancouver to play, and Lewis was 16,' recalled Alan Rae, who was like a father to Lewie. 'He was doing homework while we enjoyed a cold beer after his terrific finish. He came fourteenth behind Michael Campbell (2005 US Open Winner) and the likes of Justin Leonard and so on. He immediately ingratiated and was difficult to ignore.'

Tiger Woods

Three-times Zimbabwe Amateur champion Lewis Chitengwa Jr sprung into international acclaim after he became the first non-American to win the 1992 Junior Orange Bowl International Golf Championship in Florida, US. The younger Chitengwa made history as he defeated Tiger Woods, America's top junior golfer, the future world number one at the Biltmore Golf Course. Chitengwa, Woods and Gilberto Morales of Venzuela entered the final round tied 211.

Lewie who took his mother's maiden name because his father, Muridzo, was a professional at his home club Wingate, sensationally went on head-to-head in the final round. But only Chitengwa was able to shoot par (71) to finish at 2- under 282 – winning with scores of 72 70 69 71 (282) –three stokes better than the previous year winner, Tiger Woods! (Possibly the greatest golfer, presently with 15 Majors, 81 PGA Tournament victories, and 'Tigermania' at the time of writing), who edged Spain's Oscar Sanchez (70-285) in a playoff for second place. Morales dropped to fourth (75-286). This is the only time two black golfers have come first and second.

Looking at previous winners it was a smorgasbord of future famous golfers and a stepping-stone to the big time: Mark Calcavecchia, Carmilo Villegas, Tiger Woods, and recently Renato Paratore, while fellow competitors included Bobby Cole, Dale Hayes, Craig Stadler, Andy North, Hal Sutton, Bob Tway, Billy Mayfair, Nick Price, Jose Maria Olazabal, and Matt Kuchar.

Lewie achieved something considered impossible by the Americans; he won the Orange Bowl World Junior Championship – always held in the US – outright.

South Africans, Ernie Els, Des Terblanche, and Phil Jonas have all triumphed as world junior champions, but they were merely recipients of what is called the foreign division title – the champion golfers from outside of the US.

Yet Lewie was the first Southern African – in fact, the first player from anywhere outside of the US – to win the world junior championship outright.

1992 Orange Bowl World Junior Golf Championship — Lewis Chitengwa holding the Gary Player trophy. Lewis won the duel by three shots. His fellow competitor was Eldrick 'Tiger' Woods.

Between 1992 to 1994, Chitengwa was the top amateur in Zimbabwe winning the Zimbabwe Amateur three-times. Now two years since the end of apartheid, it was 'black power' to the fore when 18-year old Zimbabwean, Lewis Chitgenwa came to play in the fabled 1993 SA Amateur at the East London Golf Club, home to many SA Opens and rated one of the best courses in the country.

The conqueror of Tiger Woods was apprehensive about the consequences of apartheid and how he would be treated. Lewie arrived at the East London Golf Club and was immediately denied entry to the club's entrance by a gentleman who said that caddies had to enter through the back entrance.

Lewie politely insisted that he was a player and not a caddy, but the gentleman insisted caddies had to enter at the rear. Being well brought up by his mother and father, he arrived through the rear entrance and the rest is, as they say, history.

Everyone who was present that sun-drenched week in March warmed to this young man, who was not only playing sensational golf but proving to be an excellent ambassador for his country with his charming personality.

After his first practice round, he and Nasho Kamungeremu (later President of the Zimbabwe Professional Golfers Association), who also participated for Zimbabwe, went to the bar to buy some drinks and were told in Afrikaans, 'caddies are not allowed in the bar'. They replied, informing the barman that they were actually players having been invited to take part in the championship. They were then ridiculed and told a handicap of three and below was required to qualify, not six or seven. Lewie was a scratch player with a +2 handicap.

Lewie was a revelation to watch, all skill and grace, and day after day attracted the largest galleries seen at an amateur event for many years. He reminded people of Ernie Els and Bobby Locke with his unique, engaging openness and charisma.

The crowds were a mix of black and white supporters, who gave him every encouragement along the way.

Chitengwa came into the championship believing he had a good chance of winning the 72-hole strokeplay title, especially after gaining a share of the lead after the first two rounds. However, coming from dusty calm Wingate Park Golf course in Harare, and not used to wind, he had a bad day in the howling easterly wind that buffeted this seaside course for the last 36 holes.

Having fallen out of contention for a strokeplay crown, he never believed he could win the match play. 'Matchplay has always been my weakness,' he said. However, his attacking style of play was entirely suited to the East London course in calm weather, as many of the holes offered birdie opportunities.

As Chitengwa grew in confidence, he showed everyone in match-play just how talented and exciting a player he really was. He combined power off the tee with delicate finesse shots that settled close to the pin, and he putted with the confidence of youth.

In the first two rounds of the match-play he accounted for Neil Homann of Randpark who was destined to win the 1994 SA strokeplay title the following year, and the 1992 Transvaal Amateur champion, Callie Swart of Pietersburg, winning both matches comfortably 4/3.

Then came Friday morning, and another match that would be long remembered by the members of East London Golf Club. The club's last hope of producing the SA champion in their centenary year was 18-year-old Ulrich van den Berg, who was playing inspired golf.

In the first round, he had upset one of the top match play contenders, Colin Sanderson of Stellenbosch, and then the promising teenager Chad Ransby in the second round.

Van den Berg was up against Chitengwa in the quarter-finals and continued from where he had left off the previous day, playing superb golf to be 3-up after eight holes.

The East London youngster lost the 9th after hooking his tee shot into the bush, but that still left him 2-up. Eight holes later, however, he walked off the course in a daze, having been beaten 2/1 by the most incredible run of golf.

From the 10th to the 17th, Chitengwa was 6-under par, with four birdies and an eagle 2 at the 292m 16th, where he rolled a pitch shot into the hole from 60m out to go 2-up.

For the next few minutes, there was pandemonium around the 18th green. His supporters went crazy with delight, toy-toying and exchanging high fives as if the championship had already been won. Lewie himself had a grin from ear-to-ear, knowing he had all but clinched a memorable victory.

There was no coming down to earth after that, with eight birdies following in the afternoon semi-finals as he beat Rory Sabbatini of Royal Durban 4/3 (Sabbatini was destined to be runner-up 2007 Masters, third in both the US Open and The PGA, winner of the 2003 World Cup, six victories on the US Tour, with a world ranking high of eight, and inducted into the Southern Africa Golf Hall of Fame).

Chitengwa's opponent in the final was Western Province's Hugo Lombard, a 23-year-old from Paarl who had become one of the established names in amateur golf during the previous three years. Lombard had won some tough matches to reach the final for the first time.

It seemed as if it would be a tame affair once Chitengwa had established a five-hole lead at lunch, but the 36-hole came to life in the afternoon as Lombard made a brave fightback.

After playing indifferently in the morning not making a single birdie, dropping four shots and duly punished by his opponent's flawless play, Lombard became a different player in the afternoon when he had a positive 'go for broke' attitude and threw two quick birdies at Chitengwa at the 1st and 3rd. The Zimbabwean not only matched them, but came up with another birdie at the 4th to go 6-up, and then another at the 8th, his fourth of the round, and made a good half after being bunkered next to the green. It was too late — against an opponent who played excellent golf all day.

Lombard to his credit never threw in the towel, and promptly won back three holes in a row, which included birdies at the 11th and 12th, making five birdies in the first 12 holes, and now only 2-down. The pressure was then on Chitengwa, and he showed his mettle under pressure as they played the last six holes in a brisk easterly wind.

The young man with the quiet personality was up to the occasion. He replied to the challenge and never faltered. He boomed his tee shot long and straight up the 13th, 14th, and 15th fairways, and it was Lombard who cracked, missing the fairway left into the rough, failing to reach the green and not being able to get up and down for his par, and the match ended on the 16th when Lombard 3-putted.

Thus this 18-year old Zimbabwean international, Lewis Chitengwa won the Bells SA Golf Championship when he beat Western Province's Hugo Lombard 4/2 in the 36-hole final.

Chitengwa was three under par for 33 holes when the match finished. He had seven birdies and four bogeys and became the first Zimbabwean to win since Teddy Webber at Durban Country Club in 1978. The victory also earned him an 'exemption status' for the following year's SA Open.

'He became historically the first black man to win the 100-year-old SA Amateur trophy. People flocked from far and wide to witness this accomplishment, and when Lewis encountered the gentleman who denied him entry and who now wanted everything to do with him, Lewis politely shook his hand and thanked him for his hospitality,' said Rae.

His victory in SA was often referred to as the 'African golfing equivalent of Jackie Robinson, breaking baseball's colour barrier' in the US, and he was an instant hero to all who had suffered under apartheid rule and opposed the racist system.

It was entirely fitting in this first year of unified amateur golf in SA that Chitengwa should be crowned champion, the first time a black man had won in its 101-year history. His victory inspired more young blacks to take up the game. One of the stated aims of the unified SAGF, formed the previous year, was to provide opportunities for black youngsters to play golf.

But technically Lewie never knew apartheid, being born in Harare in post-Rhodesia post-Colonial days. But this remarkable 18-year-old had already seen enough of our continent to understand that a struggle has and is still taking place. As a young black man he felt for the impoverished caddies – would-be golfers, who may have all the talent in the world as players, but through lack of funds and opportunities will never get a chance to realise their potential of proving themselves as competitors.

It was, however, a momentous year for the furtherance of black golf in the country, with Chitengwa becoming the first to win the SA Amateur title, and Vijay Singh of Fiji, in winning the Bell's Cup at Mowbray, the first since 'Papwa' Sewgolum to capture a significant professional title in SA.

But that was not the end of the story ....

All this good play earned the young Zimbabwean a scholarship to attend the University of Virginia. 'He's only 20-years-old, but he's already being touted in many circles as one of professional golf's "great black hopes" for the future, and surprise, he's not Tiger Woods.' (Golfweek magazine)

His extraordinary ability with a golf club brought him across the globe from his home in Harare, Zimbabwe to Charlottesville, Va., where Chitengwa completed his freshman year at the University of Virginia on a full scholarship.

1992 Lewis Chitengwa became the first black man to win the SA Amateur title.

'While Eldrick (Tiger) Woods may be the most ac-claimed young black golfer today, Chitengwa had already made history in his homeland. He was the first black man ever to win the SA Amateur Championship.' stated Virginia University coach, Moragham, a feat that's prompted Golf Digest to liken him to the black Olympian Jesse Owens winning gold medals of golf in front of the apartheid re-gime. Chitengwa described the event as his most memora-ble. 'How I got there and how I played... that's probably the greatest moment of my life.'

Making the decision to come to the US and leave his home and family for extended periods was difficult, but not one he regretted. Fifty-two American colleges were keen on getting Lewis on to their golf team.

'I realised this sport could take you places and I was really starting to enjoy it,' he said, 'plus my dad was en-couraging me. When I first started, he would tell me I just needed to practice, and I could be good at this.'

But it was his victory at the Orange Bowl Junior Clas-sic, and Mike Moraghan, golf coach for the University of Virginia who saw him play in the 1992 British Amateur in Portrush where he shot 71, 89 (missing the cut by 2), and then in the Waterford Crystal Cup, where the conditions were brutal; 'I saw more great shots at Waterford and I knew this was the guy,' that prompted UVA coach Mike Moraghan to take notice and begin recruiting efforts. 'He's a great learner - the kind of guy I have to say something to only once for him to digest it, think about it, figure out if it's going to work for him and apply it. In many ways, he's mature beyond his years as a college freshman.'

He was a long hitter and played extremely aggressive golf, trying to drive any par-4 less than 300m. Moragham recalled a college event at Kiawah Island in South Caroli-na. 'Lewis was playing the par-5 ninth hole, lined with wa-ter hazards, and was waiting on the fairway to have a go at the green with his second shot – he was an incredibly bold player. I was alarmed though, not about the shot he had to play, but because there was an alligator in the fairway close to Lewis. Anyway he played the shot, and afterwards I went up to him and said, 'weren't you scared?' 'No, the alligator. Didn't you see it?' Lewis laughed. An alligator? We have real crocodiles in Africa!'.

Lewis made an immediate impact on the fortunes of the UVA Cavaliers. The freshman shot 67 75 67 at Osprey Point, Iowa, for a second-place finish at the Kiawah Island Inter-collegiate tournament, propelling the team to a first-place finish.

In the five tournaments he played, his average score was 72,4. Lewie's goal, as he said, was to be the best golfer ever to come out of Zimbabwe; 'Nick Price has set the target for me,' were his words.

He was also rated by Golfweek magazine as a 1994-95 'Freshman to Watch'; received an All-American Honourable mention; made the All-Atlantic Coast (ACC) Conference and All-State Virginia teams, and was named ACC Rookie of the year.

Lewie's goal was to complete his studies at UVA and then pursue life on the PGA tour, where he hoped and expected to run into Tiger Woods again. By 1995 Lewis was a top player at the inter-collegiate championship, and shot a record 67 that was adopted as an emblem at the college.

That year he won two college championships and finished seventh in the NCAA tournament. Golfweek magazine selected him as a pre-season first-team All-American. In 1996 he won the individual, and with his team, the USA Furman Inter-collegiate

Chitengwa had a flair for dramatic shot-making and a penchant for smashing enormous tee shots which earned him victory in the 1996 NCAA Long Drive Contest held at the Honours course in Tennessee, yet again edging out Tiger Woods into the second spot.

In 1997 he played in the USA Eastern Amateur, shooting 29 in the practice round of the Portor Cup Amateur at Niagara Falls CC in New York. He came third, carding 272 – second was Matt Kuchar. Lewie's third round of 63, 7-under par, was the lowest round of the tournament.

It is interesting to reflect on past winner of the Portor Cup, which includes Scott Verplank, Robert Gamez, Ben Crenshaw, Scott Simpson, and Deane Beman. In the same year, Lewis was successful in winning the USA Seminole Classic

Golf, however, wasn't his only passion. Lewie wanted to become his family's first college graduate, and in 1998 he did so, earning a degree in African-American studies. However, his overriding passion was golf, and his dream was to become number one in the world.

After turning professional in 1999, Lewie became the first African to qualify for the Buy.Com Tour finishing one-hundredth. He made it into several events on the PGA Tour competing in the 1996 Greater Vancouver Open and the 1999 St. Jude Classic.

Moving forward to 2001, he came third in the Canadian Tour Qualifying School, and found himself on the Canadian Tour, playing well, with a number of top-10 finishes in a row, and thirteenth on the Canadian Tour money list going into the Edmonton Open.

But that year, aged only 26, Chitengwa died in tragic circumstances.

Showing flu-like symptoms after the second round of the Canadian Tour's Edmonton Open – where he was tied for the fourth position after a second round 67 – Chitengwa fell ill, slipped into a coma and died of meningococcemia, a rare and deadly strain of meningitis.

No matter what Lewie could've done as a pro, his most significant achievement would've remained winning the 1993 SA Amateur. He was the first black to take that event, and he did it only two years after Nelson Mandela was released from prison and apartheid had been abolished.

'I guarantee you, he would have been a tournament winner on the PGA Tour,' Price told Golf Digest following Chitengwa's death. 'He had determination and intensity, and he had a great short game. Guys with great short games win golf tournaments.'

'I really want to see us produce the next (Tiger) Woods. And we can do it. There is a man standing here today, from Zimbabwe whose son Lewis was on his way to being that champion,' Player said.

'In fact, he beat Woods twice in America. He won the Gary Player Orange Bowl Tournament in America that is named after me. He was a collegiate champion in America, which is an unbelievable effort. He was playing the Canadian Tour and died at the age of 26. Well we will meet him in heaven one day, and I can tell you he's the leading money-winner up there right now,' he said.

Lewie had impeccable manners and was humble and generous. He gave every penny away that he didn't need to support himself, sent money to numerous charities in the US and to Zimbabwe for his brother's schooling and to help his parents

'His full ride to the University of Virginia was deserved and he became the only person I know who beat Tiger Woods to earn that coveted 4-year full ride. His inspiration is best evidenced in my sons who are both scratch players as he instilled in them the virtues of integrity, honesty and hard work,' said Alan Rae, his father-away-from-home.

Sadly as veteran local sports writer, John Kelley said in his 120-year book on The History of Golf in Rhodesia and Zimbabwe: Staying the Course, '...We will, therefore, never know whether arguably the greatest talent to emerge among the black Africans in this country at the time would have achieved his stated ambition to become world number one.'

Lewis Chitengwa Quotes:

- I think golf is one of the most exciting games to play because you've got to be focused. The reason they say it's boring is because it's real slow compared to sports like basketball and football ... but I think golf is more exciting, and if people learn to understand the game, then they'll learn to appreciate it and enjoy it – Lewis Chitengwa
- Lewis had an incredible imagination and touch around the greens and, most importantly, never lost his composure on the golf course
- At 18 years old, Lewis finished in the top 10 at the Eastern Amateur beating all of our players – and the Eastern is a very good field – Mike Moragham
- Lewis had an unbelievable go for it attitude and always played without fear. He was capable of pulling off some of the greatest shots you have ever seen at the most appropriate times, and he was a brilliant putter with an incredible short game
- Lewis was a better player than I had been at the age of 19 – Nick Price
- Lewis never forgot where he came from or those who were less fortunate than himself

Lewis was basically the first African to play in NCAA golf competition. He was a person I knew from junior golf, and the AJGA Tour and, subsequently, when we both went to college. He had a bright future ahead of him, but, unfortunately tragedy struck.

We were acquaintances more than anything else. When we were at the same tournaments, we definitely talked to each other about how everything was going in our lives. He was a fighter, an absolute fighter, and is somebody we're all going to miss.

Tiger Woods.

His legacy is kept alive through events such as the Lewis Chitengwa Memorial Championship (Canada) which helps grow the game in Lewis's memory. The competition benefits the 'Lewis Chitengwa Foundation', to help under-privileged children gain access to educational and athletic opportunities that they otherwise might not have.

Lewis Sr invited Golf World into his self-described dilapidated house, 150 yards from the academy at Wingate. The Orange Bowl trophies sit proudly in the home; Chitengwa won a posthumous award alongside three history-making golfers who included veteran Nick Price and Tony Johnstone.

'The memories are still there, but we have to show the other up-and-coming golfers that they can also reach the same heights scaled by Lewis. Lewis remains my best ever student, and among all my children, he is the one who really loved golf. Here was a guy I had to spend as much as 15 hours per day on the course with. Lewis loved it. No wonder he was the world junior champion and achieved a lot in a short space of time,' the Wingate resident pro said concerning the tragic death of his son who had emerged from a humble background to beat the world's best against the odds. Death robbed him of his son who was evidently destined to scale dizzy heights on the international golf arena.

Alan Rae together with close family members of the Muridzo family was in attendance in June 2015 when Chitengwa was recognised posthumously for his immense contribution to golf by being inducted into Southern African Golf Hall of Fame, 14 years after his death.

Chitengwa was inducted into the class of 2014 with SA golf luminaries Fulton Allem, John Fourie, A.E. Vernon, Ronnie Glennie and the SA Golf Association's Walter Conyers Kirby.

Previous inductees included Gary Player, Bobby Locke, Ernie Els, Nick Price, Mark McNulty, David Leadbetter, Retief Goosen, Sewsunker Sewgolum, Vincent Tshabalala, David Frost, Tony Johnstone, Denis Watson, Dale Hayes, Denis Hutchinson, Bobby Cole, Dale Hayes and Sally Little.

Gary Player presided over the ceremony, where he paid tribute to Chitengwa, who he said was on his way to greatness and would have been as good as 15-time major champion Woods.

Brendan Barratt, editor of Africa's leading golf publication Compleat Golfer, described Chitengwa's induction as the most humbling moment of the Southern Africa Golf Hall of Fame Induction dinner held in Cape Town.

Despite the devastation of losing the son whom he expected to conquer the world one day, Muridzo-Chitengwa, who has been coaching golf in Zimbabwe for 62 years is still waiting for another world-beater.

At 74, the veteran coach, who was presented with a 'Lifetime Achievement Award' by the Zimbabwe Golf Association, says he will not quit coaching until he has uncovered that one golfer who will make it to the top. Golf has given him great satisfaction in his life, and through it, he says he has made a number of good friends, 'now it's payback time'.

'I am waiting for that one guy who is going to win The Masters, The US Open and The British Open. I know Lewis could have done it had he lived longer, but I see that potential to produce top golfers here in Zimbabwe with the students I teach.'

'I can't retire just yet. What I want to see are more youngsters, especially blacks, taking up this game and playing as professionals. I would say Lewis is the best I have taught here in Zimbabwe and I taught him here at Wingate.'

LEWIS CHITENGWA
(Zimbabwe 1975 — 2001)

'There's no telling how good he could have been'
Gary Player

- 1985: Aged 10 Mashonaland Junior 'B' for Junior Inter-Provincial (won 2/3 singles)
- 1987: Bob Blake Junior
- 1988: Mashonaland Junior 'A' (aged 13)
- 1988: Won 7/13 club tournaments
- 1989: Tanzanian Amateur 14th (aged 14)
- 1990: Selected Zimbabwe (abroad France & USA)
- 1992: Won major Junior (9) & Senior (19) events
- 1992: Mashonaland Junior 'A' captain
- 1992: Played for the Zimbabwe Jr. Team at the World Junior Golf Team Championship in Japan
- 1992: Eisenhower Cup in Vancouver, Canada — shot 66 equalling lowest score
- 1992: Won the Orange Bowl World Junior Championship in Miami, Florida — 72,70,69,71 (282) = 6 under (three-shot victory over Tiger Woods)
- 1993: Won the Zimbabwe Men's Amateur Championship for the second time – won it three times
- 1993: South African Amateur - first black golfer to win (beat Rory Sabbatini — later ranked eighth in the world)
- 1993: Zone 6 Golf Championships (part Zimbabwe team)

- 1993: USA Eastern Amateur tournament top 10
- 1995: Top Inter-Collegiate player 1995
- 1996: USA Furman Intercollegiate
- 1996: NCAA Long Driving Contest - beat Tiger Woods
- 1997: USA Seminole Classic
- 1999: Qualified for the Buy.com Tour — first black Zimbabwean (and Africa) to play on Buy.Com Tour — also played in US PGA Tour events
- 2001: On the Canadian Tour where he had 10 top ten finishes in a row
- 2015: Inducted into the Southern Africa Golf Hall of Fame

*Ranked 13th on Canadian Tour when he died
*The Canadian Tour annually holds the "Lewis Chitengwa Memorial Championship"

(Left) Lewis's family at his induction into the Southern Africa Golf Hall of Fame in 2015 donating memorabilia to the SA Golf Museum. (Right) Lewis Muridzo-Chitengwa and his wife at Lewis's induction together with his sisters

OTHER STORIES

Meanwhile, there were others who made a mark, and whose stories also need telling.

Theophilus 'Theo' Manyama

After being denied the right to compete on the SA circuit, Theo turned his attention to refereeing and officiated as the chief rules official, tournament director, and chief referee including:

- Presidents Cup
- The Open Championship (19)
- The Masters (16)
- US Open (9)
- The PGA Championship (1)
- The Players Championship
- Numerous World Golf Championships, US and European Tour events

In 2003 he was joint tournament director of the Presidents Cup, and he received the Compleat Golf Magazine Award: 'Lifetime contribution to the golf industry'. A PGA of SA Master Professional, in 2010 Theo Manyama was inducted into the Southern Africa Golf Hall of Fame, and he received the Minister's Excellence award at the SA Sports Awards.

In 2015 Manyama completed his 'Grand Slam' by officiating at every major when he was invited to officiate at The PGA Championship, and in 2016 he was the rules official at the 2016 Olympic Games

Richard 'Boikie' Mogoerane

Mogoerane made up the five musketeers on the non-European tour, rival to Sewgolum (seven years older), Hlapo (thirteen years older), Chowglay (three years older) and Tshabalala (seven years younger).

- SA Non-European Championship 1973, 76, second '72, third '67, 70
- Free State Non-European Open 1968, 73, 74, 75, 76, 77, 78, 79, 80, 81
- 1981 established Junior Golf Development in Soweto
- 1992 Participated in negotiations leading to the unification of golf administration
- 2010 Inducted into the Southern Africa Golf Hall of Fame

Joe Dlamini

Joe Dlamini was Swaziland's first professional golfer and forged the way for the next generation of the golfers from the Kingdom.

- Lifetime head professional and coach at the Royal Swazi Country Club 1981–2006
- Won the Pro-Shop Swazi Pro-Am (268) against a top 'white' field at the Royal Swazi GC and two events on the Winter Tour
- Won nine Swaziland amateur and five TPA non-European Tour events
- Golfer of the Year 1978
- 2013 Inducted Southern Africa Golf Hall of Fame

'Ntata' Andrew Mlangeni

- Worked as a caddy from age 12 at Johannesburg GC
- Sentence as one of the five, together with Nelson Mandela, at the Rivonia trial to Robben Island
- Found three golf balls on Robben Island and hid them in his cell to remind him that one day he would be free
- Chairman of the Parliamentary Golf Club
- 2013 SA Golf Hall of Fame Harry Brews Award for his unselfish contribution to the betterment of golf.

LEST WE FORGET

Dr Zukile Luyenge,
Hon Andrew Mlangeni,
General Bantu Holomisa

Mokgeteng John Mashego

The first black player to win a tournament on the Southern Africa Tour after it lifted its white-only rule in 1991 when he won the Bushveld Classic, defeating Steve van Vuuren and Ian Palmer in a play-off.

This was his only victory, the rules having been changed too late to allow him to play on the tour through his prime, though he finished sole or tied second in at least three further tournaments, including the Cock 'o the North (Zambia).

'Star' Naidoo (–1962), considered the doyen of caddies in his time. He caddied at Royal Durban for 48 years (including for Bobby Locke in 1936 when he won the Natal Open), eventually playing off a +2 handicap. In 1935 he bet he could break 80 with one club. He chose a 2-iron with which he could also putt and scored 73 (par 76).

R.T. Singh, the unbeatable and most dominant player from around 1937 and still featuring in tournaments as late as 1961.

S. Swartz, with a handicap +2, won the unofficial SA Non-European Open champion six years in a row from 1942–47.

Ronnie Ditsebe, the SA Non-European champion in 1949 (2nd 1957), featuring in tournament results from 1947–1963.

David 'Bobby Locke' Motati, a two-time winner and runner-up of the SA Non-European Open, as well as three other victories and six second place (at least).

William Manie was the assistant pro at the Royal Winchester GC 1961, and later the club Professional Richmond (UK). He participated in The Open 1961, but back home his application to play in the SA Open was denied.

Henry Govender, whose goal was normalising golf in SA. He was the Durban Indian GC affiliate to SA(N-W)GA. the Natal GA Executive President 1981, and the SA Golf President 1980–92 (disbanded) and finally the President of the unified SA Golf Federation 1993.

...and some of the others: Bob Nkuna, Jacob Gumbi, Mark Borman, 'Polly' November, Lawrence Buthelezi, L Khatidi, Johannes Semenya, Daddy Naidoo, Reggie Mamashela, Solly Sepeng, Sammy Daniels, Samson Mnisi, Alf Magerman, Louis Nelson, Bernard Gase, Alfred Maqubela, Percy 'Fiver' Mazibuko, Atroll 'Sid Brews' Mazibuko, JM Jass, Patrick Dladla, Dick Phala, Edward 'Otto' Lee, Ronald Anooplal, Johnson Chetty, Raydmuth Rajdaw, J Ranjith, Abe van Rooyen, Mervyn Gallant.

This then is the story and history of black golf in SA and its heroes who dominated the sports pages of mainly black, coloured, and Indian-read newspapers and magazines, read by millions, and how these forgotten icons assisted the anti-apartheid sports movement and ultimately to the dismantling of apartheid.

Golf is a worldwide sport with an international audience, and as such it reaches many more countries and people than any other game played in SA. The fact that Papwa Sewgolum, of Indian descent, came onto the scene at just the time that Nelson Mandela and others were being locked away was hugely significant, not only for the citizens of SA but also the international community.

His victories in the Dutch Opens and then the Natal Opens opened the eyes of the world to the inequality of the apartheid system locally, while abroad the anti-apartheid sports movement had their figurehead when photographs of him receiving his trophy in the rain in 1963 went viral.

The fact that Sewgolum was also a hero to India's population, looking for sporting heroes outside of cricket, further drew attention to the iniquities of apartheid and their influence led to South Africa being barred from the Olympics.

Beating Gary Player in 1965, the national government's sporting icon, and South Africa's white population's favourite son as they revelled in his international exploits, threw down the gauntlet to the sporting policies of the land and the invincibility of white sportsmen. This struck further into Verwoerd's gullet, and even more so P.W. Botha, when Player, one of three SA worldwide icons at that time (the others being Nelson Mandela and Chris Barnard) launched a scathing attack on the nationalist government and their apartheid policies in 1985.

Against all the odds, those golfers of colour, competing abroad in The Open and other tournaments directly shone the spotlight on apartheid, especially when Papwa

Sewgolum won the Dutch Opens, and Vincent Tshabalala won the French Open, and led to sports boycotts, thereby stopping white golfers from competing internationally. This not only impacted negatively on the government, but also on the psyche of the population used to our golfers carrying the flag and winning abroad.

These sportsmen had a major impact in helping to break down the golf sporting barrier, and apartheid in its totality, even if they were not necessarily politically active.

Finally Lewis Chitengwa, by beating Tiger Woods and then winning the SA Amateur put the seal on the ability of black golfers to compete on equal terms with white golfers on the world stage.

RANKING

Southern Africa's

All-Time Best Black Golfers (pre-1994)

1. Sewsunker '*Papwa*' Sewgolum (1954–77)
2. Lewis '*Clever Boy*' Chitengwa (1991–01)
3. Vincent Tshabalala (1968–83)
4. Ismail '*Baby-face Boy*' Chowglay (1955–83)
5. Simon '*Cox*' Hlapo (1953–68)
6. Joe Dlamini (1983–1990s)
7. Ramnath '*Bambata*' Boodhun (1920s–34)
8. Edward '*Eddia*' Johnson-Sidebe (1951–68)
9. Richard '*Boikie*' Mogoerane (1966–83)
10. David '*Bobby Locke*' Motati (1958–67)

*Looking in – RT Singh, Mokgeteng John Mashego, Daddy Naidoo, Ronnie Ditsebe, 'Star' Naidoo, S Swartz, A. 'Polly' November, Laurence Buthelezi, Sammy 'Slamming' Daniels, David Phala, Bob Nkuna, Ram Rajdaw, Jacob Gumbi.

Southern Africa's

All-Time Best Golfers

1. Gary Player (ranked 1 – 9 majors)
2. Bobby Locke (ranked 1 – 4 majors)
3. Ernie Els (ranked 1 – 4 majors)
4. Nick Price *Zimbabwe* (ranked 1 – 3 majors)
5. Retief Goosen (ranked 3 – 2 majors)
6. Sid Brews (ranked 5 – 8 SA Opens)
7. Harold Henning (50 victories – Canada Cup)
8. **Sewsunker 'Papwa' Sewgolum**
9. Sally Little (ranked 3 – 2 majors)
10. Louis Oosthuizen (ranked 3 – 1 major)
11. Mark McNulty *Zimbabwe* (ranked 3 – 1 senior major)
12. Charl Schwartzel (ranked 5 - 1 major)
13. **Lewis Chitengwa *Zimbabwe***
14. David Frost (ranked 3 – 1 senior major)
15. Trevor Immelman (ranked 12 - 1 major)

*16-30 Denis Watson *Zimbabwe* (1 senior major), Dale Hayes (ranked top 10), Bobby Cole, Rory Sabbatini (ranked 8), Tim Clark (ranked 15), Brandon Grace (ranked 10), Retief Waltman, John Bland, Cobie le Grange (ranked 15), Fulton Allem, Hugh Baiocchi, Tony Johnstone *Zimbabwe*, George Fotheringham, Wayne Westner, Maud Gibb (1 major)

*31-50 Jock Brews, Denis Hutchinson *Rhodesia*, Reg Taylor (amateur), Simon Hobday *Zambia* (1 senior major), Bobby Verwey (1 senior major), Trevor Dodds *Namibia*, Darren Fichardt, Allan Henning, **39. Vincent Tshabalala**, Richard Sterne, George Coetzee, Douglas Proudfoot (amateur), John Fourie (1 senior major), Thomas Aikin, Lawrie Waters, James Kingston, Trevor Wilkes, Eric Moore, Hennie Otto, Barry Franklin.

65-75	**Ismail Chowglay**
75-85	**Joe Dlamini *Swaziland***
85-95	**Ramnath 'Bambata' Boodhun;** **Simon Hlapo**

*Author: Best golfer ranking based on ability and not how many majors or tournament victories

LOOKING BACK

John Petersen, 90, the former chairman of the WP(N-E)GU in 1957, played amateur golf for many years, and although apartheid prohibited him from playing professionally in a game that he first took up as a six-year-old boy.

Petersen and his family were among 20 families who lived on what is now the Mowbray Golf Course, an area known then as Raapenberg.

Although the golf course was on Petersen's doorstep, he was not allowed to play there – like all other people of colour during apartheid. He said they could not play with white people, and were denied access to the golf clubs, including its facilities. This did not deter him, however, and he found alternative ways to hone his skill on a daily basis. The ex-

JOHN PETERSEN, of our Parks Maintenance Department, with the trophy awarded to him after he had won the Western Province Coloured Golf Union's Wynberville open competition in May with the excellent score of 148 (74-74). He has won a number of tournaments in the past and will play in the Western Province Bram team at the South African non-European open tournament at Durban in December.
Picture by E. R. Newton.

ception was when the SA Golf organisers made allowance once a year, for the use of the golf course, to play the then 'Coloured SA Open'.

'Where the City Lodge Hotel is now, that used to be our home. I would have liked to play professional, but we were not allowed to. I used to practice every day by playing between the trees, as we could not use the golf course. I could not get a handicap, because you had to belong to a club, and the clubs were only available for white people. We only had an opportunity once a year to play on a golf course. And even on that day, we were not allowed to use the facilities, like the clubhouse,' Mr Petersen said.

Joe Petersen dropped out of school and was a golf caddy for a number of years, before becoming a skilled player himself. He played his final competitive game 27 years ago, at the age of 65. On this day he won his last trophy in Oudtshoorn.

As a highly skilled golfer, he travelled all over SA, playing the sport he loved, earning dozens of trophies and championship wins. Among the titles he has won, were the Beaufort West Open, and the WP Knock-Out. He also won the Midlands Club Championship eight times and captained the Western Province team twice, and on both occasions, they won the trophy. Their son, Gary, was named after the SA golfing great, Gary Player.

In acknowledgement of his achievements, Joe Petersen was presented with a Lifetime Honorary Membership at the Cape Peninsula Golf Club in 1999. It is now known as Wynberg Golf Club.

Nelson 'Madiba' Mandela on Gary Player

"The brave man is not he who does not feel afraid,
but he who conquers that fear".

Because he was a professional golfer who spent much of his career performing outside South Africa, Gary Player was always perceived as being one step removed from the world of politics. Yet, few men in our country's history did as much to enact political changes for the better that eventually improved the lives of millions of his countrymen. Through his tremendous influence as a great athlete, Mr Player accomplished what many politicians could not. And he did it with courage, perseverance, patience, pride, understanding and dignity that would have been extraordinary even for a world leader.

During my many years spent in prison, I was frequently made aware of the harsh treatment Mr Player endured as a representative of our nation. In 1969, at a very important tournament in America (the PGA Championship) a group of militant demonstrators who opposed apartheid yelled in the middle of his swing in an attempt to disrupt him. They threw ice at him. Once they even tried to rush him, but Jack Nicklaus, who is the greatest golfer of all, brandished his golf club and helped restrain them. Amid this, Mr. Player finished in second place, perhaps his finest performance ever.

On another occasion, in Australia, protesters ventured onto one of the putting greens in the middle of the night and etched, with white lime, the slogan, "Go Home, You Racist Pig" on the green. Mr Player frequently received threats against his life. There were people who thought he was partly to blame for apartheid in South Africa when in truth he was no more responsible for that policy than Jack Nicklaus or Arnold Palmer were for racial conflict in the United States. Mr Player was in danger many times, and the American FBI stayed in his company for months on end to protect him. That must have been terribly distracting, yet he endured and stood his ground.

And he always remained loyal to South Africa. Many athletes, you know, have fled their countries for the US, but Mr Player remained true to his South African heritage. He did his best to explain the complex nature of trying to invoke change in our country and always set a tremendous example for all South Africans. For instance, he successfully lobbied our government to allow golfer Lee Elder and tennis player Arthur Ashe to compete in South Africa. He established the Gary Player Foundation, which has done a great deal to further education among young black people in our country. I am proud to serve as a trustee for the foundation. Upon my release from prison, I met with Mr Player and told him, *'You have not received the recognition you deserve.'* I was very sincere in saying that.

Mr Player was voted the top athlete in the history of South Africa. His accomplishments as a golfer are extraordinary. He won 167 tournaments worldwide and compared very favourably against the greatest golfers of all time. He won tournaments in five different decades — including the Grand Slam — all four professional majors in his career.

That is impressive, but it is important to note that Mr Player also was voted one of the top five influential people in our nation's history. His accomplishments as a humanitarian and statesman are equal to, and may even surpass, his accomplishments as an athlete. That is a legacy that will last forever.

CHAPTER THIRTEEN

The Future

VISION GOING FORWARD

South Africa's black nouveau riche are now found frequenting the golf courses in our democratic dispensation, the majority of black golfers in past years were working-class citizens who learnt the game while caddying for whites and usually allowed to play on white courses on Mondays.

In moving forward from this painful reminder of our divided past, perhaps the greatest tribute we can all pay to the 'deferred dream' of past black golfers is to find and nurture a Tiger Woods from SA.

A new class of golfers who would make us all proud and smile when recalling the names of Sewsunker 'Papwa' Sewgolum, Ramnath 'Bambata' Boodhun, Edward Johnson-Sedibe, Vincent Tshabalala, Ismail 'Boy' Chowglay, Lewis Chitengwa, and Simon 'Cox' Hlapo while they now walk on greener fairways.

WHAT HAS CHANGED?

A tour of SA provides many such glimpses of a nation in transition, a nation of extremes. There are many beautiful new golf resorts; their promotional materials boast of 'electrified palisade fencing, motion detectors, infra-red and radars, and guards and armed response with dogs.'

'The whites live locked away in their fear, the blacks live locked away in their anger,' says Mandla Mentoor. 'They hold the key to unlock our anger. We hold the key to unlock their fear.'

But we are starting to find each other and to be proud of our multiracial sportsmen and women, as seen with the 1995

World Cup Rugby and the 1996 African Cup of Nations soccer tournaments. Now to unearth a golfing 'black diamond'.

As SA emerged from its pariah state, the world flocked to shower the 'rainbow nation' with international sporting events. Now it was time to show off SA golf and courses to the world with the 1996 World Cup and the 2003 President's Cup.

WORLD CUP AT ERINVALE, CAPE TOWN

The 1996 World Cup of Golf took place 21–24 November at the Erinvale Golf Club in Somerset West, Cape Town. It was the forty-second World Cup. The tournament was a 72-hole stroke play team event (32 teams) with each team consisting of two players from a country. The combined score of each team determined their results. Individuals also competed for the International Trophy.

Unlike 1976 when Vincent Tshabalala refused for political reasons to partner Gary Player in the World Cup, with the resultant backlash, this time Vincent was merely a proud spectator.

The SA team of Ernie Els and Wayne Westner won by 18 strokes over the US team of Steve Jones and Tom Lehman. Ernie Els took the International Trophy by three strokes over Wayne Westner.

1996	South Africa	Ernie Els & Wayne Westner	Cape Town, South Africa	Steve Jones & Tom Lehman

Scores

#	Country	Score	To par	Money (US$)
1	South Africa	136-144-130-137=547	−29	400,000
2	United States	146-140-140-139=565	−11	200,000
3	Scotland	139-142-142-143=566	−10	125,000
4	Germany	145-144-140-142=571	−5	100,000
5	France	144-141-144-143=572	−4	
T6	Argentina	142-147-140-150=579	+3	52,500
	Denmark	138-147-152-142=579		
T8	Italy	143-149-147-141=580	+4	28,000
	Namibia	146-146-143-145=580		
	Wales	143-149-143-145=580		

International Trophy

#	Player	Country	Score	To par	Money (US$)
1	Ernie Els	South Africa	68-72-65-67=272	−16	100,000
2	Wayne Westner	South Africa	68-72-65-70=275	−13	
3	Bernhard Langer	Germany	71-68-72-69=280	−8	
T4	Paul Lawrie	Scotland	69-70-70-72=281	−7	
	Ian Woosnam	Wales			

THE PRESIDENT'S CUP AT FANCOURT, GEORGE

Presidents Cup, Fancourt 2003:
Ernie Els, Nelson Mandela, Tiger Woods

The 2003 Presidents Cup ventured to George, SA, for the first time, fittingly, as the nation is home to Gary Player, who led the International Team for the first time in a contest against Jack Nicklaus' US Team. The host venue, The Links at Fancourt Hotel and Country Club Estate, saw the first tie in Presidents Cup history, and the Republic of SA. President Thabo Mbeki served as the Honorary Chairman.

The Presidents Cup ended in a remarkable tie and after Ernie Els and Tiger Woods battled it out for three extra holes shot for shot with some amazing pressure putts to halve the hole until darkness fell. The captains Nicklaus and Player called it a tie, which led US captain, the legendary Jack Nicklaus, to call it: 'the most unbelievable event the game of golf has ever seen.'

2003	Fancourt Hotel and Country Club	George, Western Cape, South Africa	Tied	17–17	Jack Nicklaus	Gary Player

343

**Jack Nicklaus, President Thabo Mbeki,
Gary Player sharing the President's Cup**

CHAPTER 14

Recording History

THE SOUTH AFRICAN GOLF HERITAGE TRUST

But that's not the end of the story, as the SA Golf Heritage Trust recognised the performances of those involved with golf under a category 'disadvantaged' to take into account the challenges faced by people of colour when being inducted into the Southern Africa Golf Hall of Fame.

Induction criteria:

'Golf Hall of Fame Inductee: Person who, by their actions or achievements, has made an extraordinary contribution to the development of golf in Southern Africa or to the standing of Southern African Golf in the eyes of the international golfing community.'

SOUTHERN AFRICA GOLF HALL OF FAME INDUCTION

Harry Brews (son of Sid Brews) and Barry Cohen collaborated to fund the launch the SA Golf Museum in 2010, with Cohen designing and building the museum at Oubaai GC, George. Following Brews's passing, Cohen relocated this heritage centre to Cape Town.

One of the functions of the SA Golf Heritage Trust is to induct those from the golf industry who have contributed in a significant manner, also taking into account those disadvantaged by colonialism and apartheid. The minimum age limit for induction being 40 years old.

Following his passing in 2012, it was decided to introduce an additional category, 'The Harry Brews Award' for those 'who had unselfishly contributed to the betterment of golf'.

The induction committee presently consists of Sally Little, Denis Hutchinson, Dale Hayes, Harry Brews (deceased), Barry Cohen, Peter Sauerman, and Dorian Wharton-Hood.

Barry Cohen

Harry Brews

Johann Rupert and Gary Player being inducted into the Golf Hall of Fame, and Hugh Baiocchi.

'BLACK' HALL OF FAME INDUCTEES & AWARD

Induction

Class 2009
Sewsunker 'Papwa' Sewgolum

Class 2010
Vincent Tshabalala
Richard Mogoerane
Theo Manyama

Class 2011
Peter Louw

Class 2012
Simon 'Cox' Hlapo

Class 2013
Joe Dlamini

Class 2014
Lewis Chitengwa

Class 2015
Ismail 'Boy' Chowglay

Harry Brews Award

Class 2013
Honorable 'Ntate' Andrew Mlangeni

Those who may be considered for future Southern Africa Golf Hall of Fame Induction or for the Harry Brews Award may include Ramnath 'Bambata' Boodhun, Edward Johnson-Sedibe, Mokgeteng John Mashego, Daddy Naidoo, R.T. Singh, Louis Nelson, Graham Wulff, Alfred Magerman, Fred 'FM' Paul, and Rodney Hess.

Raymond Ackerman congratulating the Hon. Andrew Mlangeni on the receipt of the Southern Africa Golf Hall of Fame 'Harry Brews' award 'for his selfless contribution'

Golf Hall of Fame 2010 Induction: Hugh Baiocchi, Duggie Donnely (famous European Tour commentator) ,Vincent Tshabalala, Dale Hayes, Louis Oosthuizen

2010 General Bantu Holomisa together with Richard Mogoerane and Vincent Tshabalala at their Southern Africa Golf Hall of Fame Induction invitational golf tournament, Oubaai.

2014 Induction: Dan Retief, Joe Dlamini, Senator Mike Temple

Honorable Andrew Mlangeni receiving the 2013 Harry Brews award with Wendy Warrington, Bobby Cole

SOUTH AFRICAN GOLF HERITAGE CENTRE

In 2009 December, the SA Golf Heritage Trust hosted their first annual Southern Africa Golf Hall of Fame Induction awards at the Hyatt Regency Oubaai, George, where among other honours, Sewsunker 'Papwa' Sewgolum was inducted.

The following year the SA Golf Museum was opened by Gideon Sam (SASCOC) at Oubaai, built and funded by Harry Brews and Barry Cohen.

'There are displays of memorabilia at the SA Museum of Golf that can only be bettered at the R&A museum at St. Andrews and at Royal Blackheath. It should be compulsory for all young golfers to pay the museum a visit so that they can stroll through the history of the game in South Africa' — Dale Hayes.

In 2015, at the specific request of their sponsor, Mercedes-Benz, this heritage centre was relocated to the V&A Waterfront, Cape Town, again built and funded by Cohen, and where it was opened by Gary Player, Deputy Minister of Tourism Tokozile Xasa (now Minister of Sport), and Mayor Patricia de Lille.

This heritage centre specifically featured a subset on black golf, including special sections on the TPA Tour, the iconic black golfers, and the lost history of black golf.

Records of black golf and the TPA tour were not usually recorded, so there are gaps in the history.

Executive Mayor
Patricia de Lille

Gary Player, Minister of Sport
Tokozile Xasa

Gary Player, Minister Tokozile Xasa, Helga and
Lewis Muridzo-Chitengwa Snr.

Fulton Allem and his wife Jennifer watching a documentary on Papwa Sewgolum

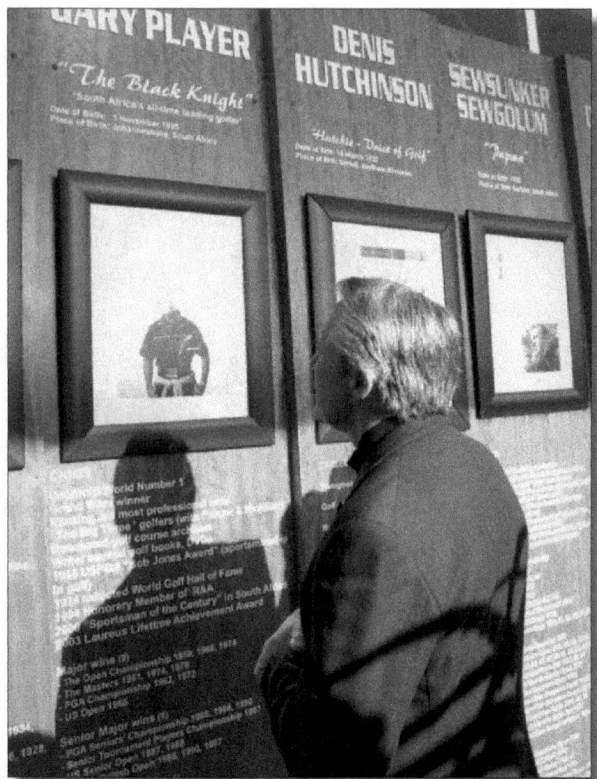

Gary Player reading his citation in the Hall of
Fame (right) Papwa Sewgolum's citation

TIMELINE OF CHANGES
Pre-unification: The Struggle

1878/86: Beginning of golf in SA – work for caddies

1927: Indentured caddies earn 3 pounds per month with free schooling, rations, board, clothing, medical.

1927: Formation of the Durban Indian Golf Club at Indian Recreational Grounds (Curries Fountain).

1929: Ramnath 'Bambata' Boodhun plays in the British Open

1936: Caddies Jack Nathan and A Seepersadh defeat Ryder Cup players Alf Padgham (The Open champion) and Alan Dailey 2/1

1937: Peter Louw establishes Sunningdale Park GC (near Royal Cape GC)

1938: Unofficial SA Non-European Open won by J. Dyasi

1947: Formation of the SA Non-European Golf Association

1948: Formation of the Western Province Coloured Golf Association

1949: Official SA Non-European Open won by Ronnie Ditsebe

1953: Publication of The Golfers Annual

1950s: Emergence of black golf champions – Johnson-Sedibe, Hlapo, Chowglay, Sewgolum.

1957: Sewgolum shoots 59 in a non-white competiton – not recognised as he was not affliated to the 'white' golf body

1957: Sewgolum shoots 62 to break the Beach wood course record

1959:	Johnson-Sedibe and Sewgolum play in 'The Open'
1959:	Sewsunker 'Papwa' Sewgolum wins the Dutch Open mobbed by 100 000 supporters on his return
1960:	Milnerton GC, a white club, opens to black tournaments with the SA Non-European Open
1960:	Sewgolum ineligible for SAPGA member ship becomes a member of the British PGA so he could play in Europe
1960:	Sewgolum wins the Dutch Open for the second time
1961:	Sewgolum becomes the first player of colour to play in a white tournament – SA Open – but a permit required with restrictions and only granted periodically
1961:	First SA Non-European Ladies Open won by Dr Moeti
1963:	Sewgolum wins the Natal Open beating Bobby Verwey and Denis Hutchinson
1963:	Sewgolum 2nd in the SA Open
1964:	Sewgolum wins Dutch Open for the third time
1965:	Sewgolum beats Gary Player and Harold Henning head-to-head to win the Natal Open for the second time
1966:	Sewgolum survives an assassination attempt
1966:	Sewgolum banned from playing in 'white' SA professional golf tournaments
1967:	Sewgolum turns down Royal Calcutta Golf Club club professional job offer
1967:	Sewgolum runner-up in the Dutch Open

1970:	Government revokes and cancels Sewgolum's passport
1971:	International pressure leads to Sally Little withdrawing from British Ladies Open, and Bobby Cole banned from playing in the Volvo tournament
1971:	Concept of 'Open International' tournaments introduced where Lee Elder and Mr Lu plus four black SA golfers participate
1972:	Open International golf sees SA Amateur open to all races
1973:	Challenge Matches against international black players introduced
1974:	Sewgolum wins the SA Non-European Open for the 10th and last time
1975:	First multi-racial Open tournament
1976:	Vincent Tshabalala wins the French Open
1976:	Vincent Tshabalala refuses to partner Gary Player in the World Cup – consequently his SA Open entry is refused
1977:	Non-White amateurs can play in all SA national and provincial events, and clubs can play matches against white clubs and enter the same leagues
1978:	Clovelly CC opens to all races, sets precedent such that all sports clubs can now choose their membership
1978:	Sewsunker 'Papwa' Sewgolum dies
1980:	Mini Circuit for Non-European golf introduced
1981:	Million Dollar Challenge at Sun City introduced to overcome sport boycotts
1982:	Nine black golfers given full membership of the Tournament Players Division of the

SAPGA but TPA not consulted over
selected players

1985: Gary Player scathing attack on apartheid
and the Government

1985: Phalaborwa Classic boycott by black
players when 40 overseas players given
automatic playing exemptions

1986: TPA Gary Player sponsored tournament
for record R100 000 purse – criticism of
reverse apartheid leads to Player
resigning as president of the SAPGA

1986: TPA boycotts Germiston Centenary
Classic which was celebrating 100 years
of the black man's oppression

1987: Sammy Daniels becomes the first person
of colour to win a provincial open when he
wins the Boland Open

1990: Vincent Tshabalala elected captain of the
SAPGA

1991: John Mashego becomes the first winner
of colour on the Sunshine Tour

1992: Unification – struggle over – one golf
body for all golfers

Post-unification: Finding a Black Champion

1992: Lewis Chitengwa wins the World Junior
Golf Championship beating Tiger Woods

1993: Lewis Chitengwa becomes the first black
man to win the SA Amateur (includes
victory over Rory Sabbatini)

1996: SA's Ernie Els and Wayne Westner win
the World Cup at Erinvale

1997: Vijay Singh wins the SA Open

1990s:	Various golf academies opened to the disadvantaged in the hope of finding a black golf champion
2003:	Presidents Cup at Fancourt ends in a draw with Ernie Els and Tiger Woods involved in a playoff
2009:	Sewsunker 'Papwa' Sewgolum inducted into the Southern Africa Golf Hall of Fame
2010-15:	Additional black players inducted into the Southern Africa Golf Hall of Fame
2015:	The SA Golf Museum relocates to the V&A Waterfront and includes a subset dedicated to Black golf

CONTROVERSY

1958:	Barkley East caddy strike over increase wages.
1963:	Sewsunker 'Papwa' Sewgolum receives the Natal Open outside in the rain with the white players looking on from inside the clubhouse. This photo goes worldwide and sparks an outcry, with 'Papwa' unintentionally becoming the symbol of the anti-apartheid sport movement.
1965:	Following Sewgolum's victory over Player to win the Natal Open – mixed racial sport galleries banned
1966:	Sewgolum banned from playing in 'white' Open tournaments.
1970:	The government cancels Sewgolum's passport.
1972:	Papwa Sewgolum boycotts the Oros Stroke-Play Championship at Houghton GC due to the direction in which the organisation for non-white golf was heading.

1973:   Daddy Naidoo and 16 other golfers refuse to play under the politicised Non-White Professional Players Association after it insists that all non-whites become members of that association or be barred from their tournaments. Being a member could get themselves barred from multi-racial tournaments. The SAPPA then suspends 8 professionals and fines Sewgolum.

1975:   Split among black professional golfers as two rival controlling bodies are formed, namely the SA(N-E)GA and the SA(N-E) NGU.

1976:   Vincent Tshabalala refuses to partner Gary Player and play for SA in the World Cup as he says it is a political selection which he does not deserve. The SAPGA bans him from playing in white tournaments, while the TPA bans him for having played in a white tournament. He forms the Bantu GU to get around these bans.

1981:   George Blumberg resigns from organising black tournaments following Tshabalala's statement that he is being discriminated insofar as white tournaments.

1981:   160 Black golfers walk out of a Grahamstown GC tournament as a result of the humiliating racial incident involving white caddy, Clive Marx.

1982:   Gary Player called to emergency meeting following SAPGA granting full PGA membership to nine black players without con sulting the TPA concerning the selection of the players.

1985: Gary Player makes a scathing attack on the government and apartheid.

1986: Gary Player resigns as SA PGA President due to criticism within the SAPGA surrounding his organisation of a R100,000 tournament for blacks only – seen as 'reverse apartheid'.

1986: The TPA boycotts the Germiston Centenary Open because of its association with the celebration of 100 years of black man's oppression. Daddy Naidoo expelled from the TPA for ignoring the boycott.

1986: Phalaborwa Classic boycotted by black players following the SAPGA extending 40 automatic exemptions to overseas players.

1988: Lexington PGA boycotted as black golfers are not allowed to play on whites course prior to events, few black professionals invited to play in the pro-am tournaments, and the excessive influx of overseas professionals allowed to play on the circuit.

1999: Tshabalala accuses the SA PGA of anti-black sentiment after it suspends John Mashego and Solly Sepeng following conflict concerning the introduction of a new policy reducing the number of black invitees from ten to five, giving preference to youth.

2000: Tshabalala hits out at anti-black sentiment in the game at the Dimension Data Pro-Am.

Statistics

TOURNAMENT RECORDS

Note: The more important tournaments were often played at the end or the beginning of the year such that they may have been designated as the tournament for that year or the following year. I have only surmised the actual year based on my research and newspaper articles.

SA NON-EUROPEAN OPEN

YEAR	FIRST	SECOND	THIRD	FOURTH	FIFTH	COURSE
1938	J Dyasi	Michael Swartz				Wynberg
1942	S Swartz					
1943	S Swartz					
1944	S Swartz					
1945	S Swartz					
1947	S Swartz					
1949	R Ditsebe				*first official SA N-E Open	Kimberly
1950	J. Gumbi (317)					Bloemfontein
1951	E Johnson-Sedibe					
1952	E Johnson-Sedibe *play-off	K Madlanga/ J Jass				Johannes-burg
1953	Bob Nkuna 70 75 79 73 (297)	D Phala	R Ditsebe			Kimberley
1954	L Khatidi 74 75 77 74 (300)					Bloemfontein
1955	S Hlapo					

YEAR	FIRST	SECOND	THIRD	FOURTH	FIFTH	COURSE
1956	A (Polly) November 78 77 73 77 (305)	I Chowglay				Thornhill
1957	S Hlapo 72 66 74 78 (290)	R Ditsebe/J Mazibuko		R D Phala		Bloemfontein
1958	David Motati	D Phala				Bloemfontein
1959	S Hlapo 67 70 67 69 (272)	D Motati	R Ditsebe & D Harrison			Kroonstad
1960	S Sewgolum (308) 80 80 74 74 (308)	RL Brown (310)			*played first white course	Milnerton
1961	S Sewgolum 75 73 76 73 (297)	S Hlapo (305)	I Chowglay/ PL Paul (307)		J.Semenya (311) / RT Singh(314)	Kloof & Royal Durban
1962	I Chowglay 72 74 74 77 (297)	F Mazibuko 73 74 76 78 (301)	J Simenya 79 72 72 79 (302)	PL Paul/ S Hlapo/ R Ditsebe	*8th S Sewgolum (308)	Kimberley
1963	S Sewgolum 75 77 75 74 (301)	I Chowglay 74 77 80 83 (314)	S Chakane 75 84 75 82 (316)	R Ditsebe/D Motati/R Tiney (318)		Walmer *par 75
1964	S Sewgolum 71 72 70 75 (288)	E. Lee & J Semenya (309)		I Chowglay (310)	S. Hlapo (315)	Glendower
1965	S.Sewgolum/V Tshabalala 77 74 69 71 (291) 74 74 73 70 (291)		I Chowglay (292)			Alexander
1966	D Motati (292)	V Tshabalala				Bloemfontein
1967	S Sewgolum 70 69 72 71 (282)	I Chowglay (289)	S Mogoerane	S Hlapo		King David

YEAR	FIRST	SECOND	THIRD	FOURTH	FIFTH	COURSE
1968	S Sewgolum 70 70 71 74 (285)	V Tshabalala (293)	S Hlapo			Circle CC
1969	S Sewgolum 71 76 73 75 (295)	A Hartzenberg				Athlone
1970	S Sewgolum 77 67 69 74 (287)	V Tshabalala (295)	R Mogoerane (302)	J Ranjith	Solly Sepeng	Benoni & Ohenimuri
1971	V Tshabalala (292)	S Sewgolum (293)	D Naidoo	R Anooplal	J Chetty	Benoni
1972	I Chowglay 74 74 75 74 (297) *62 qualifying record	V Tshabalala & R Mogoerane (301)				Kroonstad
1973	R Mogoerane	I Chowglay	R Anooplal			Wedgewood
1974	S Sewgolum 77 69 75 70 (291)	V Tshabalala 70 70 72 80 (292)				Glendower
1975		John Thetele	John Baxter			Kimberley
1976	R Mogoerane					
1977	V Tshabalala 73 75 73 70 (291)					Durban
1978	L Govender (313) *playoff	R Naidoo & J Chetty (313)				Durban
1979	Willy Lewis	Ismail Chowglay				King David
1980						
1983	V Tshabalala					

SA BANTU CHAMPIONSHIP

YEAR	FIRST	SECOND	THIRD	FOURTH	FIFTH	COURSE
1939	Simon Nchoeu 80 75 70 70 (295)					

SA NON-EUROPEAN AMATEUR

YEAR	FIRST	SECOND	THIRD	FOURTH	FIFTH	COURSE
1965	Joe Manana (311)					
1969	Godfrey Zwane (310)					
1972	Reggie Mamashela (308)					
197?	Shan Dorasamy					
197?	J Baichen					

LADIES

SOUTH AFRICAN NON-EUROPEAN LADIES OPEN

YEAR	FIRST	SECOND	THIRD	FOURTH	FIFTH	COURSE
1961	Dr N Moeti	D. Xaha				

SA MIXED FOURSOMES
first mention women in the record books

YEAR	FIRST	SECOND	THIRD	FOURTH	FIFTH	COURSE
1958	Miss Langa & M. Boice (78)	Mrs S. Tau & D. Mashigo (79)				

PROVINCIAL RESULTS

TRANSVAAL NON-EUROPEAN OPEN

YEAR	FIRST	SECOND	THIRD	FOURTH	FIFTH	COURSE
1948	B Nkuna (324)	JM Jass (326)	A Matsili	D Tlale	J Nkosi	
1953	B. Nkuna 75 74 74 73 (296)	D Mashigo	S Hlapo			
Pre-1957	J Gumbi					
1957	S Hlapo					
1958	Johannes Mahlatsi	S Hlapo				Boksburg
1959	S Hlapo					
1960	Bobby Tshabalala 67 68 65 68 (268)	J Mazibuko 67 67 68 68 (270)	S Hlapo (273) *63 2nd round		J Semenya	
1961	S Hlapo 68 70 67 69 (274)	D Motati 68 71 66 70 (275)	P Mbuyisa			
1962	S Hlapo (274)	S Mdeni				Wynberg
1963	S Hlapo *65 course record	E Borman				Benoni
1964	S Sewgolum (284) *65 course record	E Borman (304)				Benoni
1965	S Sewgolum 70 70 71 71 (282)					Glendower
1966	S Sewgolum 69,70,70,73 (282)	S Hlapo	R Mogoerane	D Motati	J Gumbi	
1967	R Mogoerane (302)	S Sewgolum	S Hlapo			

YEAR	FIRST	SECOND	THIRD	FOURTH	FIFTH	COURSE
1968	I Chowglay 73 69 73 73 (287)	N N'kosi (307)				
1969	S Sewgolum	I Chowglay				Benoni
1970	S Sewgolum	V Tshabalala/ S Sepeng/ R Anooplal				
1971						
1972	V Tshabalala (295)	S Sewgolum (297)				Ohenimuri
1973-79						
1980	Obed Matlou					
1982	Daddy Naidoo					
1983	I Chowglay					
1984-86						
1987	Mervyn Gallant	Peter Mkata	Joe Dlamini			

O.F.S. NON-EUROPEAN OPEN

YEAR	FIRST	SECOND	THIRD	FOURTH	FIFTH	COURSE
1959	D. Motati					
1960	S Hlapo (272)					
1961	S Hlapo (268)	D Motati (272)				
1962	S Hlapo 67 74 68 72 (281)	D Phala & G Diamond (285)				
1963	S Hlapo 76 76 77 75 (304)	D Motati 78 73 83 76 (310) / John Mazibuko 77 80 80 73 (310)				Bloemfontein
1964	I Chowglay					
1965	Jacob Gumbi 74 75 81 84 (314)	Edward Lee (319)	B Nkuma (320)	E Ngidi (322)	G Sonanizi (322)	
1966	S Sewgolum 69 70 70 73 (282)	S Hlapo 69 76 75 71 (291)	R Mogoerane 73 75 75 76 (299)	D Motati 77 77 73 74 (301)	J Gumbi 75 77 75 75 (302) / Z Mavundla 74 77 74 77 (302)	
1968	R Mogoerane (302)	S Sewgolum (304)	S Hlapo (306)			Bloemfontein
1969	S Sewgolum	R Anooplal				Bloemfontein
1973	R Mogoerane					
1974	R Mogoerane					
1975	R Mogoerane					
1976	R Mogoerane					
1977	R Mogoerane					
1978	R Mogoerane					
1979	R Mogoerane					
1980	R Mogoerane					
1981	R Mogoerane					

NATAL NON-EUROPEAN OPEN

YEAR	FIRST	SECOND	THIRD	FOURTH	FIFTH	COURSE
1954	S Sewgolum					
1955	S Sewgolum					
1956		S Sewgolum *lost playoff				
1957	S Sewgolum					
1958	S Sewgolum					
1959	S Sewgolum					
1960	S Sewgolum 74 72 75 73 (294)	RT Singh 76 79 79 79 (313)	S Hlapo & P Mazibuko			Royal Durban
1961	S Sewgolum 73 73 71 73 (290)	PL Paul 77 76 79 71 (303)	J Semenya 80 77 73 76 (306)	C Shakane 76 80 74 79 (309)	RT Singh 78 78 78 75 (309)	
1962	S Sewgolum					Kloof
1963	S Sewgolum	J Semenya				Circle
1964	S Sewgolum 72 71 73 75 (291)	D Motati 76 76 74 75 (301)	L Buthelezi 75 74 79 78 (306)		R Rajdaw 79 72 76 80 (307)	Maritzburg
1965	Raydmuth Rajdaw (293)	S Sewgolum (294)	S Hlapo (297)			Kloof
1966	S Sewgolum 70 71 73 74 (288)		V Tshabalala			
1967	S Sewgolum 71 76 69 70 (286)	Ram Rajdaw 69 80 72 75 (296) *69 course record	Reggie Naidoo (am) 78 77 72 76 (303)	L Polagadu 74 80 70 80 (304)	D Motati 79 78 71 78 (306)	Maritzburg
1968	S Sewgolum 71 76 69 70 (286)	J Ranjith 74 72 74 79 (299)	M V Naidoo 76 75 75 76 (302)	V Tshabalala 80 75 69 78 (302)	D Motati 72 75 78 78 (303)	Maritzburg
1969	S Sewgolum *by 21 shots					Stanger
1970	S Sewgolum					
1971	V Tshabalala	S Sewgolum				Maritzburg

YEAR	FIRST	SECOND	THIRD	FOURTH	FIFTH	COURSE
1972	V Tshabalala 73 69 69 71 (282)	Johnson Chetty 81 69 68 70 (288)				Windsor Park
1973	J Dlamini					
1974	S Sewgolum					Maritzburg
1975	S Sewgolum 73 73 77 71 (294)	I Chowglay / R Rajdaw 78 75 76 74 (303)		A Collins (306)	I Ranjith (307)	Circle
1976	I Chowglay *play-off	S Sewgolum				
1977	S Sewgolum					
1983	J Dlamini	R Mogoerane	Peter Mkata/ Daddy Naidoo			Circle

WESTERN PROVINCE NON-EUROPEAN OPEN

YEAR	FIRST	SECOND	THIRD	FOURTH	FIFTH	COURSE
1949	A (Polly) November					Somerset West
1950-53						
1954	A November 76 78 (154)					Somerset West
1955					I Chowglay	
1956	I Chowglay					
1957						
1958	A Roman					Thornton
1960	S Sewgolum	RL Brown	Alex Njokweni			
1961	P van Dieman	I Chowglay				
1962	A November					
1963	I Chowglay					Westlake
1964	S Sewgolum 68 65 72 70 (275)	I Chowglay / P van Dieman (302)				Royal Cape
1965	I Chowglay					

YEAR	FIRST	SECOND	THIRD	FOURTH	FIFTH	COURSE
1966	I Chowglay					
1967	I Chowglay	Willy Lewis	D Motati			King David
1968	I Chowglay (297)	S Sewgolum (305)				Athlone
1969	S Sewgolum 74 74 76 72 (296)	V Tshabalala (298)				Athlone
1970	Abe van Rooyen 284	R Mogoerane	Vincent Tshabalala	Daddy Naidoo		Athlone
1971	I Chowglay 79 76 72 75 (302)	Abe van Rooyen (306)	Wally Johannesen	Percy Lendis		Athlone
1972	A 'Polly' November					Athlone
1973	I Chowglay					Athlone
1974						
1975						
1976	S Sewgolum 78 70 76 77 (301)	J Chetty (307)	S Dondashe (309)	Noel Maart (310)		

EASTERN PROVINCE NON-EUROPEAN OPEN

YEAR	FIRST	SECOND	THIRD	FOURTH	FIFTH	COURSE
1961	A Njokweni					
1962	B Maselwa	A Gxekwa	W Malangeni	M Hector		Walmer
1963	I Chowglay (309) *course record	S Sewgolum (310)				Walmer
1964	S Sewgolum	I Chowglay				Walmer
1965-67						
1968	I Chowglay	S Sewgolum				

GRIQUALAND WEST NON-EUROPEAN OPEN

YEAR	FIRST	SECOND	THIRD	FOURTH	FIFTH	COURSE
1959	Ronnie Ditsebe					
1960	S Sewgolum 69 72 72 72 (285)					Kimberley
1961	S Sewgolum 75 68 69 73 (285) *68 course record	Jacob Gumbi (308)				Kimberley
1963	S Sewgolum (285)	I Chowglay (293)				Kimberley
1964	S Sewgolum 77 72 74 72 (295)	I Chowglay 75 75 73 78 (301)	S Hlapo 80 76 77 77 (310)	P Mbuyisa 83 77 77 76 (313)	D Motati 83 82 76 75 (316)	Kimberley
1965	S Sewgolum 71 69 70 71 (281)	S Hlapo 75 69 71 71 (286)	J Semenya 75 77 73 78 (303)	S Sepeng 80 74 78 77 (309)	D Mcumola 79 79 77 77 (312)	Kimberley
1966	S Sepeng	S Hlapo				
1967	S Sewgolum (300)	S Sepeng 78 78 75 72 (303)	S Hlapo 78 79 74 76 (307)			
1969	S Sewgolum 78 78 75 69 (300)	R Anooplal				

NATAL AMATEUR

YEAR	FIRST	SECOND	THIRD	FOURTH	FIFTH	COURSE
1946	S Sewgolum					Curries Fountain

OTHER NON-EUROPEAN TOURNAMENTS

TRANSVAAL MATCHPLAY

YEAR	FIRST	SECOND	THIRD	FOURTH	FIFTH	COURSE
1946	Bob Nkuna					
1947	B Nkuna	R Ditsebe				
1961	D Motati 8/7	Phineas Mbuyisa	S Hlapo			Zola
1966	V Tshalalala 5/4	Atroll Mazibuko				Pimville

VIKING ROUND ROBIN

YEAR	FIRST	SECOND	THIRD	FOURTH	FIFTH	COURSE
1952	R Ditsebe					
1953	R Ditsebe					

NORTHERN TRANSVAAL OPEN

YEAR	FIRST	SECOND	THIRD	FOURTH	FIFTH	COURSE
1953	E Johnson-Sedibe 79 79 (158)	B Nkuna	E Lee	R Ditsebe / M Boice		Viceroy

EAST RAND OPEN

YEAR	FIRST	SECOND	THIRD	FOURTH	FIFTH	COURSE
1953	B Nkuma 79 77 (156)					

SOUTH WESTERN OPEN

YEAR	FIRST	SECOND	THIRD	FOURTH	FIFTH	COURSE
1953	L Khathide 82 83 (165)					

EAST RAND OPEN

YEAR	FIRST	SECOND	THIRD	FOURTH	FIFTH	COURSE
1953	B Nkuna 79 77 (156)					East Rand Central

SOUTH WESTERN OPEN

YEAR	FIRST	SECOND	THIRD	FOURTH	FIFTH	COURSE
1953	L Khathide 82 83 (165)					Homicide

N. OFS & N.E. TRANSVAAL

YEAR	FIRST	SECOND	THIRD	FOURTH	FIFTH	COURSE
1953 Inter Club	S Hlapo (playing for Wynberg)					
1959	S Hlapo					

NORTH EASTERN OPEN

YEAR	FIRST	SECOND	THIRD	FOURTH	FIFTH	COURSE
1957	S Hlapo					
1958	Johannes Mahlatsi (141)	S Hlapo	L Shezi	S Hlapo		Kwa Thema

GREAT KAROO OPEN

YEAR	FIRST	SECOND	THIRD	FOURTH	FIFTH	COURSE
1954	John Petersen 78 74 (152)	P J Duimpies 72 81 (153)				Beaufort West
1958	John Baxter	P J Kleintjies				Beaufort West

LITCHFIELD-BORMAN

YEAR	FIRST	SECOND	THIRD	FOURTH	FIFTH	COURSE
1957	J Fiver Mazibuko	A Mazibuko				Bethal
1958	S Hlapo (145)					Homicide

OFS SPECIAL STROKEPLAY

YEAR	FIRST	SECOND	THIRD	FOURTH	FIFTH	COURSE
1958	D Motati 70 70 (140)	D Phala 69 72 (141)				
1964	S Hlapo (214)	D Motati	I Chowglay			

BORDER OPEN

YEAR	FIRST	SECOND	THIRD	FOURTH	FIFTH	COURSE
1958	W Batyi 74 79 74 79 (306)	A Njokweni	Nonyama *play-off	N Malangeni		Queenstown

EAST LONDON OPEN

YEAR	FIRST	SECOND	THIRD	FOURTH	FIFTH	COURSE
1958	S F Makhubalo (150)	S Fufu (156)	F N Johnson	B Mntima		
1961	Solomon Dondashe (156)	S William Malangeni				
1963	H Mtombeni (312)	B Mgeni (317)				Ziphunzana

WESTERN TRANSVAAL

YEAR	FIRST	SECOND	THIRD	FOURTH	FIFTH	COURSE
1959	A Mazibuko 66 71 (137)	S Hlapo				Richmond

NATAL MIDLANDS

YEAR	FIRST	SECOND	THIRD	FOURTH	FIFTH	COURSE
1959	S Sewgolum *play-off	Laurence Buthelezi				
1960	S Sewgolum					

OFS OPEN R200

YEAR	FIRST	SECOND	THIRD	FOURTH	FIFTH	COURSE
1959	S Hlapo 68 68 (136)	D Motati 70 70 (140)	R Ditsebe 72 69 / D Harrison 68 73 (141)			

FAR NORTH & EAST OPEN

YEAR	FIRST	SECOND	THIRD	FOURTH	FIFTH	COURSE
1959	P Mazibuko (145)	S Hlapo (146)				
1966	S Hlapo *playoff	V Tshabalala				

KROONSTAD OPEN

YEAR	FIRST	SECOND	THIRD	FOURTH	FIFTH	COURSE
1959	S Hlapo 68 68 (136)	D Motati 70 70 (140)	R Ditsebe 72 69 (141) D Harrison 68 73 (141)			Kroonstad
1960	S Hlapo		I Chowglay			
1964	S Hlapo (214) *67 course record	D Motati (218)	I Chowglay (223)			

EAST LONDON INVITATIONAL OPEN

YEAR	FIRST	SECOND	THIRD	FOURTH	FIFTH	COURSE
1959	Alex Njokweni					
1960	Alex Njokweni					
1961	Alex Njokweni					

YEAR	FIRST	SECOND	THIRD	FOURTH	FIFTH	COURSE
1962	W Malangeni 80 78 77 (235)	Alex Njokweni (239)				West Bank & Alexander

MIDLAND OPEN

YEAR	FIRST	SECOND	THIRD	FOURTH	FIFTH	COURSE
1960	W Batyi (219)	N Tyobeka / S V Makubalo		V F Jonas		Adelaide

PORT ELIZABETH OPEN

YEAR	FIRST	SECOND	THIRD	FOURTH	FIFTH	COURSE
1961	A Njokweni	N Malangeni				Redhouse & Walmer

GREEN VALLEY OPEN

YEAR	FIRST	SECOND	THIRD	FOURTH	FIFTH	COURSE
1961	S Hlapo					

F.O.S.A OPEN

YEAR	FIRST	SECOND	THIRD	FOURTH	FIFTH	COURSE
1961	Shan Poonsammy 71 74 (145)	Ceasar Shakane *play-off	S Sewgolum			Umgeni
1966	Collin Appalsamy 68 72 (140)	S Sewgolum 68 73 (141)	Phillip Mhlongo 70 77 (147)	L Buthelezi 75 72 (147)	R Tiney 76 74 (150)	Springfield
1970	Daddy Naidoo 68 71 (139)	Harold Sukraj 142	J Buchen 144	A Collins/L Buthelezi 146		Springfield

TRANSVAAL INVITATIONAL

YEAR	FIRST	SECOND	THIRD	FOURTH	FIFTH	COURSE
1962	S Hlapo 69 72 67 66 (274)	S Mdeni (276)				Wynberg
1966	S Sewgolum (273)	S Hlapo (275) *65 third round	Israel Khumou			Wynberg

R2000 SPONSORED INVITATION

YEAR	FIRST	SECOND	THIRD	FOURTH	FIFTH	COURSE
1964	S Sewgolum 72 70 (142)	A Collins 75 70 (145)	PL (Fred) Paul 78 71 (149)	Daddy Naidoo 75 76 (151)	C Skakane 75 77(152)	Durban

BAMBATA MEMORIAL TROPHY

YEAR	FIRST	SECOND	THIRD	FOURTH	FIFTH	COURSE
1965	S Sewgolum					Springfield
1966	Ramphal Tiney 69 68 (137)	S Sewgolum (138)	Daddy Naidoo 73 74 (147) Philip Nhlongo 77 70 (147)		DL Solanki (148)	Springfield

THUNDERBIRD R500 CLASSIC

YEAR	FIRST	SECOND	THIRD	FOURTH	FIFTH	COURSE
1965	S Sewgolum 70 72 72 72 (286)	A Collins 76 6972 74 (291)	PL Paul 75 73 76 76 (300)			Springfield

GARY PLAYER TROPHY

YEAR	FIRST	SECOND	THIRD	FOURTH	FIFTH	COURSE
1967	S Sewgolum 69* 71 (140) – won R40 *course record	R Mogoerane 74 71 (145)	I Chowglay (148) R Tiney 79 69* (148) *course record	8th (152) L Buthelezi, H Lewis, Percy Mazibuko	D Motati 77 78 (155)	Paarl

KIMBERLY OPEN

YEAR	FIRST	SECOND	THIRD	FOURTH	FIFTH	COURSE
1968	S Sewgolum					Kimberly
1969	S Sewgolum					Kimberly

SWAZILAND SPA OPEN

YEAR	FIRST	SECOND	THIRD	FOURTH	FIFTH	COURSE
1968	S Sewgolum					Swaziland
1970	V Tshabalala					Swaziland

GARY PLAYER INVITATIONAL OPEN

YEAR	FIRST	SECOND	THIRD	FOURTH	FIFTH	COURSE
1968	S Sewgolum (218)	S Hlapo				
1969	S Sewgolum					
1970	S Sewgolum					Benoni

SPECIAL 72-HOLE TOURNAMENT

YEAR	FIRST	SECOND	THIRD	FOURTH	FIFTH	COURSE
1968	S Hlapo (291)	R Mogoerane	J Sithole	V Tshabalala		Dundee

ST MICHAELS OPEN

YEAR	FIRST	SECOND	THIRD	FOURTH	FIFTH	COURSE
1968	S Sewgolum					St Michaels
1971	S Sewgolum		S Hlapo			St Michaels

LUYT LAGER

YEAR	FIRST	SECOND	THIRD	FOURTH	FIFTH	COURSE
1972	S Hlapo	S Sewgolum	I Chowglay	R Mogoerane		Ohenimuri

LTA MASTERS

YEAR	FIRST	SECOND	THIRD	FOURTH	FIFTH	COURSE
1974	S Sewgolum (218)	R Mogoerane (219)	V Tshabalala (220)	I Chowglay (221)		
1975	D Naidoo	S Sewgolum				

GRIQUA GOLD CUP

YEAR	FIRST	SECOND	THIRD	FOURTH	FIFTH	COURSE
1974	S Sewgolum					

COCA COLA OPEN

YEAR	FIRST	SECOND	THIRD	FOURTH	FIFTH	COURSE
1975	D Naidoo	S Sewgolum				Durban

TOURNAMENT OF CHAMPIONS

YEAR	FIRST	SECOND	THIRD	FOURTH	FIFTH	COURSE
1974	S Sewgolum					

MARLEY CLASSIC

YEAR	FIRST	SECOND	THIRD	FOURTH	FIFTH	COURSE
1982	D Naidoo					Nigel
1988	J Dlamini 73 73 68 (214)	Theo Manyama 76 72 70 (218)				

3M CLASSIC

YEAR	FIRST	SECOND	THIRD	FOURTH	FIFTH	COURSE
1983	S Hlapo					Soweto
198?	T Manyama					

NOTABLE PERFORMANCES

1937	Jack Nathan/A Seepersadh bt. Alf Padgham (British Open & Ryder Cup 1934-37)/Allen Dailey (Ryder Cup) 2/1	
1957	Shoots 59 in caddy tournament	Papwa Sewgolum
1959	Dutch Open - 1st	Papwa Sewgolum
1960	Transvaal Open 2nd round shoots 63	Simon Cox Hlapo
1960	Dutch Open - 1st	Papwa Sewgolum
1960	Italian Open - 26th; Portuguese Open - 30th	Edward Johnson-Sedibe
1961	Spanish Open - 26th	Edward Johnson-Sedibe
1962	Ballentine Bigger Ball *Round 1 - 65 leading	Edward Johnson-Sedibe
1962-63	Oxford Blue for golf	David Phiri
1963	Natal Open - 1st	Papwa Sewgolum
1964	Cock o' the North (Zambia) - 1st	Papwa Sewgolum
1963	The Open - 13th	Papwa Sewgolum
1963	SA Open - 2nd	Papwa Sewgolum
1964	SA Open - 3rd	Papwa Sewgolum
1964	Dutch Open - 1st	Papwa Sewgolum
1964	Grand Prix Series 1st Leg - 1st	Papwa Sewgolum
1964	Grand Prix Series 2nd Leg – 2nd	Papwa Sewgolum
1965	Natal Open - 1st	Papwa Sewgolum
1964	SA Open – 3rd	Papwa Sewgolum
1965	SA Masters – 3rd	Papwa Sewgolum
1966	Bata Bush Babes (Rhodesia) - 1st	Papwa Sewgolum
1966	Dunlop Tournament (Rhodesia) - 5th	Papwa Sewgolum
1966	Natal Open – 4th	Papwa Sewgolum
1967	Bata Bush Babes (Rhodesia) – 4th	Papwa Sewgolum
1967	Dunlop Tournament (Rhodesia) – 4th	Papwa Sewgolum
1967	Carling World Championship - 6th	Papwa Sewgolum
1967	Dutch Open – 2nd	Papwa Sewgolum
1967	Indian Open - 6th	Papwa Sewgolum
1968	Swaziland Open - 1st	Mark Borman
1968	Swaziland Spa Open - 1st	Papwa Sewgolum
1970	German Open - 6th	Ismail Chowglay

1970	The Open Qualifying round (St Andrews) - 64	Papwa Sewgolum
1971	Coca Cola - 1st	Papwa Sewgolum
1974	SA Non-European Open – 10th victory	Papwa Sewgolum
1976	French Open - 1st	Vincent Tshabalala
1976	SA Masters – 5th	Vincent Tshabalala
	Goodyear Classic – 2nd	Joe Dlamini
1989	Royal Swazi Classic – 2nd	Joe Dlamini
1989	Pro-Shop Swazi Pro-Am (record -20 (268)) - 1st	Joe Dlamini
1991	Bushveld Classic (Sunshine Tour) - 1st	John Mashego
1992	Belfast Telegraph Irish Masters -2nd	Vincent Tshabalala
1993	World Junior 'Orange Bowl ' - 1st	Lewis Chitengwa
1993	South African Amateur - 1st	Lewis Chitengwa
1994	J&B All African-Classic - 3rd	Vincent Tshabalala
1996	Newcastle Classic - 2nd	John Mashego
1996	FNB Pro Series 5 (Botswana) - 2nd	John Mashego
1997	Kenya Open - 2nd	Vincent Tshabalala
1997	Shoots 61	Thabang Simon
1997	FNB Botswana Open - 1st	Nasho Kamungeremu
1997	Vodacom Series (Gauteng) - 2nd	John Mashego
1998	Vodacom Senior Classic - 1st	Solly Sepeng
2000	Cock o' the North (Zambia) - 2nd	John Mashego
2003	Seekers Travel Dainfern Pro-Am - 1st	Vincent Tshabalala
2004	Nelson Mandela Invitational - 1st	Tshabalala (with E Els)
2005	Nelson Mandela Invitational - 1st	Tshabalala (with T Clark)
2006	SAA Pro-Am Invitational - 1st	Tongoona Charamba
2006	Zambian Open – 2nd	Madalitso Muthiya
2006	First Zambian & African to play US Open	Madalitso Muthiya
2007	Samsung Royal Swazi Sun Open - 2nd	James 'Cobra' Kamte
2007	Vodacom Origins Tournament - 2nd	James 'Cobra' Kamte
2007	Kenya Open - 2nd	James 'Cobra' Kamte
2007	Vodafone Challenge (Germany) - 4th	James 'Cobra' Kamte
2007	Seekers Travel Pro-Am - 1st	James 'Cobra' Kamte

2007	AfrAsia Bank Mauritius Open - 1st	James 'Cobra' Kamte
2007	Finance Bank Zambia Open - 2nd	Lindani Ndwandwe
2008	Metmar Highveld Classic - 1st	James 'Cobra' Kamte
2008	First black SA to qualify to play the European Tour since Vincent Tshabalala 1976	James 'Cobra' Kamte
2008	Dimension Data Pro-Am 1st – first black SA to win an event on the summer tour since Papwa Sewgolum 1965	James 'Cobra' Kamte
2008	MTC Nambia PGA - 1st	Tongoona Charamba
2009	Qualified for US Open	James 'Cobra' Kamte
2009	Qualified for Asian Tour International	James 'Cobra' Kamte
2010	Mylan Classic (Nationwide US Tour) - 7th	Madalitso Muthiya
2011	BMG Classic - 1st	James 'Cobra' Kamte
2016	Vodacom Origins of Golf - 1st	Madalitso Muthiya
2017	Cape Town Open - 3rd	Keenan Davidse

Author's Notes

I started playing golf one Sunday afternoon as a 12-year old, after going to watch my father play bowls at Clovelly CC where the 1964 WP Open was in progress, won by Retief Waltman, from Gary Player, Harold Henning and Bobby Locke. Being very popular with the Clovelly members, Locke responded to calls for his ball after he putted out on the 18th green, by throwing his ball into the crowd.

This looked like fun, and I went home and swopped some pram wheels I was using to make into a go-cart for a friend's late-father's wooden-shafted set of right-handed clubs (Locke later encouraged me to change to playing left-hand) and a canvas bag.

Soon I was caddying at Clovelly for pocket money, and playing prentice golf with Sally Little. I was lucky enough to play against many memorable names such as Dale Hayes, Peter Sauerman, and David Frost, while Bobby Locke took me under his wings for a while.

At university I was involved with the 1972 student demonstrations for free black education at St George's Cathedral, carried off UCT's Jameson stairs by police, met Steve Biko at Fort Hare, and studied law with Anton Lubowski.

I also became very friendly with the Clovelly caddymaster, Ismail Chowglay, who took the juniors under his wing, playing and coaching us. Later I recall Raymond Ackerman opening the club to all races, and I was friends with Moses Mooi, and Abe van Rooyen. Consequently, I was one of those in the gallery watching the challenge match between Player, Chowglay, Sewgolum, and Tshabalala at Athlone GC in 1974.

I was living in New Zealand during the 1981 Springbok rugby tour debacle, where my extended family included Maori national rugby players and plenty of debate.

I finally decided to turn professional at age 39 – something I had always wanted to do, only to fall into my swimming pool the night before my first tournament and break my wrist.

Upon returning to Cape Town in 1994, again playing off scratch, I played in the SA Amateur, (the year after Chitengwa won), but after watching Darren Fichardt, Tim Clark and Rory Sabbatini hit the ball at least three clubs further than me, I vowed never to play competitively again.

Having returned to law my path crossed with Tony Buirski, I also devised and launched Fantasy League (later called SuperSport Dream League) for various sports including golf, and later launched the Springbok Supporter Clubs worldwide (for SARFU). After that, as the CEO of CANSA, I was involved with the Sanlam Cancer golf fundraising tournament.

I subsequently heard that Ismail Chowglay had died in poor circumstances and wrote a letter to Compleat Golfer remembering him, which became the 'letter of the month'. This drew the attention of Harry Brews, who in 2006 asked me to head up the 'Sid Brews Golf Development Trust' with its stated objective being to build a golf museum and honour those who had made a contribution to the game. This offer of becoming involved with Harry Brews drew on my passion for the sport and especially golf

When the trust ran out of funds in 2008, I took over the funding, hosting our first induction event in December 2009, and after researching, designing, and opening the museum in 2010, I became aware that there was not much recorded concerning black golf and I set out to research this subject. At the same time, the induction committee decided to introduce a new category for induction, namely 'disadvantaged', where different criteria were used for induction. Through this project, I became friends with Vincent Tshabalala, Rajen Sewgolum, Alan Rae, and Lewis Muridzo.

Finally, I relocated the museum to the V&A Waterfront, where I designed a subset of panels within the museum on black golf, being both the history, as well as the results of black golf including the TPA Tour.

Interesting how a small pebble and the ensuing ripples by stumbling across the 1964 WP Open at Clovelly and watching Locke and Player would lead me all the way to this book. This then is their story ...

I would like to especially thank Dennis Bruyns for filling in the blanks while I was out of the country during the 1980s, Jeremy Wightman for all his advice and kicking my butt to re-write this manuscript when I erroneously thought it was complete.

Further, Christopher Meister for information concerning Edward Johnson-Sedibe, Alan Rae, Lewis Muridzo-Chitengwa, Sujatha Boodhun, Bernnedett Hlapo, and for his advice, Duncan Cruickshank, Selvan Naidoo (1860 Heritage Centre) and Rajen Sewgolum for their encouragement and photographs, Peter Sauerman and Tony Buirski (who both assisted our trust), and Abe van Rooyen for their input.

Of course, it also helped to have access to the most extensive book, magazine, and manuscript golf library in Africa at our SA Golf Museum.

And then Craig Urquhart for his encouragement and advice, Marion Pfeiffer for her suggestions and editing, and both Bridgit King and Neville Humphreys from Office National Hout Bay for all their hard work cutting photos, and recording and designing the museum wallpaper and other assistance, as well as the staff at the National Library in Cape Town.

Finally my old rugby and law friend, Hannes Wessels (Rhodesian war and golf author) who assisted further with the editing, and for all his advice

Putting together the historical results I relied heavily on R.G. Fall's writing in SA Golfer magazine, as well as newspapers, and for the stories, books, magazine articles, and the internet, chats over the years with various of these personalities, as well as Peter Sauerman's writing on the SAGA website and his Peter Louw induction speech.

This then is the story and history of black golf in South Africa, and its heroes who dominated the sports pages of mainly black-read newspapers and magazines, read by millions, and how these forgotten icons assisted the anti-apartheid sports movement and ultimately the dismantling of apartheid.

I hope this story will encourage those holding any records or information to come forward so that the missing links may be completed. I have also taken the liberty of selecting my top ten black players pre-the new democracy – I trust this is not too controversial.

Barry Cohen

*I took one liberty of including the musical King Kong in Sewgolum's narrative. In fact, this musical only reached the West End in 1961 (not 1959), as this popular heavyweight boxer's tragic life story 'musical' was being performed to mixed-race audiences in SA at that time.

Bibliography

Books

Bell, T. (2005) *Papwa Sewgolum – From Pariah to Legend, News & Views by Terry Bell by Christopher Nicholson* (Wits University Press, 2005) reviewed by Terry Bell.

Black Sash Records (1974) *Everyone's guide to the pass laws.*

Brews, H. *South African Golf, Volume One: Blazing the Trail, The Story of South Africa's First Internationally Famous Golfer*, Cape Town: Published under the auspices of the Sid Brews Golf Development Trust.

Canale, N. (2013) *Snakes in the Garden of Eden*, Cape Town: Don Nelson Publishers.

Case, M. (2015) *Papwa: Golf's Lost Legend.* Kwela Books.

Chitengwa, L.M. (2016) *My Life and my love for the great game of golf.*

Corcoran, M. (2010) *Duel in the Sun: Tom Watson and Jack Nicklaus in the Battle of Turnberry*, Simon and Schuster. ISBN 9781439141922.

Fall, R.G. (1958) *Golfing in South Africa.*

Fall, R.G. (ed.). (1960) *How far the underprivileged have advanced in the game?* South African Golf.

Joyce, P. (2014) *The rise of the phoenix*, Zebra Press.

Kelly, J. *History of Golf in Rhodesia and Zimbabwe*

Kerr, W.M. (1997) *The History of Royal Durban Golf Club.* Durban: Colorgraphic.

Mallon, B. and Jerris, R. (2011) *Historical Dictionary of Golf.* Scarecrow Press. p. 864.

New York Times (1966) *'Gary Player ties for Second'*, AP. 20 February. [Retrieved 20 April 2017.]

New York Times 1966. *Player shoots a 72 for 286 to take South African Golf.* The New York Times. AP. 7 February. [Retrieved 20 April 2017.]

Meister, Christopher: Golf Historian & Writer - Hamburg Area, Germany. (correspondence)

Muir Ferguson, R. *The wonderful golf of Ramnath B. Bambata.* 1929

Pariah to Legend by Christopher Nicholson, (Wits University Press, 2005) News & Views reviewed by Terry Bell.

Norval, R. (1951) *King of the Links: The story of Bobby Locke*, South Africa: Maskew Miller.

Norval, R. (1965) *Gone to the Golf*, Citadel Press.

Norval, R. (1954) *King of the Links*, Bailey & Swinfern.

O'Donnell, P. (1973) *South Africa's Wonderful World of Golf*, Cape Town. Don Nelson Publishers.

Partridge, Ted: *The World of Golf.*

Player, G. *Gary Player World Golfer.* (1974)

Player, G. (1966) *Grand Slam of Golf*, London: Cassell & Company.

Player, G. and McDonald, M. (1992) *To be the Best.* London: Pan Books.

'Presidency Communications Research Document: *The National Orders Awards*, October 2004' [online] Available at: info.gov.za [Accessed 31 March 2009]

Rae, E. (2007) *A Gentleman's Game: The Life and Legacy of Lewis Chitengwa*, Echo Memories Ltd.

SA History – *Sewsunker 'Papwa' Sewgolum.* www.sahistory.org.za/people/sewsunker-papwa-sewgolum

Sauerman, Peter: Premier Golf Historian writing – Various discussions.

The Compleat Golfer Guide to Golf 2000. Cape Town: Ramsay Son & Parker (Pty) Ltd

The Mercury (2018) *A talent apartheid tragically denied - Honouring Papwa's memory* [17 April 2018] / Selvan Naidoo.

Urquhart, C. (2013) *The Kings of Swing*, Zebra Press.

Vlismas, Michael (2012) *Extraordinary Book of South African Golf*, Johannesburg: Penguin Books.

Webb, Richard: Narrative Media SA. Various discussions.

2005 Documentary film *'Papwa: The Lost Dream of a South African Golfing Legend'*.

Clarence Harry Moore & Heather Heath: *Autobiographical Anecdotes of the SA War; Growth of Golf in Natal & Transvaal*; South Africa's first Golfing Dynasty 1900 - 2000 (2018)

Newspapers, Magazines, and Interviews

Abe van Rooyen – Various discussions

The Bantu World: October – November 2015

Bernnedett Hlapo – 'Cox' Hlapo's daughter – Various discussions

Cape Times: July – August 1960; January 1964; March – April 1964; 10 January 1965; 19/01/1965; March – April 1965; 23/07/1967;

City Press: March 1963; March 1965; May 1976

Compleat Golfer: Various Articles

Daily Despatch – 1992

The Daily News: July–August 1959, '60' 64; February 1963, '65, March 22'93

Drum: February 1964; 30 January 1966

Drum: August – September 1959; September 1960; February 1963; March – April 1963; March – April 1965; May – June 1965; September 1964; September 1967; January – February 1975; January – February 1978

Evening Post – 1963 March 2; 1964 March 15; 1993 March 22

Fall, R.G. *South African Golf Magazines*, 1960

Fiat Lux: August 1979

Golden City Post: 1937 pages 55-65

Golf 15 Augustus 1959 & 1960 – *Officieel organ van her Nederlandsch Golfcomite*

Golf Digest: Various Articles

German Golf Magazine 'Plock' (Delius Clasing Verlag, Bielefeld) 2006 article

Golf Digest: 06/07/2015, various others

The Golfer's Annual 1953/4

The Golfer 1926-1978

Leader: July 1929; February – March 1937

The Leader: March 13 1959; July – September 1960; March 02 1963; November 1963; July 1967, '70, '77

Longhurst, H. '*South Africans at Muirfield*' in Sports Illustrated (America) 13 July 1959

Maandblad: *First indentured Indians Durban*

The Masters Golf Society: 10th Anniversary Celebration, pp 7

The Mercury: 15 January 1973

Mercury: February – March 1963; March 1965

Mercury: August 1959; August 1960; August 1964

The Post: 29 November 1964; Various Articles

Rajen Sewgolum 'Papwa' Sewgolum's son – Various discussions

Selvin Naidoo, CEO, 1860 Heritage – Various discussions

South Africa Golf magazine: Various 1926 – 1982 – Editor R.G. Fall, later P Sauerman

Sports Illustrated

Sujatha Boodhun – Ramnath 'Bambata's grand-niece – Various discussions

Sunday times – Various Articles

The Star 19/11/38

Sunday Tribune: 24/01/1993

Tony Buirski Various discussions

Trust: August 1959; August 1960; August 1964

Zonk: July-August 1959, September 1959 pg 27, 29, 1960, January-February 1963, February 1964 pg 29

Websites

www.abaphenyi.co.za/news/2018/05/04/department-of-sports-ruled-offside

https://allafrica.com/stories/201609051428.html

Articles.sun.sentinel.com>Collections>Orange Bowl

https://athlonsports.com/golf/golf-course-review-wintergreen

https://www.athlonenews.co.za/news/golfing-great-reminisces-about-his-career-15226813

https://www.athlonenews.co.za/wp-content/uploads/2018/05/102989507.jpg

https://www.athlonenews.co.za/wp-content/uploads/2018/05/102989510.jpg

Baileys Africa History Archive www.baha.co.za

Blackenterprise.com/1998-black-enterprisepepsi-golf

Books.google.co.za/books?id.vol29no2-magazine

www.brandsouthafrica.com/tag/gary-player

catdir.loc.gov/catdir/samples/simon031/2002025156.html

Connection.ebscohost.com/c/articles/5202568/life-death-lewis-chitengwa

Dailypress.com/news/dp_xpm

Thefreelibrary.com>Business>Black Enterprise>September1, 1998

www.thefreelibrary.com/Star+profile+Lewis+Chitengwa

From Caddying for to Playing With Player October 15, 2014

www.golfclubatlas.com/courses-by-country/netherlands/royal-hague

www.golfclubatlas.com/courses-by-country/south-africa/durban-country-club

https://www.golfdigest.com/story/papwa

www.golftheunitedstates.com/story/235

Hitting Apartheid for Six? The Politics of the South African Sports Boycott – Douglas Booth https://doi.org/10.1177/0022009403038003008 - 01/07/2003

https://www.imdb.com/title/tt5847770/?ref_=fn_al_tt_1

Infoplease.com/people/lewis-chitengwa

www.theopen.com

http://papwasewgolum.com/index.php/media/photos/

Passing on Ambition from Father to Son by Paul Spencer Sochaczewski and International Herald Tribune Aug. 25, 1998

www.pgatour.co.za

Presidents Cup www.presidentscup.com

https://www.nytimes.com/1998/08/25/opinion/meanwhile-passing-on

https://www.sahistory.org.za/dated-event/nelson-mandela-free

www.saga.co.za

www.scribd.com?...?344558583/The-Casbah-40-1977-April-1977

www.sochaczewski.com/2009/08/30/my-kids-gonna-be-a-star

South African Golf Association website: *History of Non-European Golf.* www.golfrsa.co.za

https://www.thestandard.co.zw/2017/04/23/zims-black-golf-trailblazer

www.sun-sentiner.com/news/fl-xpm-1992-12-31

Wikipedia – Various Articles

https://en.wikipedia.org/wiki/File:John_Vorster.jpg

https://en.wikipedia.org/wiki/File:Dennis_Brutus_(1967).jpg

South African Golfers http://en.wikipedia.org/wiki/list_of_African_golfers

https://twitter.com/GolfDigestSA/status/871436464126558209/photo/1

World Cup http://en.Wikipedia.org/wiki/1996_World_Cup_of_Golf

Yesteryear profile with Daniel Nhakaniso / Munyaradzi Madzoker

www.ingramcontent.com/pod-product-compliance
Lightning Source LLC
Chambersburg PA
CBHW062357090426
42740CB00010B/1310

* 9 7 8 0 6 2 0 8 2 7 7 9 9 *